"Spark's in the

Anthony **David** Crawford

David was born in Haverton Hill, County Durham. His father worked in the local shipyard & his mother looked after the house & her father, David grandfather a retired salt worker originally from Winsford in Cheshire. David was educated at the local state school before qualifying to attend the Technical College in Stockton on Tees. From here he started work at Dorman Long Steel Company as an Apprentice Engineering Draughtsman. Over the years he has worked for a number of companies, building Blast Furnaces & Nuclear Power stations before becoming a freelance designer in the oil & gas industry. He & his wife Margaret were married in 1973 & live in Marton in Cleveland.

1

Dedication

This book is dedicated firstly to my very understanding wife Margaret who has eagerly awaited the finished book commemorating a much loved and greatly missed friend. She has for the last ten years had to watch as I listened & re-listened to my recordings of Jack Spark recounting his life both civilian & military. There were also the reams of documents I found that had to be checked before inclusion. This was followed by hours of typing the results onto my computer & checking the validity of the content.

I then added George Silva's content interweaving both stories in a date order. During this time I came into contact with some of the families of the American Crew members who provided information of their individual lives both civil & military. The largest contributors were Gloria & Art Silva Mack who provided a document written by George Silva himself which added to my own content enormously.

Then from Holland there has been a great contribution by Adrian van Zantvoort who provided letters exchanged between Jack & himself. It was Adrian that actually found Bob Cook the pilot of the B17 Fortress which culminated in contact between Jack Spark & George Silva.

Foreword

by Doctor William S (Bill) Hossack

In his role as oral historian, David Crawford has assiduously and painstakingly researched and recorded the life and times of Jack Spark, dating from his origins in Cumbria. The end result is a comprehensive biography, encompassing his life in peacetime and in war.

My initial encounter with Jack in the mid-nineties was in relation to R.A.F. Elsham Wolds Association, in which he was an active member at the time and of which he subsequently become President. Tall in stature and easy in demeanour, Jack was always smartly attired. He was an excellent raconteur and had an engaging sense of humour. Although he had experienced personal sadness and distress in family life, including the loss of his brother, a pilot with the R.A.F, he remained unbowed and resilient.

In civilian life Jack was, by his own definition, 'involved in the cloth trade', eventually becoming store manage at Burton Tailors. In the Second World War he took up arms against the aggressor by volunteering for aircrew, in the course of which he acquitted himself with distinction. Such men were a race set apart. His relating of events of his time with the forces, in his own inimitable style, was informative, educational and frequently laced with benign humour.

On a personal note, we both shared a love of music. A defining moment and lasting memory for me is of a Reunion event in the Village Hall at Barnetby when he and I, with no prior practice, embarked on a harmonica duo rendition of Lady Nairne's famous 'Will Ye No' Come Back Again?'. The haunting melody and lyrics of that number linger with me as a reminder of my times with Jack, whose existence touched the lives of so many who knew him along life's journey.

Forward

by Group Captain Donald (Don) Hiller RAF (Retired)

David's thoroughly researched biography of John Robinson "Jack" Spark is a fitting tribute to a man who was well liked and held in great respect by all who knew him. My wife and I met Jack, and other survivors of the raid in France, on the coach trip to the commemoration of the costly RAF air raid on the German Panzer training camp at Mailly-le-camp. Here 42 Lancaster's were lost in one hour, on an "easy" raid that counted as only "one third of an Operation".

Our friendship developed from this. We would drive up to Gateshead to spend time with Jack, and he would travel down by train to stay with us in Grantham. Jack was in a reserved occupation and used his initiative to get released to volunteer for aircrew. Early in his tour as a Wireless Operator, Jack's initiative would be instrumental in saving his aircraft when it was badly damaged over Germany, as David's biography records.

David's biography also reveals that fate dealt Jack some massive blows that would have broken the spirit of many. We were proud to call Jack our friend, and proud that he called us his friends.

The Bomber Command Spire

In the glorious fields of Lincolnshire

From where our Bombers once flew

They have built a Spire, remembering the crews

In sight of the Cathedral, it will be seen for years

But the reason it's there, will bring you to tears

It's a tribute to the flowering Commonwealth seeds

Who came to defend freedom, in its hour of need

All across Europe, these seeds lay scattered

In the hope that their sacrifice, really mattered

There were fifty-five thousand, who never went home

Into the face of the Memorial, their names have been honed

So, let's stand in silence, and remember their loss

Then try to make a World, without another Cross

David Crawford (Watching)

Introduction

This is the story of young men fighting the air war against Germany in 1944. The first is a Cumbrian Wireless Operator Jack Spark, flying with his seven-man crew in RAF Bomber Command by night. The other is a Californian Radio Operator George Silva, flying with his ten-man crew in the 8th Army Air Force by day. Though they never met during this period their paths crossed in March 44, when Jacks Lancaster crashes into Georges B17 Flying Fortress the "Passionate Witch" on Dunsfold airfield in Surrey. Fifty years after the war Jack was prompted to find out if the crew of the Passionate Witch had survived the conflict. What he finds is a story of courage, tragedy and suffering by the American crew.

The original Wireless Telegraphy Operators Morse keys had a small voltage running through them, this produced a visible spark from the contacts as the dots & dashes were tapped out. This resulted in operators being called "Sparks". The RAF Wireless Operators Sparks Badge is in fact a Clenched Fist holding three Lightning bolts.

In the beginning

Mathew Wilkinson Spark was born in 1883 at Alston in Cumberland. He was the son of a lead miner, the grandson of a lead miner, with a surname as prolific as the Cumbrian raindrops. Alston the highest market town in England was also the center for the lead mining industry in this country. There were two local mines within reach of Alston, one at Nenthead the second at Killhope. The working conditions for miners were grim; there was the dampness combined with the cold of the mine workings. In addition, there was the lethal lead ore dust, created when dynamite blasting in the shaft takes place. Then when you were working above ground, there was the highly poisonous atmosphere given off by the ore smelters. All would take its toll on their health, the longer they worked at the mine. Mathew started work in the mine as a drilling machinist, but by the age of nineteen, he is not happy to spend the rest of his days there. He quickly realised that the life of a lead miner was a hard one, but more importantly it would be a short one. Headstones in the local cemetery, bear witness to the average life expectancy of a miner to be only some forty-five years, this was not for him. Other work in the area was limited to hill farming, mainly sheep which was as poorly paid as lead mining. So, he would have to leave home, as the local economy had little to offer, in the way of job opportunities.

Casting his eye about for alternatives, he realised that Carlisle the nearest large town, with its growing railway industry was a likely place to begin looking. A visit to Carlisle resulted in an offer of a start with the railway company, which became the London North Eastern Railway Co. Although at the bottom of the ladder as a cleaner in the engine sheds, the opportunity for improvement was all he needed to accept the job. The company were true to their word as Mathew through hard work, he found himself advancing through the ranks. A period as a fireman, shoveling coal into the firebox of a train, he finally ends up as a driver.

Life was not all work as Mathew meets Ellen Robinson an accounts clerk who was working for a local provisions merchant. He did not let the grass grow under his feet either, marrying Ellen Robinson in 1912 in Carlisle. They set up home at 24, Herbert Street, in what was then the small village of Harraby, on the south side of Carlisle.

This was during the hard times of the early 1900's, but it did not stop them from starting a family, Thomas William Spark was born in September 1913 at home.

Thomas grew up in Harraby, playing in the streets or surrounding countryside, before attending the local primary school.

Then at the age of nine, he suddenly finds he has a new brother. John (Jack) Robinson Spark came into the world, on Thursday the 19th

Oct 1922. At the age of 40, his mother was very surprised by his arrival as was his dad. The fact that he was mum's little accident, she would jokingly relate to Jack, on many occasions during his life. But despite his unexpected arrival, he grew up in a loving home, with an older brother to look after him should the need arise.

School Days

At the age of five, Jack was introduced to the joys of education at his local school, Brooke Street Primary. One Monday morning accompanied by his mother, he reports to his first teacher Miss Hodgson who introduced him to his new class mates. Arriving back home, in Herbert Street, Ellen Spark busied herself, with the everyday chores of a housewife, on a Monday morning. There was washing to be done, meals to be planned, a house to be cleaning. The morning came and went, then a break for a bite to eat at midday, was interrupted by the sound of the front door slamming shut. Young Jack appears in the kitchen, to his mum's amazement he pronounces "School is all right mum, but I don't think I will go back". But back he went, as he is promptly marched off to school again, no doubt with a flea in his ear. His older brother Thomas had by this time passed through junior school, where he qualified to attend 'Creighton Central Secondary school'.

During the school holidays Jack with his pals, would explore the local countryside, enjoying the adventures, everyone who was young once, should remember. One of these attractions was Harraby Mill, (on the river Petteril) a small but essential provider of badly needed jobs for local men. Horse racing week in Carlisle (end of June) was a holiday, which saw the mill close for two weeks coincidentally with the school break. This closure meant the Mill-race sluice gates were shut, leaving the mill pond a safe place to swim for Jack and his friends. But as the sun shone, the pond water drained away over a few days, revealing a number of trout, trapped in the shallow water. Quickly, these trout were seen as a free lunch by these young lads, if only they could be caught. Charging about in the shallows proved to be fruitless; no fish were caught and the water being reduced to a muddy haze. At this point, Jack decided to wait for the water to clear. Then armed with an old brass stair rod, he stepped back into the pond, slowly stalking the trout. The stair rod flashed through the air, to come crashing down on the fish. In a short time, he had enough for the group of pals to take home; a memorable day was had by all. As all young boys remember, growing up meant joining the big boy's gang, at a time when this was a totally innocent group, without the modern connotations of violence. To join, you had to undergo an initiation ordeal, Jack would not be exempt. Behind the village of Harraby stands Gallows Hill, atop of the hill lie's the Gibbet stone. Here the near do wells or Border

Reivers of the past had been summarily dealt with, in a bloody brutal way. This was Jacks test; on a dark night he had to climb the hill, watched by the other gang members to sit for thirty minutes on the stone. When he was out of sight, the other gang members would climb the hill unseen from opposing sides. From the bushes they would rattle chains or howl, like demented souls, to try to unnerve him. But undeterred, he stayed for the required time coming down, a fully-fledged member of the gang.

As young lads we would spend hours at weekends searching for bird's nests to identifying the different marking on the eggs. Other times we would be turning over large stones near ponds or looking under building foundations for Newts or Toads. One evening I remember gathering with the rest of our gang; we had acquired an old wallet to which we tied a length of fine twine. This wallet was then carefully positioned, on the pavement, outside one of the local Pubs. Here it would be readily visible to anyone, going in or out of the front door. We did not have long to wait, though the first man to leave turned left away from us, so he did not see it. Then the next one who stepped out spotted the wallet, looking about to check if he would be seen he swooped to pick it up; gotcha!. The twine was pulled to take the wallet out of his reach, it would often take two or three tugs, before some of them realised they were being fooled.

One of the members of our gang was Albert Bargett; his father worked and lived in a house within the grounds of the Mill. He was employed as a caretaker cum general handyman, which including locking up at night then opening up each morning for the workers. Young Albert was a Down's syndrome lad, who mixed happily, with the rest of us kids in the street. He played football with us, romped through the woods, joining in our adventures; his only fear was the dark and bats. As his home was at the end of a dark lane, through the woods, he would disappear early to be home in daylight. One night I found Albert at the end of the lane afraid to continue home, so I walked with him to protect him. From that moment on, it would be 24 Herbert Street he would call at, to ask Jack to take him home if he was out late. "But I was the one who had to walk back, on my own through the woods with my hair standing on end" recalls Jack.

Guy Fawkes Night was one time in the year, when the gang came together as a group, to outdo other gangs in the area to build a bonfire. The village of Harraby is divided by the main A6 road to Carlisle running through its center. The children living on the west side would compete with those on the east side, to build the biggest bonfire.

I remember scavenging, with the rest of our gang, for waste wood, to heap on the growing pile that was our bonfire. Because of the competition with the east side of the village, evenings would be spent guarding our bonfire, for as late as possible. Both sides were not above raiding the opposition's bonfire, to enhance their own. Came the evening of the fifth a torch was put to the bonfire by one of the adults, though I don't remember many fireworks disturbing the night sky. Later as the fire started to die down, we would gather round the embers to roast potatoes on long sticks, "Oh boy did they taste good". Life was so much simpler then, what we had you could not buy, but our lives were enriched all the same. As young lads we were always hungry, so when the apples start to ripen in the vicar's orchard, the inevitable happened. Lookouts were posted, others were hoisted over the fence to grab as many apples as they could, before the vicar may spot them. What a waste of stealth on our part, it turned out the vicar was away on two weeks holiday. We were not rich as kids, but I remember there were always a few coppers for sweets. There were liquorice sticks, tiger nuts, locust beans (carob pods) plus other treats you just can't get now. I also doubt if modern youngsters would want to chew on a length of liquorice stick root as we did then.

In the 1930's money was always in short supply, so being self-sufficient was the order of the day. My father, along with many other men in the area, would stretch their income by growing their own food on allotments, close to our homes. Hoping to nurture Jack's interest, he took him along to help with the weeding or watering of the vegetable plots. A small patch of ground was set aside for me; I had to cultivate it before sowing it with vegetable seeds. I carefully planted them in rows, before watered them under dad's direction. The picture on the front of the seed packet looked wonderful, as I imagined the full-grown vegetables on a plate, with gravy drizzled over them. Two days later, I returned to the allotment with dad to be disappointed, there was nothing sticking out of the ground. His explanation that it would take weeks for them to grow came as a big letdown, I lost any interest in gardening I may have had. Competition amongst these gardeners was very keen; every year there would be a local flower and vegetable show. Dad would be carefully eyeing up his best vegetables or flowers for possible entry into this show. When it came, he would be cleaning or preparing his entries. After the show when judging had taken place, his reward would a first in one class or another. In the summer of 1931, I remember he really hit the jackpot with a first for his Leaks, Celery, Onions, Rhubarb plus two firsts in the flower sections. My father was never a vain man, but these wins put a smile on his face, that lasted for weeks. Though for my part, I thought the prize vegetables tasted just the same as the rest.

In 1933 aged eleven, Jacks term at Brook Street primary was coming to an end. Like his brother before him, he sits the secondary school exams, to his parent's delight he passes with flying colours. Jack now transfers to Creighton Secondary School, which involves a bus trip to the other side of Carlisle each day. The school was Dickensian in its approach to education, where the teachers were held in awe, if not downright fear. Here he becomes involved, in the sporting side of his new school, playing rugby, tennis, running and boxing, a sport which would come back to haunt Jack in the R.A.F. Of all the sports, he took part in, the high jump is the one he remembers most, enjoying some success at it.

Transferring with him from Brooke St was his pal Dennis Langhorne who lived on the North side of town. We had been friends sharing a desk throughout junior school. At Creighton Dennis and I struck up a friendship with another young school pal Bob Raven. We became inseparable as friends, in our future we would all three join the RAF, Bob became a pilot, Dennis an air gunner with me a wireless operator.

During 1933 we had to come to terms with a personal tragedy when young Albert Bargett took ill and died suddenly. His death was the main topic of conversation among us young lads, trying to understand why it had happened. This was my first experience of death which left me with lots of unanswered questions. We never found out what had been the cause of Albert death, as parents were always protective when it came to discussing things like that.

On weekends, we young lads would gather, in the woods to climb trees, tying ropes onto the high branches. Johnny Weissmuller (Tarzan) was our hero at the time, so we tried to emulate him by swinging, from tree to tree. Jack also remembers, becoming a member of the Boy's Brigade where we were instructed in signalling, using flags. At weekends there were group hiking trips round the Lake District where we would be instructed in map reading. This beautiful area of Cumbria is one that Jack has many happy memories of; early morning bus rides from home to Keswick. Then long walks, round the shores of Derwent Water, to catch the late bus home, somewhere along the way. The ride home was usually spent, slumped against each other on the back row of the bus fast asleep. Fortunately, Carlisle was our terminus, so we could not miss our stop. There were also, school trips to Windermere, with our teachers, climbing in the hills with them, to awaken our knowledge, of the big world outside Carlisle.

Weekends at home were also a time when we would visit, or be visited, by relatives. Mum's sister, Aunt Lillian was a regular visitor with her daughter, my cousin Lillian, I remember she was a similar age to me. On one visit I recall, because we were all poshed up in our best clothes, we had our photo taken in the yard with my brother Thomas.

I remember the snowy winters in Harraby, when we would use Gallows Hill as our sledge run, which was very steep. Plummeting down the hill, our speed could be hair rising at times, with a change in the slope near the bottom, very exciting. This would launch our sledges into the air, for what seemed like miles, before crashing back to earth, most times without the rider. All of our sledges were homemade from spare lengths of wood; these were nailed together; with any strip of metal we could find for runners. There was also the local attraction of Hammonds Pond, named after the brick works owner. When they froze over, we would spend our afternoons or weekends skating about on these ponds. Any bent piece of wood was put to use as a hockey stick with a flat stone for a puck, our imaginations knew no bounds. Though I remember, even in those far off days, the thickness of the ice was always checked first by parents, before anyone was allowed to skate. There were less welcome memories of winter in Harraby, our old houses still had outside toilets. So, a trip to the loo, was not a happy or long experience. Each evening I had to make sure that a lighted candle was positioned on a shelf beneath the water tank. This was the only way to ensured it did not freeze up overnight.

When Christmas came round, we looked forward to receiving those luxury presents, we all hoped for. But I doubt if a leather football and boots or the pair of roller skates we got, would be considered a luxury by today's youngsters. There was also the obligatory selection of Walnuts, Brazil and Hazel nuts in the bottom of the stocking, hanging from the mantelpiece over the fireplace. Then if you were really lucky there was a large round Orange in the stocking plus a few toffees.

During the summer school holidays, my father ensured we kept in touch with our grandparents and the extended family, back home in Alston. My Aunt Meg ran a general dealers shop on the market square; it was here I would stay with my brother Thomas. Early on a morning, Meg would make up a packed lunch for the two of us, with a Billy can of tea to wash it down. Then off we went to the river below the town with our fishing rods in hand. The South Tyne River, on the west side of the town, is joined by the river Nent, below the railway station. Today we are headed for the South Tyne, with its grassy banks and pebbled shallows. This river varies from, narrow deep channels to wide shallows, still deep enough for fish to swim, but ideal for wading to fish. Thomas was a dab hand at fly fishing; he would spend hours showing me how to develop my casting technique. We started out on the river bank, perfecting my casting action; only when this is correct, can I hope to accurately hit a chosen point on the water at will.

Even after I start to get the casting right, there was the art of reading the river. Each day it can be different, the favourite pools change from the morning to the afternoon. The natural fly's, the fish rise for varies month to month with the weather changing their moods, making them lazy or lively. It's this variability that changes fishing from a challenge, to the passion Jack enjoys today, "Though I still never eat anything I catch". We spent, so many happy times together fishing the river. There were the hills rising up, on both sides with only the sound of the water, to break the silence, it was a magical time. My brother taught me everything I know about fishing plus a lot of other things beside; we were great pals. Both my brother and I were tall, by the age of 15, I was 5 foot 10 inches and still growing, my brother at 24 was the same height. Our father was much shorter than that, but he would often retort "If my legs had been straight, I would be 6 foot tall", he was quite bow legged. Mind you, I remember he had a good turn of speed when he needed to run, so it was not that much of a handicap to him.

In the 1930's depression, Mathew, Jack's father, was one of a small number of men in the street, who were in regular work. One of the perks of his job on the railway, were the free trips each year for the whole family, to anywhere in the country. This also included the ferries serving the Islands, around the coast of Scotland. So, Oban and Dunoon were a favourite holiday destination for the Spark family. Leaving home neighbours would jokingly comment, "There go the Spark's off cruising again". I loved to sail around the Islands on the West coast of Scotland the scenery was as dramatic as the Lake District. As we passed between the Islands you could almost believe you were sailing on Windermere or Derwentwater. Then when we were home again my school pals were left wishing they had a dad, who was an engine driver. In the school holidays, Jack would spend many happy hours, on the footplate of his dad's engine while he was shunting, in the local goods yard. Today's health and safety experts would have nightmares at this scenario. My father was a patient man, who spent his spare time talking to my brother and myself, apart from when he was down at his allotment.

He would talk about his trips away, places he saw along the length of the country, especially when his work took him to Scotland. There were stories of the mountains then trips along the east coast, over the Forth Bridge then up to Aberdeen.

Thomas, Jack's older brother, having passed through Creighton School nine years earlier, had left his own mark on the teaching staff. Jack recalls his brother had a passion and a remarkable talent for water colour painting, which began at school. So, when I arrived for my first art lesson Mr Shackleton, who was making up the new class register asked. "Mr Spark do you have a brother Thomas".

My "Yes Sir", was followed by his "Thank goodness, we have another Spark painter, in the school". I was quite surprised and a little embarrassed by this unexpected attention. Four weeks later he took me to one side to retort; "Sadly Spark, any artistic talent in your family, went into your older brother", this was something I already knew. Though Jack comments, "I can't see, what he had to complain about; I always put a title on my paintings, so people would know, what they were". My own talents were the ability, to play the piano by ear plus the self-taught harmonica quite well. There were occasions, when I would accompany my brother on his painting excursions, often into Carlisle's City Centre. Here there was a wealth of subjects for Thomas to paint; 'The Castle, the Old Town Hall, our beautiful Cathedral' plus a multitude of other scenes.

I would sit watching for hours as he sketched a Cathedral scene in pencil, then painted in the grass, the sky then the building stonework. Not satisfied with one painting, he would return another day, then do it all again from a different viewpoint. Occasionally people would stop to watch Thomas at work, which would then attract others, who would come over to see what was going on. I was always a bit embarrassed at this attention, but Thomas just continued to paint on, oblivious to the crowd. He had a talent for a representation of the scene in front of him; it was never an exact copy, but his artistic interpretation. I often wished I had that vision, the ability to see things so clearly then commit them to paper.

Our math's master at school was Mr Garrigon, a Scotsman who never missed a trick; he knew all the dodges and was a strict disciplinarian. Most nights of the week, we were set homework, to be completed within a few days. Amongst schoolboys, there is always, an amount of collusion with each other, to complete our homework. Jack remembers one incident, when a school friend, two years older than himself, who lived in the same street, helped him with his math's homework. On the morning, the homework was to be checked, I sat at my desk, full of confidence, waiting to be called, by Mr Garrigon. When it came, I walked forward to his desk with my math book, in my hand; six questions had been set; I had answered them all. There was a silence, as he went down the list, slowly checking each answer, before placing a large tick beside them. As he reached the final question, there was a pause, before he placed the last tick in place, slowly he closed the book picking it up he said. "Do you take me for a fool laddie; ye never did any of that work", he promptly hit me about the head, with the homework book. My ears rang for an hour or so, but I always did my own homework after that. Today his actions would have landed him in Court or could have cost him his career; though I am sure it did me no harm. One of Mr Garrigon's other party pieces, was to suddenly, ask a question of the class then, look around to see who was to answer it, usually me. My class mate Dennis Langhorne, was always one of the first to raise his hand, to answer any question. So when I asked, how he always knew the answer he replied he didn't, but if you raise your hand he won't ask you, because he thinks you know. I tried it; it worked most of the time, but not always.

One of Jacks interests was rugby, but unfortunately for him it was coached, by Mr Garrigon. I took great pleasure in playing Rugby for the school, but was not really built for the game. Being tall with a very light build, I was no match for the shorter heavily built opposition. Though they

14

did not always have it all their own way, Jack was very quick on his feet, able to change direction in a flash. This often left the opposing backs, struggling in his wake, trying to lay a hand on him. During the winter when the ground was frozen, Mr Garrigon would as a concession allow us to play football, but only with a rugby ball. You have to experience this first hand to believe it, the unpredictable bounce of the ball made kicking or passing a nightmare. There was also the inevitable temptation to pick the ball up then run toward the goal. This teacher's attitude to rugby football was, we take no prisoners, wimps are not tolerated, nor did they stay long in his team.

French classes at Creighton were under the tuition of Mr Bennett, who was a tall gangly man; this earned him the Knick name of "Big Ben". The class room was a large one, with an open fire in one corner, which we were all glad of during the winter months. Mr Bennett would often set the class a written test, then stand, in front of this fire, warming his rear, while we completed the assignment. This fire was fed quite often, with waste paper, from the litter bins which led, to one of the class, plotting a prank. His father had a starting pistol, which he used at local athletic club events. He took five, of the blank cartridges, from his father's stock which he then brought into class. They were carefully wrapped, in paper then thrown into the waste bin. Unsuspecting, Mr Bennett picked out these bundles, then threw them onto the fire, replacing the guard in front, he stood warning himself. The first blank went off with a loud bang which startled him, but the other four going off together sent him scurrying to the other side of the room. Fortunately, the explosion was put down, to something, in the coal, so the culprit was never brought to book for this prank.

Wood working was one of the other classes we attended; here we learned to mutilate pieces of timber, under the direction of Mr Rowland. This teacher was a stickler, for accuracy in sawing, planing or making joints in wood. He always carried around a two foot long (600mm) steel rule which if, he caught you fooling about, he would slap you across the legs, with the flat side of it. By Jove, it did smart, this quickly earned him the nickname of Killer Rowland.

Every morning he would arrive, in his old car which he parked, under a lean too in the school grounds. Then as he climbed out of the car, we would shout "Morning Killer" from a place of hiding. The curriculum, at Creighton Secondary was varied and difficult, but despite Jack claiming not to be studious, he did well. His examination passes included, Mathematics, Geography, English, Art plus French. His only failure was Chemistry, this subject was a complete mystery to me, I knew I would never make a sorcerer's apprentice. In fact, the only chemical reaction I was familiar with was, hot water poured on tea leaves. My desk mate

Dennis however was quite the opposite, doing well in the subject, he would qualify, in time as a pharmacist. Later in life he would work for 'Halloway's Chemists' in the town where he met his future wife, Cecilia Jardine.

Thomas by now had completed his term, at secondary school, enrolling at a Teacher Training College in Cheshire. When he qualifies, he returns to Carlisle looking for a teaching post. Because he is newly qualified Thomas has to take temporary teaching positions, moving from school to school. He buys an old car which he uses to take Jack, Dennis and Bob Raven, to the Lake District, dropping them off, for a couple of weeks camping. Jack remembers, "We spent a few of our days trying to dry out our wet clothing, or struggling, to cook something edible. Most of our time, we just enjoyed the sunshine, swimming in the lakes or climbing in the hills, it was quite an adventure for the three of us." It was great times like this that laid the foundations, for the lifelong friendship for these three young men.

When it came to holidays there were trips to Edinburgh with my parent, to see my Uncle George Mather and his wife Edith; he was the Member of Parliament (MP) for Leith, a very safe Labour seat. We all went canvassing with him, attended some of his election rallies, listening to him speak. Later in his career he would be appointed 'Keeper of the Keys' at Hollyrood House in Edinburgh, a most prestigious appointment. I remember one of our trips to Scotland, coinciding with a country fair at South Queensferry, there was fairground rides and side shows. Though for me, seeing the Forth Bridge for the first time was just fantastic, the fact that my Dad drives trains over it was even better. Edinburgh itself was special; we have a castle in Carlisle, but the one overlooking Princes Street, was incredible by comparison.

During this period at secondary school, Jack comes into the possession of a Morse code set. He and a pal, spend hours practicing with this set to finally master it. We also had the advantage that our school held a night class course in wireless telegraphy which we both promptly signed up for. This episode, set's the course for his future career in the R.A.F, though at that time he was not to know it.

Thomas having returned home enrolls at Carlisle's 'School of Art', in Tullie House to continue his love of painting. Here he meets Doris Wild, an accomplished artist in her own right, their friendship blossoms as they become engaged. Working locally in his temporary posts, Thomas applies for and obtains a teaching position, at a school in High Wickham near London, which prompts their decision to get married. The ceremony takes place in Carlisle, with Jack officiating as best man, his first introduction to public speaking.

Work and Play

In 1938 Jack reaches the age when he will be leaving school; he begins thinking about what he wants to do for a living. One opportunity that presents itself is a job in a gentleman's outfitters, (the rag trade) as Jack knows it. He applied for a position with, 'Prices the Tailors' a well-known and long-established company in the Carlisle area. The interview goes well with the offer of a job in the post, which he accepts. He now had to report to the shop to be measured for his business suit; a black jacket, waistcoat, pinstriped trousers, a white shirt with a wing collar. Standing at the front door, of the family home, booted and suited, for his new job. Jack remembers his mother standing there, on the doorstep, watched with pride as her young son prepares to set off, for his first day at work, "What a smart little fellow you are", she remarks. A tear in her eye is dismissed as windblown dust, which she wipes away, with the corner of her apron. Arriving early on his first day at work, Jack introduces himself to one of the assistants; he is taken to an office at the back of the shop. Here he meets George Russell the shop Manager, "Ask Mr Jones to step into my office", he tells the assistant. A young man slightly older than Jack duly arrives, introductions take place. "Take Mr Spark downstairs; show him his cupboard then inform him of his duties". A cupboard thinks Jack, my first day at work and I have my own cupboard. He follows Arnie to a door opposite the manager's office, then down the stairs to an enormous cellar below the shop. Arnie could hardly contain his delight, he finally has a replacement, he is on his way up, Jack is now the new junior. The cupboard Jack has inherited, contains a myriad of brushes, mops plus cleaning materials, his new world as a junior, in the Prices Empire. I recall my second day at work, down on my knees on a small mat, stoning the shop door step to whiten it. Then I had to polish the brass nameplate followed by the other door furniture. Twice a week or more, I would have to clean the shop windows inside then outside. How I came to hate the rain, which would mean having to do the windows again. This new world also required my attendance at evening classes, where I was taught, the art of, window dressing, salesmanship plus book keeping.

The working week at Prices shop was, Monday - Thursday 9.00am to 7.00pm, Friday 9.00am to 8.00pm and Saturday 9.00am to 9.00pm. A total of 55 hours each week; all for the princely sum of 7/6p (37.5p), however we did not work Sundays, unlike today's businesses. This late finish, on a Saturday, sees Jack and Arnie changing out of their work suits before popping into the local dance, straight from the shop. During the working week, Jack learns about the different types of cloth used for suiting, their individual strengths or weaknesses. There are also the style options to consider, single or double-breasted jackets, the types of lining to use, when to suggest a waistcoat. Each day, he would watch attentively the older men greet customer's, take them through the latest styles in suits followed by their cloth options. He watches, as one assistant measures a customer, with another, taking down the measurements, which would be repeated back, as a check. He listens as little code words, are exchanged between the two assistants, which would convey, a slight lean, in a customer's posture, or the natural droop, of one shoulder, or the other.

In a period when, being frugal was a virtue, Jack would spend the dark evenings, standing in the doorway of the shop. Here he could operate, the switches, which controlled the lights, in the shop window. When shoppers stopped, to look in the window, he would switch the brighter light on but when they walked away, he switched them off again. This doorway was in the center, of two large shop windows; on the left was Price's, on the right Burtons the tailors. Jack quickly realised that, when people stopped to look into Burton's window, if he gestured to them, from the doorway, they would walk into Price's, thinking it was the same shop.

This business acumen was not appreciated, by the manager of Burton's who many a time would be complaining to Jacks manager, "Your lads enticing my customers away again". Despite the complaints from the opposition, which would do Jacks career no harm at all, he continued to grow in confidence and ability. His friendship with the previous junior was cemented by the fact that both he and Arnie play the harmonica. Together they would practice in the cellar during lunch breaks to become proficient as a duo. But in the background, the world was moving into troubled times that would have a profound influence on many people's lives, including Jack's.

One day on the way home from work, Jack passes a second-hand shop, in Carlisle, where he spots, a "Roy Smeck" Banjo in the window. The price, three pounds fifteen shillings, (about £3.75p today) was more than he could afford, but into the shop he went to examine it. Later at home, after Dad had finished his evening meal, Jack broaches the chance of a loan to buy the Banjo. "How much" is dads Reply "That's almost a week's wage, you will have to save up for it". Returning to the shop next day and after a long discussion the shop keeper takes pity on Jack, he agrees Jack can pay a few shillings every week. Then when it is paid for, the Banjo will be his to take home. My Christmas and Birthday present money was used in payment; It took me a number of weeks to reach the total needed. But pay up Jack did and he took his Banjo home. This instrument would accompany Jack throughout the war, providing music during that period, but that was to be in his uncharted future. During this time, he expands his outside interests, he joins the Cumberland County Motor Club, attending motor cycle trials meetings in the area. This sport was popular in the Cumbrian hills, where Jack watched with admiration the skills of local riders, wishing he could be one of them. Then Jacks world comes apart; "On 3rd September 1939, War was declared", business confidence collapses. Everything from food to clothing became rationed. In response, Prices Tailors reduced the number of shops they own, including the people they employed. This results in both, Jack and Arnie losing their jobs in the June of 1940. The shock of becoming unemployed did not dent Jack's confidence, as he quickly found a job at No.14 Maintenance Unit. This new RAF depot's construction had started in 1937 to the north of Carlisle where it was growing quickly to become, the Main spare parts store. Eventually, it would become one of the largest, in the country, with six individual sites, within its boundary. The chief clerk there was Mr Sorrell who puts Jack to work in No.5 site, as a junior store man under a friendly Forman, called Charlie. Here Jack becomes busy with the processing, of the huge amount of equipment, arriving on a daily basis for Britain's war effort. The spares stored at the depot, were varied and numerous ranging from, barrage balloon cables, to parts for just about every aircraft, in the RAF's armoury. His intention is to sit out his time at 14 M.U. until he reaches the age when he can enlist as a wireless operator in the R.A.F.

At about this time, his brother leaves his job as a teacher to join the RAF, where he is accepted for pilot training. Because of the war, Carlisle has become busy with soldiers; where local theatres are being used to entertain them. Two volunteers to perform for the troops are Arnie and Jack; they had borrowed two accordion cases as props for the show. They march on stage to great applause, where they ceremonially opened the cases to remove only their small harmonicas. Their cheeky start to their performance is greatly appreciated by the audience, as was the standard of the music that followed. This early display, of Jacks comic side, he still retains, as an octogenarian (Old Git as he prefers to describes himself).

On the 4th April 1941 enlistment day arrives, Jack promptly joins up, passes the medical without any problem, he is raring to go. But when he presents his documents to the recruiting officer, they spot his job at 14 M.U. "Sorry young fella, you are in a reserved occupation, we can't take you", I was totally devastated. Arriving back at work, Jack tries to convince his boss that he wants to join the RAF stating there are plenty of people who can do his job. Sadly, Mr Sorrel is not to be moved, "You can't leave we need you here". Back in the depot, Jack is disgusted, he decides to take action; he arrives late for work every day then leaves early, to make his protest. His Forman, Charlie, takes him to one side, "Nice try Jack, but you won't get your cards that way, just accept it you're stuck here for the duration of the war". For a while he settles down, but is still thinking about, how to resolve the situation. Then one weekend, he is spurred on by his families news, Lillian his cousin has beat him to it by joined the Navy as a Wren. This is the final straw; Jack makes his mind up to take the bull by the horns.

Every day a truck leaves his depot, for the Headquarters of 14 M.U. So next morning Jack is a passenger aboard this truck, on his way to see the head of the whole site, Mr Moon. A long passage leads to an Oak door on which the gold writing reads, V.H. Moon O.B.E., Jack is anxious but determined, he leans forward to knock. Suddenly the door opens and Mr Sorrell is standing, in front of him, "Where the bloody hell do you think you're going Spark". "In there to see Mr Moon", came the reply, "You can't just go in to see Mr Moon", "Well, you ask him to see me, or I will go in to see him, unannounced". Shaken by Jack's manner, Sorrell re-enters the office he had just stepped out of.

A few minutes elapse, then a subdued Mr Sorrell reappears, he motions to Jack to enter the lions den. The room appears vast; in it is a large man with a pale complexion and dark hair, greying at the temples. He stands behind an equally large desk, so this was Mr Moon. Jack's bravado has started to wane as he steps forward, "Have a seat Mr Spark, what's the problem" asks Mr Moon. "Well sir, I have been trying to get my cards", "You want your cards" comes the reply. "Yes sir you see",……. Jack relates his attempt, to join up, as aircrew but fails as 14 M.U., is classed as a reserved occupation.

In silence Mr Moon listens, then when Jack has finished, he calls Mr Sorrell back into the room. In a calm voice he informs him, "Mr Spark, wants to join the R.A.F; I am not about to stand in his way, see that he gets his cards as once". Later back at our Depot Mr Sorrell is still upset at losing me. "You would have made a good stores man Spark, you could have progressed to a much more senior position given time. But if you are set on joining the RAF, then I will have to abide by Mr Moons decision, I only hope you don't regret it". There were times in my future, when his words would come back to haunt me. Usually when there were bullets flying about my ears, or I was looking death in the face. Having got my own way, It suddenly dawned on me, I would now have to tell my parents I was joining up. Back home mum was strangely quite at my news; she told me she was not happy, but understood why like my brother I was joining the RAF. Dad was away at the time, when he returned, he said he had been expecting my news, his only comment "Keep your head down".

RAF Training

On 13th May 1941 Jack enlists, retakes the very rigid medical which he thankfully passes. Now he has to go before the selection board, here he expresses his wish to be a wireless operator. In his favour is the signal training he received at school, "I never wanted to be anything else". At this point, his reserved occupation resurfaces; it causes a delay in his enlistment, until confirmation of his release from 14 MU is obtained. When this is clarified he is promptly sworn in to be accepted for aircrew training, I was now in the RAF. However there came a shock. I was being sent home on deferred service until such time as a place became available on the wireless course.

Sitting at home, three months went by before eventually, a letter came. Enclosed was a rail travel warrant for Jack to report to RAF Padgate in Cheshire for kitting out. I arrived at Padgate wearing my suit holding a small suitcase containing my pyjamas, underwear and tooth brush. This was all replaced with a uniform a service number; all of the paraphernalia, he will need in the RAF. I will never forget the way we were issued with our uniforms, the stores Corporal looked at me, walked away then came back with a bundle. "Next" he shouted and as far as he was concerned, I was served. To my surprise most of it was a close fit especially the hat, until the camp barber got to me. By the time he had finished cutting my hair, I had what we called at school, a three penny all off; it was almost a shave, my hat no longer fitted. Now it's time for our jabs, we were inoculated for every imaginable disease, plus a few that had not been invented yet. Some of the recruits took these jabs badly; a few fell over before they got to the Doc and were placed on a bed. Here a nurse completed these airmen's jabs, while they were still unconscious. Shortly after this we were paraded to be informed that our pay, for being an AC2 (Aircraftsman 2nd Class) would be 2/0p (10p) a day with a bonus of 6p (2.5p) a day, war pay.

Then on the 28th Nov with all the formalities completed, Jack is transferred from Padgate to a wireless operator's training unit, in Blackpool. As we stepped down from the train at Blackpool Station, (all three hundred of us) there was a welcoming party, headed by a Flight Sergeant. This immaculately dressed man, "The smartest man, I have ever seen" Jack remembers; lining up the new recruits he introduces himself. He promptly walks past the line of men, muttering, "What a bloody shower". The last lot were worse than the previous lot, but you are the worse I have ever seen. Now he said "My name is Bill, Bill the Ba**ard" and when you have been here five minutes you will know why".

Our squad was promptly marched into town and deposited at their respective billets, to be collected, the following morning at 07.00 hours sharp. A small hotel at 27, Reeds Ave with five single beds to a room is to be Jack and his new pal's home during their stay in Blackpool. Sure, enough next morning, a troop of service men, wends its way through the streets of Blackpool, growing in number at each stop. At the head of this squad, is Jack Spark the tallest of them all and a marker for the rest to form up on.

Their destination is the now defunct Billiard Hall, above Burtons the tailors, which has been converted into a wireless training room. Here they will be taught, the basics of wireless telegraphy, up to a speed of twelve words a minute. In addition to this training, there is "THE BULL" of saluting and marching, usually along the sea front. Marching seems to have been, the local mode of transport, for trainees. So, it comes as no surprise that rifle training, at "Cleveley", requires everyone to march there and back. Any opportunity these airmen had, to enjoy free time in Blackpool, was restricted by the money they have in their pockets. At twenty-eight shillings, a fortnight (£1.40) there was no possibility, that we young airmen would be painting the town red. A visit, to a local picture house, or maybe, nip into the nearby pub for a pint and game of darts, that was about their limit. One new oasis was provided by their host, at Reeds Ave, they are members of the local working men's club, with affiliation rights for their guests. This clubs cheaper beer and cigarettes proved just the right place, for these hard up young airmen.

Something that became apparent quickly was the distinction between uniforms; there was of course corporals, sergeants, flight sergeants etc. But there was even a difference between the AC2's, the aircrew W/ops forage caps had a white flash at the front. But the ground based W/ops did not have the flash, which led to a bit of a problem for the aircrew lads. The ground based W/ops quickly put it about to the local ladies that the white flash was a warning. It indicated the airman had an unspeakable disease. This meant we were completely shunned by the local girls until we found out the reason why. There was also other restriction to our nocturnal activities; we had to be back in our billet by 22.00 hrs. So, when we spent the evening at the Tower Ballroom, which ended at 23.00 hrs, we had a big problem. Getting back to the billet meant running the gauntlet of the Military Police, who patrolled the streets of Blackpool looking for curfew breakers. I remember coming back, very late from a night on the town and having taken a young lady home. Slowly wending my way back to Reeds Avenue, I suddenly spotted two MP's standing in a shop doorway, having a crafty smoke. The street was almost empty, with only three cars parked at the kerb side (unlike today) so I had to wait to see, what they would do next. When they decided to move on, I was horrified to see them turn toward me, I had to move fast.

Slipping into the front garden, of one of the houses, through the open gate, I laid down on the grass, close as I could, under the small hedge. Hardly daring to breath, I waited as the two MP's approached, listening as they grumbled about having to spend the cold night chasing servicemen. When they were a safe distance away, I sat up then watched until they disappeared round a corner, before I continued on my way. Next morning though I had to be up early, to give my uniform a good brushing down to remove any soil marks.

Our Flight sergeant Bill is one smart man who never misses a trick; he always see's everything, even when you think he is not looking. One incident highlights his all-seeing eye; we were marching from the billets, into town one morning. Christmas was approaching, so some of the shops had decorated their display windows. Because of his previous employment, in this industry, Jack gave one particular window a casual glance. From the rear of the column, booms the order, "Squad halt" and it does, just that. Standing in his normal position, at the head of the column, Jack thinks to himself, "Some poor buggers in bother", as Bills footsteps, come closer and closer. The hot breath on his neck tells Jack it's him as Bill enquires, "You like looking at shop windows Mr Spark", Jack splutters out "Yes Flight". Without further ado, Bills command, "Squad, left turn" is carried out and everyone is now facing the shops. "Well Mr Spark I want you to go over there, have a good look in the shop window, 'WE' will wait for you here". Jacks reply "There is no need thanks Flight" is ignored as Bill repeats his command to look in the shop windows. Realising there is nothing left for it; Jack walks over to the shop front. A quick glance at the window display, then he is back in line with the rest of the squad. Bill slowly walks up to Jack, here despite his height disadvantage he looks him squarely in the eye. "If you ever, he bawls"…*!*…. the rest will be remembered, by every serviceman who wore a uniform, so needs no further explanation here. New Year 1941 was my first ever away from home; as usual I was almost skint. Payday was a week away, but new years eve was tonight; eventually I ventured out with another skint W/op to the local working men's club about nine o'clock.

Between us we had enough for a couple of half pint's each to drink very slowly to reach midnight. As we sat chatting happily with the locals a few of the older men came over to ask how we were doing on our training.

These hard-working Lancashire lads immediately recognised our situation, "You lads waiting for pay day", we both nodded. "Well then young fella's have one on us, as two pints of bitter were put down in front of us". We thanked them profusely, but they replied "We have lads in the forces, let's hope one of your family is buying one of ours a pint somewhere". What a New Year that was, the generosity of these ordinary working men left a lasting impression. Blackpool's famous Tower had an enormous ballroom below it, plus a circus, though I don't think the circus was open during the war. The ballroom on dance night was something to behold, the room was packed with servicemen, "On the pull" as they say today. I remember the fog of cigarette smoke hanging over the crowd of dancers but the sound of a big band playing was unforgettable.

Some of the young men on the course found it hard to take the discipline, but at the end of training we had to accept and act on an order without question. It is this strict discipline that can save our lives, when the bullets start to fly. Sitting in our billets on an evening, we start to notice some of our fellow recruits have become very quiet. Homesickness can affect anyone, you can be as brave or as tough as the next man, but you can still be homesick. One lad in our group suffered this way, he was an only child who had never left home before, so we all rallied round him to keep his spirits up. Or should I say we kept the spirits down him, we showed him everything he had been missing. By the time we left Blackpool, he had matured considerably and was enjoying his new found freedom. Though I often wondered what his mum thought about the changes in her baby boy, on his next home leave.

Standing six foot three (1.91M) Jacks height makes him a target for instructors, one day during training for unarmed combat he suffers. The instructor spots him immediately, "Step out here lofty"; today you are to learn how to disarm a sentry. Handing him a rifle he pronounces, "I will come at you from behind and you must defend yourself when I touch you". Standing tensed waiting for that first touch Jack only feels the short flight through the air then the crash as he lands on his back. Now barks the instructor, just in case, everyone did not see what happened, I will demonstrate it once again. Determined to give a better account of himself this time, Jack still fly's though the air landing with a thud, "But I did feel him grab me that time".

Thinking back though, you don't get much call for disarming sentries, at twenty-five thousand feet. Having reached the required wireless standard, the squad now transfers on the 1st April 1942, to RAF Yatesbury, for advanced training. Here our basic Morse output will be improved, to a minimum level of eighteen words per minute. Arriving at the main gate, I remember the weather was foul, the wind was blowing a gale and the place looked like a POW camp. But we were there to be trained to do a job, so the sooner we completed it, the sooner we could move on.

During his time in wireless training, Jack remembers one or two occasions, when the intense concentration of the course, comes to a crisis for some individuals. A few operators, found the stream of Morse dots and dashes, just too much for them to take in. Their reaction displays itself, when an operator would stand up, remove his headphones then start to talk incoherently. Instructors quickly lead the confused operator away, for a little quite time in another room. Here he will recover his grasp on reality then continue another day, to become a competent operator. In reality not all operators did make the grade, the squad of thirty-eight I started out with, was whittled down to twenty-six by the end of the course. Being a competent wireless operator was not only the ability to send and receive Morse code, there was also the fault finding. Once in the air you can't just call a wireless technician to fix your duff set, you have to find the fault then rectify it yourself. In the aircraft we carried spare valves but our ability to fix sets was limited once you left the ground. At the end of June we were gathered together, for our official squad photo. We were all stood in the road outside the photographer's studio, with Corporal Adams in the center with the street houses as a backdrop. While we were at the studio, a number of us took the opportunity to have individual portraits taken, to send home to our families.

You're In the Army Now

In July 1942 as a qualified Wireless Operator, Jacks expectation is to be posted to an RAF Squadron then go on Op's. He was therefore very surprised to be assigned, to the British Army at Bulford Camp on the south of Salisbury Plain. The Army's Royal Corp of Signals, had posted a number of its wireless operators to fight overseas, this had left them short at home. Here at Bulford, Jack and the other RAF operators who were on loan, had to assist on army exercises in the area. It was here at Bulford, I noticed a change in my appreciation of being a wireless operator, listening to an incoming message one day. When I handed the message to an army operator, I mentioned that I thought the message was from a particular operator I knew. He then complemented me by saying, "Once you start recognising a particular Morse hand, you are becoming accomplished". Because of their unusual situation, the RAF lads were excused army parades and marching. However, one morning, an army sergeant appears in our billet with Enfield rifles, which he proceeded to hand out. Pleading ignorance we claimed, never to have had rifle training, these trained W/Op's pulled a flanker on this sergeant. One lad, pulls the bolt out of his Enfield, proclaiming, "Sergeant this one's broken"; "Have you lot never used a rifle" asks the sergeant, "No sir, is the reply but they're smashing aren't they, when do we get our bullets". The sergeant went pale; the rifles went back to the Armoury and the RAF lads chalked up a victory. Sadly, this ruse backfires, when they were told to report, for rifle training, on the army ranges. There additional work on the ranges, following so soon, after their training in Blackpool, resulted in a shock for the army. The final order for the rifle shooting course found the first three places, being filled by the RAF W/Op's. (Practice makes perfect). Because they were RAF, they had to put up with the usual taunts of the army lads in the Naffi or the Mess. "Here come the Brylcream boys, get the mirrors out, so they can comb their hair", was just one, of the more polite comments, they endured. Then one night, as they arrived in the mess, one comment proves one too many, for a slightly built Scot's RAF W/Op. Climbing onto a table he proclaims, "You Para boys think you're so dammed special, well your not do you hear".

Jack is by this time pulling at the corner of his jacket, "Sit down man, you're going to get us all killed", but the young Scot continues undeterred. "Find the hardest man you've got, I'll fight him here and now; come on then, or are you all as full of wind as your chutes". A deathly silence falls over the room, then a large Paratrooper steps forward, walking up to the small RAF airman. "You're not short of guts Jock, I'd like to buy you a drink" he proclaims, "If you don't mind drinking with a windy Para". In that brief moment, the tension dissipates, the airmen are treated more as 'Comrades in arms' than interlopers from another planet. This change in attitude however, did not extend to the American Army, when the Brits came into contact with them, in Salisbury. Their big bucks, draws the ladies to them like bees to honey with the poorly paid Brits, being left in the cold by the femme fatale in the area. Therefore, when the two forces come together it sometimes ends, in both sides discussing things with knuckles, leaving the Red Caps caught in the middle. Subsequently the town was divided, with different evenings being designated as, 'Brit' or 'Yank' nights to keep them apart.

While at Bulford Jack finds, because of his previous school boxing experience he has been selected, to represent the camp in a tournament. At first, he is successful winning the first bout on points, the second by a knock out, but then he is drawn unknowingly against an ex professional. Stepping into the ring to the cheers of the RAF contingent, the referee introduces him to his opponent; they touch gloves then Jack wakes up in the dressing room. I still don't remember much about it, but someone gave me two black eyes; it also put a finish to any aspirations I had of a career as a pugilist. This boxing tournament came at the end of 1942 Jack recalls a few days later spending New Years Eve on guard duty. With his fellow guards, he celebrated the arrival of 1943 with a hot mug of tea and a biscuit, wondering what the New Year would bring. His answer comes in February 1943; as aircrew losses grow the RAF have their own need of the Wireless Op's, who are recalled back to their own service. Their secondment to the Army is over they are transferring to RAF Bridgnorth, in Shropshire.

Return to the Fold

The Severn Valley Railway wound its way through the Shropshire countryside, before bringing us to Bridgnorth Station. Here we were met by an N.C.O. with a booming voice, who was quick to remind the assembled company, they are the lowest of the low. We are all bundle into the back of a Bedford Lorry with the usual uncomfortable slatted wood seats, then driven to the camp at Stanmore Village. We are some three miles to the East of Bridgnorth.

At No.18 Initial Training Wing, we take a refresher training course, to re-acquaint us with RAF standards and of course to march. One morning we are assembled on the parade ground for another session of 'BULL'; standing at ease waiting for the officers to appear, it starts to rain. After ten minutes, the officers have not come out onto the parade ground, the rain becomes heavy. Spontaneously, someone in the ranks starts to sing, "Why are we waiting" this lone voice is joined by others, but the officers still do not appear as the rain becomes torrential. It was then the squad break ranks we scatter en-mass to their billets, to dry off. Jack recalls, this was the nearest thing to a mutiny, he had ever seen; "Why we weren't court marshalled, I still don't know". My first off duty trip into Bridgnorth was an eye opener, it was actually two towns. There is high town and low town with a generous selection of pubs in both. Dancing was also well provided for with both 'The Palace Ballroom' and the 'Rose Marie Dance Hall'. Drinking in the Pubs was also an unusual experience, Low town Pubs closed at Ten O'clock (22:00 hrs). But High Town Pubs closed at Ten Thirty (22:30 hrs) this resulted in the usual rush, up town when time was called in the Low Town. There was also the rush back to camp to report to the main gate, as passes expire at midnight. After midnight you would have to climb over the hedge at the back of the camp to avoid being in trouble. For those airmen with a more Methodist upbringing Bridgnorth had its own YMCA. Here to be truthful a good sing song could be found, along with a cheap cup of tea plus a biscuit.

Off camp entertainment for airmen usually means the trip into Bridgnorth for dancing, or a bit of female company. One such night ends with Jack and two other airmen, walking back to camp.

When we were half way home, the volume of beer that had been drunk necessitated a stop. Finding a break in a hedge, the trio stepped off the road into the field; "Why we did I don't know" remembers Jack. "It was pitch black dark we were miles from anywhere, on a lonely country road with no traffic". Then doing what comes naturally behind the hedge, they are surprised by a torch, shining out of the darkness. "Put that light out, there's a war on" shouts one airman, as a war reserve policeman steps forward, who promptly books all three for a public nuisance. Preparing to fight for their country, these young men still have to appear in Bridgnorth

27

Magistrates Court to answer the summons. On 29th March 43 they are each fined £2.00, by the most miserable looking corpses behind a bench, I have ever seen. This offence will remain, on all three airman's records, for the rest of their air force careers, because of this petty jobs-worth. That bobby did not realise, just how lucky he was that night, many another group would have put his lights out, in quite another way.

Then in April 43 Jack is transferred back to the RAF's No.2 Radio School at Yatesbury. Here for the first time, we were taught how to use the Aldis lamp. This lamp was like a torch, but it's very narrow beam could be flashed on and off to send Morse over reasonable distances. It was more use in making contact with Navy ships from the air as it could not be picked up by the enemy as radio signals could be. Yatesbury was also our first taste of flying, with the stations De-Havilland Dominie or the Percival Proctor aircraft. Part of this training course is to send or receive signals in the air, with the accompanying noise and movement of the aircraft. I remember the Proctor was a small single engine aircraft which had a very cramped cockpit, with all the Radio Gear fitted, so different from the classroom. The pilot, Flt Sgt Keating had to fly a cross country route while I used the D/F loop to locate ground signals with the aircraft bobbing about all the time. Then it was time for F/O Wiltshire to check us out in the Dominie which was a different kettle of fish, six trainees an instructor plus the pilot. Under Sgt Browns eagle eye, each trainee would take a turn at using the single wireless set, while the pilot flew a cross country route. We had to be checked out on frequency changes along with the Direction Finding Loop procedure (Q codes). It was this sort of training that reveals the trainee's, who were afflicted by air sickness.

Sitting in an aircraft looking out of the window, while it bobs up and down is often not a problem. However, when you have to concentrate on an incoming signal then write it down on a pad, the movement can become quite disorientating. If aircrew suffer with severe airsickness, they can be removed from flying to be placed on ground duties only. Fortunately, this is not something that affects Jack; in early June 1943 he completes the course, to receiving his much prized Sparks badge.

He now has thirteen and a half daylight flying hours in his logbook, seven and a half in the Dominie with another six in the Proctor. As the training at Bridgnorth comes to an end, Jack is transferred, to No.7 Air Gunnery School Stormy Down on 30th June 43. Arriving in the billet, I find myself next to another W/op called Reg Tailby from Sussex. We sit chatting about our homes and families; Reg was married to Moira with a one year old son Ian. I said I had not taken the plunge yet but my brother Thomas who has had a daughter Corel about the same age as his son. It's nice to talk about our families; it reminds us of why we are here. Next day it's back to the course; the range itself is at Margam, we were there until the 20th July, it rained every day but one. The gunnery area was amongst the sand dunes, comprising a narrow gauge rail track set in a large oval. A trolley ran round this track with a mast rising from it, a large model of an enemy aircraft was mounted on the top. Pupils sat in a powered gun turret positioned to one side of the track. We had to follow then fire at the moving aircraft, allowing for changing position and speed. Some of the training took place at night, to familiarise us with firing tracer rounds, it also makes dismantling the gun to clear blockages, more difficult.

The one day off we were allocated during training saw the rain stop; the sun came out, so we all headed for the coast at Porthcawl. Here another trainee, Smithy and I met up with a couple of young ladies, from the local munitions factory. They decided to show us round the places of interest, I remember the Pavilion and Promenade with a long street of shops. Eventually we all ended up in a rather posh looking café; where the girls ordered tea, sandwiches with cakes for the four of us. Smithy and I started to become worried, we could only muster about ten bob (50p) between us, but when the bill arrived the girls snatched it away. No matter how hard we protested, they refused to let us pay. These ladies declared they were making good wages in the factory, while we were risking our lives, I felt very humbled.

Next day back at the camp the rain started again, but so did the training, water dripping into the turret becomes an added distraction when you were taking aim. My logbook shows my score for the gunnery course was 83.25%, but how they arrived at this figure I have no idea. The gunnery leaders note in my logbook, described me as a hard working pupil, with a good working knowledge of the subject. Fortunately, I was never called upon to fire a single round during the rest of my RAF career, so I never got to put my training to any use at all. Thankfully, having reached the required standard, we passed out as Air Gunners, and are now transferred to No.3 (Observers) Advanced Flying Unit, at Bobbington/Halfpenny Green. Here in July 43, I was informed of my promotion, to temporary Sergeant with a small increase in pay. At this unit we flew all of our exercises, in the Avro Anson aircraft; there were about a dozen of them on the base. This well liked aeroplane had windows, down both sides of the fuselage which made it light, draughty and very cold. There was also its infamous undercarriage which had to be manually retracted, by cranking a handle in the cockpit. It required 140 turns to retract the wheels, then another 140 turns to put them down again. The wireless part of the course was under the watchful eye of Sgt Leech, who checks everyone out on air operation of the D.F loop, QDM3 fixes. This was followed by a series of navigational exercises, with the wireless operator working with the navigator. While the Navigator plotted his route, I used signals from known transmitting stations, to check our position using the D.F. equipment. Some of these cross countries also included cine camera recording, of our practice bombing runs.

The observer's part of the course involved being shown silhouettes of aircraft of all nationalities. We were expected to be able to identify them, having been shown an individual card for only a few seconds. By the end of the course, I have a total of 34 Hours in my log book, which includes 9 hours of night flying. Then on the 16th August 1943, the good news comes through, I am being transferred to an Operational Training Unit. I am one step closer to going to war.

O.T.U.'s 17/08/43 – 14/11/43

The unit I have been assigned to is, No.81 O.T.U. at Tilstock in Shropshire equipped with Anson twin engine trainers. I only stayed for four days making three flights with Flt/Lt Main-Smith, all of them navigational exercises. This added another 9 flying hours to my log books which included 3 hours night flying. Once again we are on the move, when No.81 OTU is transfers to Sleap, which was previously a satellite of Tilstock, but is now the primary airfield.

Our aircraft are also being changed, gone are the Anson's to be replaced by the Armstrong Whitworth Whitley a twin engine Bomber. My logbook now has the grand total of 32 hour's daylight plus 12 hour's night flying. Arriving at Sleap, I was allocated a billet and unpacked my kit, there were other aircrew arriving doing the same. Later we all sloped of to the village pub for a pint; here I met up with a Flight Sergeant pilot who had also just arrived at Sleap. We shared a few beers chatted about our training, then at closing time we walked back to camp together. This encounter was to be one of the most fortunate meetings of my RAF service. Next morning, we are all assembled together in a hanger, here we are left to form up into five men crews. As my first priority is to find a pilot, I start looking for people with wings on their uniform.

One man catches my eye; it's the older looking flight sergeant from the pub, 'Fred Brownings'. I approached this pilot, introduced myself then ask if he has a wireless operator, "I have now" is Fred's answer; Jack has become part of a crew. Standing with Fred is 'Norman Barker' a Bomb Aimer from Canada with his fellow country man 'Ron Walker' the Navigator, Jacks new crewmates. Introductions and handshakes are followed by talk of training, home then what's the gen on this O.T.U. I immediately spotted that both of these Canadians were commissioned, they confirmed that all their country men were assigned Officers. This meant that they had to eat in a different Mess, sleeping in separate billets which they thought was a bit 'Us and them'. But rules are rules, though as we did not spend all our time on camp, it was not too much of a bind. Other airmen approach Fred, only to be turned away, because the crew position had been filled.

The last vacant station air gunner, is finally taken by a 19 year old young man, 'Bob Thomas'. Fred Brownings now has a full compliment. New crews once formed up tended to stick together for nights out, just as any normal family would do, but within these families are the pre-existing groups. These were the trade families who had been through training together; they knew each other's abilities. They would still keep in touch, helping to resolve any problems within their own group, during the forthcoming training.

The five man crew we had formed are as follows

Fred Brownings Flt/Sgt Pilot, from Brighton England
Ron Walker, Plt/Off Navigator from Toronto Canada
Norman Barker, Plt/Off Bomb Aimer from Toronto, Canada
Jack Spark, Sgt Wireless Operator from Carlisle, England.
Ronald (Bob) Thomas, Sgt Rear Gunner from Chippenham, Wiltshire.

Once crewing up had been complete, the job of welding the crew into a fighting unit starts, with Fred instilling the need for discipline in the air. No unnecessary use of the intercom, a need for clear warnings of fighter attacks from the gunners; our skipper knows what he wants. Flying begins with the twin engine Whitley; this already obsolete aircraft is a safe training option, but lacks the glamour of four engines. The Whitley aircraft is easily identified from miles away, by its characteristic nose down flying attitude; like a bloodhound, sniffing the ground. When Fred Brownings is asked about the Whitley by Jack, his response is, "It's like flying a ruddy warehouse". I remember being tall I banged my head, on every fuselage rib when I walked down the Whitley, to my radio position. Bob also commented that, he was sat higher in his rear turret, than every other crew member once in the air. This was due to the aircrafts unusual flying attitude. My location, in the Whitley, was directly behind the pilot facing forward, with Ron the Navigator, facing the rear, behind and below my position. After a long day's training the crew liked to find a pub to relax with a drink to continue that process of bonding, necessary for survival in the air.

Everyone has his own personality, but we have to learn to mix with the others to form into a single unit. The very first night our crew spent in the billet, is embedded on Jacks memory; we were unpacking our kitbags getting ready for bedding down. There was general chit chat going on from airmen sprawled on beds when, Bob Thomas our young air gunner stops, he kneels at the foot of his bed. Here he spends a few minutes praying; a hush fell over the room, with the rest of the airmen waiting for him to finish. When he does, he stood up and climbed into bed; nothing was said by his crewmates, if this was something Bob did, his beliefs would be respected. The sight of him at his nightly prayers brings a certain comfort to the rest of his crew, who became very protective towards young Bob Thomas.

Each morning, the crew would be preparing for the day, washing and shaving in the ablutions block, with a little horseplay thrown in. While these young men were either of scrawny or brawny, it was noticeable that Fred Brownings was particularly muscular. He had a broad pair of shoulders with very well developed arms; his hands were so big you could shovel snow with them. Before the war he had been a member of an offshore rowing team, which had competed successfully in coastal rowing competitions. At that time it did not seem important, but in our future it would be a life saver for the crew. Our daylight flying in the Whitley started on the 11th Sept 43, with three days of doing circuits and bumps. The instructors were Pilot officer Knight or Flying officer White, who were keeping a watching eye on Fred's progress at the controls. This was followed by a four hour cross country, then a high level bombing exercise to test the Navigator, Wireless Operator and Bomb Aimer.

During the bomb run the control of the aircraft is in the hands of the bomb aimer, looking through the bomb sight he calls course corrections to the pilot. Left, Left a bit, Right, Steady, is the sort of commands the pilot has to follow, to ensure the bombs to be dropped in the right place. This particular night we had completed a number of runs on a practice target and were about to do another. Running up to the target again, Norman's calm voice on the intercom is giving Fred our pilot instructions. "Left a bit, Left a bit, Steady, Right a bit, Steady, Steady, **Back a bit"**. This last instruction is heard in silence, before Fred's laughter can be heard over the intercom. This spontaneous moment was something we would all laugh about on occasions in our future dark days.

Later we flew a series of high and low level bombing exercises, to the Fenns Moss range including live air to air firing. On a few occasions Bob our rear gunner, had to use a cine camera gun to check on the accuracy of his efforts. Then on the 26th Sept the night flying started, with seven nights of nothing but circuit and landings. Again the instructors were, P/O Knight, P/O White and F/O Hewitt, to ensure we did not damage the RAF's valuable antique aeroplane. It's Tuesday 19th Oct my twenty first birthday, but a pint in the mess with my crew mates is the only celebration we have. There was the occasional daylight gunnery exercise thrown in to check on Bob's progress then, on the 6th November the course comes to an end. We are being transferred to 1656 HCU. at Lindholme near Doncaster, to fly the Halifax, our first four engine Bomber. My logbook now has a grand total, of 77 hours daylight plus 51 hours night flying. As the course ends, we are given eight days leave, after which we will have to report to Lindholme.

Settling in at home, Dad is keen to hear how things are going, I think he is a little surprised to hear I am still in training. Mum though is relieved to find I am not risking my life over Germany. She is concerned for me, as the local papers are regularly reporting losses, of RAF aircrew from the Carlisle area. I also find that Dennis, my old school mate had called to see my mum, when he was home last week on leave. He asked how I was and told her he was flying with coastal command, at Thornaby in North Yorkshire. She in return mentioned I was still in training at an O.T.U. It was nice to hear about how my old pal was and that he had taken the time to visit my family. It's good to be home even if it's only for a week. Simple things like walking into town, or sitting on a bench at Dads allotment, watching him tending his vegetable patch are so refreshingly normal. I would like to get out of my uniform for a change to go into town, but Mum won't hear of it. She wants to show me off, to her friends and neighbours in my uniform, I dutifully accede to her wishes. Though as I walk about in town in uniform, people I have not seen for a while, stop me to chat. They often talk about family who are also in the RAF asking if I have come across them. Strangely one of the first questions they ask is "When do you go back", I am sure every service man will remember that remark. Then all too soon my leave is over, I head to the station for the long train trip to RAF Lindholme.

1656 H.C.U. 14/11/43 – 05/02/44 Lindholme
Arriving at RAF Lindholme on the 14th November Fred Brownings takes part in another crewing session, to bring our compliment to seven men. The four engines of the Halifax require the addition of a flight engineer, plus a second air gunner for the mid upper gun turret. The two new bods Fred has picked are.

Arthur Richardson. Flt/Sgt. Flight Engineer from Penrith, Cumbria.
Ken Smart. Sgt. Mid Upper Gunner from Mitcham, Surrey.

Settling in at the HCU, the last thing on anyone's mind is evader practice, but that is what's about to take place. The occasion Jack remembers clearly was when about thirty aircrew, were gathered together in uniform with flying suit's over the top. In the ops room they were made to empty their pockets of absolutely everything, then they were informed of their fate. They will be transported in closed trucks in the dark, to be dropped in one's or two's, at undisclosed locations. It is their task to return undetected back to base, by any means available to them as soon as possible. However, the local police, home guard and the army had been informed we were out there, they would be looking for us. Off into the darkness we went, then after what seemed an awfully long time, the truck starts to unload. Airmen are being littered onto the country bye ways at random. When Jacks turn comes to be unloaded, he recalls being accompanied by another airman. Standing there in the narrow lane with the truck disappearing into the night, he remembers the feeling of, where on earth do we go from here.

Initially they set off in the direction the truck had come from, in the hope of finding somewhere recognisable, but the lack of signposts put paid to that. The stars provided a North point, but north of where; a local high point we found provided just a vista of a dark landscape.

Gone is the pre-war glow from the large towns, which would have provided some direction. At the next crossroads Jacks companion disappears in the opposite direction, leaving him to tread his own course. Another few hours of trudging the lanes, a village looms out of the darkness but reveals nothing of any help.

Weary and foot sore he sits on a grass verge to take stock; a police station opposite brings back the officers instructions, "If you are completely lost, report to the police". Knocking on the door of the station, a head appears at an upstairs window in a broad Yorkshire accent he is asked "What's thee want lad", "I've come to give myself up" is Jacks reply. "Gi thee sell up, why what's tha done". Clearly everyone is not aware of tonight's exercise; the bobby now standing at the open front door, beckons Jack in to explain his predicament. A phone call produces transport back to the airfield; here he mixes with those who have successfully completed the task. He listens to their stories, lifts hitched in trucks, unsecured bikes borrowed from unsuspecting owners. One group had come together on the road where they meet up with other airmen along the way. Finding they were north of the Humber River they head upstream looking for a bridge. Unfortunately, when they find one, the home guard are in place to protect it, so how to get over was the question. The group now numbering about a dozen airmen promptly took off their flying suits, tucking them under their arms they formed up into a column. Marching up to the bridge with its home guard sentries, with a smart salute they cross unchallenged, to head back to the airfield they had set out from.

The Halifax's we are to train on are tour retired aircraft, which to put it bluntly are clapped out old crates. They also have a reputation for being vicious, unforgiving aircraft which need to be flown carefully, if you want to stay alive. Their only saving grace is they will not be required to carry a bomb load, or a large fuel load, which will help take the strain off the tired engines. We are first expected to become accustomed to this new steed on the ground; with the extra complications of a large four engine aircraft. There are the location of the escape hatches, fire extinguishers, dingy placement plus how to use it. My position, in the nose, with Norman the bomb aimer, means that we are the first out, in an emergency. When the instructors are happy, we know what we are doing on the ground, the flying will commence. Today is Boxing Day but we are about to start flying in the Halifax, our instructor is Pilot Officer Clark. We begin with circuit and bumps for two days, then its straight in at the deep end with three engine flying including landings, still under instruction. Fred quickly takes to the Halibag so we are left to spend the next day, doing solo circuits and landings, without the instructor. This is followed by a check on Fred's progress, by Pilot Officer Gibb who continues, with the three engine instruction. There is now a navigation exercise to complete, followed by a five hour cross country trip.

As a final test for Fred and Arthur our flight engineer, we have to complete a session of flying on two engines. This also entails Arthur practicing fuel transfers between tanks to simulate battle damage on operational flying. The day time flying comes to an end so we start all over again, with night flying circuit and bumps, under Pilot Officer Banks watchful eye. As our training is going well, we are tasked to do a "Bullseye" on London, followed by another five hour cross country. Our final trip; is a one hour fighter affiliation flight, after which we are told of our transfer to No1 Lancaster finishing school, still at Lindholme. As a crew we were really coming together as a unit, I remember it was about this time at O.T.U. someone suggested a proper crew photo. So, one weekend we all troop into Doncaster, hair combed uniforms brushed all spruced up, to a Photo Studio to have the job done right. When they were printed, they were promptly sent off to our families back home. As the weeks pass our crew becomes more of a team, even though the two Canadian members, as Officers were separated from the NCO's.

One surprise for our crew came at Christmas, when the two Canadians each received large parcels, from home. These boxes were stuffed full with a selection of foods, not seen in Britain since the start of the war. Without hesitation the contents were shared, among the rest of the crew, a gesture that was greatly appreciated by them. There were tins of fruit, bags of nuts, boxes of chocolates plus tins of maple syrup. This was spread on slices of bread or toast; oh it was lovely, we were like kids again, pigging out on all of these treats. The festive season allowed us to let off a bit of steam; Doncaster the nearest town was the place to do it, there are plenty of pubs and dance halls. One of the favourite places to dance was called the 'Sweat Box' because Its ceiling was very low with a very crowded dance floor. In the thick of it I asked one young girl up to dance; we had a couple of Waltz's, then as we started the third, she suddenly went limp. It was so hot she had just passed out, in my arms in the middle of the floor. It was so crowded; I had to wait for the end of the dance before I could carry her to a seat, before taking her into the fresh air. My crew mates were all joking about what I had done to her to make her faint, whatever I said only made their comments worse. Being six foot three, I always had trouble finding a dance partner tall enough to enjoy dancing with. Then one night I spotted this young lady looking a bit sad, she was lounging in a chair behind a long table, talking to her friends. So, I went up to ask her to dance what a shock I was in for, when she stood up she was three inches taller than I was, even in her flat shoes. I could now see why she had not been asked to dance. Thankfully she was a good dancer so I had a great time, plus nobody else came to ask her to dance, I had her all to myself. It also meant I didn't need to break my back bending over when I kissed her goodnight either.

Back at Lindholme I remember catching sight of my first Lancaster close up, its size was impressive. The Wellington was much smaller than the Halifax which to me always looked a little agricultural. By comparison with the Whitley's or Wellingtons, the Lancaster was a huge aircraft. But the main impression was of a machine designed, to do a job and do it well. Our pilot Fred takes to the Lancaster, like the veritable duck to water, "Only a bird fly's better", was one of his comments. In training Fred Brownings quickly masters, all aspects of flying this new steed save one, "Landing". No matter how hard he tries, he just cannot put the aircraft down, smoothly. Time after time, there would be rebounds, before the wheels touched the runway to stay there. We used to pull his leg, on how many it would be; three or four bounces or maybe one for each crew member. Jack recalls a night time cross country trip; we were flying over the Welsh Hills, with the weather deteriorating. Fred instructs me to report the worsening conditions back to Base, warning other crews who may be coming into the area. I had just sent the message, when Ron the Navigators hand appears from under the curtain, holding a slip of paper with the one word "FIX" on it. Jack realises he must be lost so he proceeds to request a fix. As there is a lot of traffic on the airways, he receives a wait signal; after a few minutes, another note appears from under the curtain, in large letters is '"FIX". A further attempt to obtain a fix, results in the wait signal again, finally Ron's head appears, round the curtain, "Where's my fix, we're lost". "If it's urgent I can request a priority fix", says Jack, knowing it took a lot for Ron to admit he was lost, "Just do It" pleads the Nav. The Lancaster, at this point, emerges from cloud, Fred reports, the lights of a town ahead, in the distance. Ron's fix is obtained which from the heading we are flying, identifies the lights as Ireland. Then a recall signal is received; all aircraft are to return to Base. Ron now with his fix, gives Fred a new heading that brings them back, eventually over Lindholme. Next day training on the Lancaster continues when Fred is called to see the C.O. we are being transferred to 103 Squadron at Elsham Wolds; an Operation unit at last.

George Silva Mendocino California U.S.A

George Silva was born on the 15th September 1920 at 31, Ukiah Street, Mendocino a small fishing and lumber town, 150 miles North of San Francisco. His father Hercules was Portuguese, born in the Azores while Mum Laura was born in California. "Our family was a large one I had five brothers and four sisters". In the 1940 Census 19 year old George is living at home with his parents plus five younger brothers. There was Edward 13, Robert 11, Joseph 7, Laurence 4 and David 2. This Census also shows they owned the family home which was valued in 1940 at some $600. My early education was in the local school which was an easy going sort of learning. Later I attended the high school; to finance this I worked in the Saw Mill of the logging camp. We all had jobs of one sort or another, to help support the family. During the hard times of the 1930's Dad would supplement our food by growing what we could at home. Our other means of providing extra food was fishing on the Big River to the south of the town. None of my brothers or I liked to go fishing, as it meant we had to sit in the back of the boat, while dad rowed slowly up or down river. Inevitably it was me, that ended up with the job of fishing with Dad. So it was up to me to look out for half sunken logs or obstructions floating down stream toward us. Dad would sit facing me to watch the two fishing pole lines we trailed behind the boat waiting for the fish to bite. As a family we were brought up to stand on our own two feet, nobody was owed a living. In any spare time we had, we would help dad to build row boats, for anyone who had the lumber or the cash to pay for us to make one. Sadly, when dad could no longer fish, or row the boat on the river, I began to miss those Saturday's that I had tried to avoid.

After graduating from high school, I worked at the lumber yard for a while, before moving to Oakland across the bay from San Francisco for a better job. This new job was in a Naval Shipyard, working on submarines and involved fitting the batteries. These battery packs weighed some 1200lbs each, with the space to work in, very restricted and hot. So when the Japanese attacked Pearl Harbour and war was declared, I joined the Air Force right away. Unfortunately, it would be 14th December 1942 before I was accepted into the air force; such was the volume of people volunteering to fight. The country had not only to cope with all these recruits; they had to decide who would fight in the Pacific war or fight in Europe. Even then it was the 15th February 1943 before I was actually called to duty.

37

George Silva had enlisted in the US Air Force, as he thought they did not do much marching. On 14th December 1942 I boarded a bus going to the Presidio of Monterey to join the United States Army Air Force. On arrival we were taken to a barracks and shown our bunks. We were told that we would be going to several meetings in the next days or so. These would relate to us some of the things we would be doing, or learning to do that we would be different, from what we did in civilian life. The following day we would be taken down to the clothing shed, to be issued with our uniforms. We were given the choice of sending our civilian clothing we were wearing on enlistment back home, or to donate them to a goodwill box. It would be our choice but it had to be done quickly. I wore a pair of Oxfords that I liked very much, so as soon as we were issued our uniforms, I boxed up my shoes to send them home. Getting our uniforms was quite an experience; we formed a line then started down the clothing racks. The first man gave each of us two pairs of underwear, two white T-shirts, two pairs of socks, two pairs of slacks, one a pair of OD plus a pair of khaki pants. The OD called Olive drab were for dress up, the khaki pants were mostly for summer wear. Last were the shoes, one pair were dress shoes with the other for everyday use, if you were lucky, they were the correct size for your feet. I have to say that I was fortunate to get shoes that fit me very comfortably.

Next, we had classes on military protocol, as to the way we had to greet all officers without exception. We were informed that should we miss saluting an officer, he would stop us then ask why we had not shown him the proper courtesy. Here for the first time we came into contact with a Sergeant Major. This man seemed to believe that all recruits were hard of hearing, and needed to be shouted at otherwise they would not understand him. He also had to totally intimidate us, so that when he issued an order, it was carried out instantly no matter what. After we had absorbed that information, we had a couple of days before we started to learn how to do Marching Cadence. That was hup, one, two, three, four. There are many manoeuvres to learn, and we must always keep in step. It was strange how some men found marching very difficult, but after hours of practice, we learned. The next program was how to fold our clothes then store them properly in a foot locker that stood at the end of our bed. It had to be done in a precise manner, to not only reserve space for other clothing, but to keep our clothing fresh and un-wrinkled.

Finally, after the protocol of marching, clothing disciplines etc, they gave us exercises after roll call every day, now we are ready for our next assignment. After a few more days of training, I was told that I was shipping out, but not where I was going. Boarding a bus, I found that we were heading to Basic Training Unit number eight in Fresno California. Formerly a Japanese Internment camp, it had become a medical examining facility for the Air Force. It was still very much a military unit, where we marched and exercised as much as we did at Monterey. This was purpose built accommodation, but some of the features left a lot to be desired. I remember the latrines were back woods basic; there was a long trough with a plank on top into which were cut four or more holes. At the end of the trough was balanced a large barrel with water running into it. As the barrel filled it became top heavy, then it upturned dumping the water down the trough. Anyone sat down had to stand up or risk getting a wet bottom; this was something you learned to do very quickly.

When the training officers thought, we could tell left from right, we were sent for personnel selection. This involved aptitude testing to determine our best role in the U.S.A.F. Because of my previous work in the Shipyard building submarines, I had an aptitude to be a Mechanic/Air Engineer or a Radio Operator. I expressed an interest in being a Mechanic/Air Engineer; they said I would be assigned a training school in a few days. Two weeks later, I was informed to get ready to ship out, so I go pack my clothes for travel. No one said where we were going, so I asked to be informed about what was going to happen to me, they just said I was going by train to Belleville, Illinois.

Radio School

We left Fresno, California by military train which took four days and nights to get to St Louis Missouri. The train was using soft coal which made a lot of soot that infiltrated all of the cars, including all of our clothes. It was very difficult to get everything cleaned. In St Louis we were collected by a military bus to take us to Belleville. When we arrived at the gates of Scott Field, there was a huge sign beside the gateway that said, "Through these gates pass the best damn radio operators in the world". At first I thought someone must have stamped the wrong category on my orders. But then I realised maybe they needed Radio Operators more that Air/Mechanics. Because it was late in the day, we were taken to our rooms then told to report to the office after breakfast in the morning. In the office next day, we were introduced to the man who would be our instructor for this first phase of radio school. He gave us literature about the theory of the effects of air currents on radio waves. The next morning, we would start building our own radios, to send or receive Morse code signals. As our days at school were very short, we were given other things to do, just as everyone else had to do KP, scrubbing pots and pans, serving food or general ground cleaning. At times we were given the weekend off the base, so we took a bus into St Louis.

Back in the classroom each one of us was given a box, each filled with radio parts that we would have to put together to make a working radio. In the box there were resistors, connectors, a soldering iron plus a printout on how to build a working transmitter. There was also a schematic with all the information one would need to complete the task of building a radio. You could take all the time you needed to follow the instructions until everything was connected. So when power was applied you would turn on the switch you should have a working radio. You had to complete building a working radio before you could move to the next phase, which was sending and receiving Morse code. Morse code was very interesting; we had to change the alphabet as we knew it, converting the letters into dots and dashes. For instance, the V as in Victor was dot dot dot dash, then the international distress code SOS was dot dot dot dash dash dash dot dot dot. Every one of the letters of the alphabet had its own code. It was interesting when beginners were on a bus travelling into town, they could be seen converting the street signs into Morse code. You could see what that was like as they were tapping out the code letters with their fingers at the same time. Nevertheless it was good practice, it was also a great help in getting to the qualifying speed for receiving code which was at least 30 words a minute. I graduated from Radio School in July 1943 which meant I would now be sent to gunnery school.

Randolph Field, Texas

After finishing radio school we were flown to the Air Force Base at Randolph Field. Here I was taught to use a 50 caliber machine gun, by first taking it apart then putting it back together again in proper order. After a few days of ground to ground target practice, I was told that I was ready for air to air shooting. I was then taken to the airfield where I met the man who was going to be my pilot for the day.

We boarded a two-seater fighter plane; I was in the rear seat facing backwards. After I was strapped in we took then, flew around the field, soon another aircraft came by in the opposite direction pulling a sleeve target, my purpose was to shoot at the target as it went by the opposite direction, the first two tries were negative as I could not hit the sleeve. I had to learn about leading a target especially when it was going so quickly in the opposite direction; after a few more tries the pilot thought that it was enough for the day.

After we landed the pilot sat down with me, then he explained why I had failed to hit the target, he told me the proper way to shoot at a moving target. When we went up the next day, the target came by I put into practice information that the pilot had told me, I was able to score a hit right off on the target as it went by. That was my practice session. Tomorrow I would have to hit the target at least three times in order to qualify to continue. The bullets used in the test were painted green which would leave a green smudge on the target sleeve being used in the test. After three passes I hit the target at least three times each pass so I could move on to the next phase. After the sleeve was examined on landing I found I had indeed hit the target at least three times as it went by. I was happy to learn that I had qualified for air to air shooting. We now flew to the Alamogordo, New Mexico gunnery range, it was the same as Randolph Field except that the planes were much faster they also did not always fly in a level fashion, it was not unusual to find yourself upside down suddenly or sideways as well as straight up. It was very difficult to keep the target in your sites as it went by. I only had to hit the target once in three tries which I accomplished. The strange part of this course was, I never experienced any air sickness and maybe it was because I was concentrating so hard on hitting the target. Now I was ready for my next training course, whatever that was to be.

Moses Lake

My next assignment was to Moses Lake Air Force Base in Washington. When I arrived there the pilot of my aircraft circled the field a couple times so that I could see it from the air. There were many large planes parked there, it looked like a very busy field. It was also a tent city, the only buildings that were not tents were the hangers. I was taken to a tent near the airfield that had six bunks or army cots made up with foot lockers. The driver of the Jeep that took me there said that I would probably be the only one there for a while. In fact looking into some of the other tents, where I found they all had one man in them, a Radio operator. The driver came back at meal times to take us down to the mess hall, the rest of the time I spent on my own just wandering around the area. On the second day a fellow arrived at the door, he said his name was Larry Koon he was an engineer/ top turret gunner. After introductions to each other, I told him I was a radio operator/gunner. We exchanged ideas about why we were there in this huge tent with four empty bunks. The next day a third fellow arrived who said his name was S/Sgt Robert A Andrews our B.T. Gunner. The same afternoon two more fellows arrived who said they were both Waist Gunner T/Sgt Frederick Buckingham with Sgt Kenton H Anderson. We now expected that we should have a sixth person but after two days he still had not arrived. On the third day he finally arrived, he said that he was sorry he was late but he had to train back from Iowa, his name was Sgt. Sujowski, he was our tail gunner/armourer.

We were now a crew. Several days later four Lieutenants came to our tent, after introductions and salutes they told us that Lieut. Young was our pilot, Charles Clark was our co-pilot, Lieutenants Farr and Wodicka were our bombardier and navigator. Now for sure, with four officers plus six enlisted men we were now a crew of a B-17 Flying Fortress. The next day we were taken down to the office where the enlisted men were given our crew members "Wings". Before we saw the inside of a B-17 let alone fly one, there were many hours of schooling and instructions, at times all six of us together, other times we were instructed individually for each of our positions in the aircraft. As a radio operator I had especially long sessions of 2 to 3 hours at a time.

I was paired with Lt. Wodicka, (navigator) because I was the radio operator, who was needed to aid in direction finding. Between classes we were pretty much on our own, we could wander about the complex freely, except of course we could not leave. We spent a lot of time sitting around in our tent, talking about when we would actually start flying, which we hoped would be soon.

Just the thought of flying was very exciting, but when we did start to take to the air I found that each time we were up, I became airsick. Six times I became airsick. It was of course very bothersome because after we landed each time, I had to clean up before I got to go back to our tent. After the sixth time Lt. Young came to me, he said that because each time I flew I got airsick he would have to report it, with the possibility that I could be grounded.

We were due to take a cross-country flight around San Francisco to Salt Lake City, then over the mountains back to Moses Lake which was quite a long flight. It was very strange that at no time during gunnery school, where I would often be flying upside down, did I ever suffer air sickness. They say that air sickness is partially a mental thing; thankfully my brain finally woke up. In the next few days our crew would have many short training flights around the area. A long flight was from Moses Lake across to San Francisco; here as we circled the city we observed the World Series baseball game that was being played there. We then continued our flight making our way to Salt Lake City Utah. After a brief touchdown, we all got out of the airplane to stretch our legs a bit, before taking off over the mountain back to Moses Lake again. It was a great training flight; we all look forward to our next long flight.

All of the trips we took afterwards, I never got airsick again thank goodness; our crew was then given the next three days off before our next classes.

Ellensburg

In the city of Ellensburg Washington there was a "Young Ladies School". Every Friday afternoon from 1 PM to 4 PM the students had an afternoon dance, anyone from our base could attend should they desire. Since the school was not an especially long bus ride away the Air Force provided buses for transportation to the dances. Of course there were many partners to dance with, the music was provided by recordings which were always the latest tunes. At approximately 2:30 PM the ladies served cookies and tea they also provided soft drinks. It was all very nice as it gave us a chance to visit with the students, but it was cut short as the bus had to leave early enough, to get us all back in time for our evening meal. Since this was the first time that I had attended a dance there, I enjoyed it very much, so I was looking forward to getting another Friday off sometime soon.

So now it was as they say back to work, since our visit to Ellensburg my friend and I decided to take another trip somewhere on our next time off. We decided we would visit the Yakima Valley Apple centre. On July 12, we caught a bus from Moses Lake, after a ride that was not long we arrived in Yakima. True to its name, there were apples everywhere which we were free to sample any of the fruit that was on display. The people were very friendly; they demonstrated how the fruit was packaged for shipping to places all over the globe, without any damage or bruising whatsoever. It was a very interesting process. We were then invited to a local Cafe for lunch, where the food was delicious; we had a very good time. But all too soon it was time to get on our bus to go back to the base, but we promised to come back for another visit. We arrived at our base headquarters from Yakima to find that we had order's to preparing to fly overseas. In our group there were 12 crews, each one would fly their own aircraft. Six of us were going in one direction the other six going in another direction; of course we were not allowed to disclose even if we knew where we were going or when. There were rumours that we were going to prepare our aircraft for a long trip, but there are always rumours many unfounded, I was remain very sceptical until I heard official orders. Since these orders were not forthcoming, we continued to do what we do best, study, study. We continued to take a lot of short flights, with many landings and takeoffs, followed by the occasional long country flights of three hours or more. Eventually we began to realize all this extra training was for a purpose, which caused a lot more excitement among our crew.

It was on November of 1943 that we were told that we were going to be given 10 days furlough so that we would be able to go home for a short visit. My family lived in Mendocino California, so I decided I would go home for a couple of days. At this time of the year the state of Oregon had had the heaviest rainfall for many years. There were floods everywhere including the local train station which could not operate in or out. The Greyhound buses were consequently filled to capacity, with people trying to get out of Portland. With no seats available to me until at least the next day there would not be time for me to get home. I sadly, was just about to call my folks to give them the bad news, when good fortune came my way. I was still at the Greyhound station hoping that someone would cancel their trip as I was next in line for a seat.

Then fate smiled on me as a seat became available, I would be able to get to Sacramento California, where I could transfer to a bus for San Francisco. Here by a previous arrangement, one of my brothers would pick me up in his car. So despite the floods and the temporary disappointment, I was able to visit my folks and family thanks to the good man who gave up his seat for me. At the end of my furlough I was able to get back to Moses Lake without any difficulty, the rainstorm had passed on through, everything was wet but normal.

Grand island, Nebraska

On December 14, 1943 we left Moses Lake at 7:45 AM, we were a group of six B-17 bombers each with 10 crew members, six enlisted men plus four officers. We were flying our way to Grand Island Nebraska, one of our stops on the way to Great Britain, to meet our 452nd Bomb Group who was already there. We set off as a group of six aircraft but each pilot was tasked to get there on his own merit. We were all scheduled to stop at designated places on the route to Great Britain. We arrived at Grand Island for an overnight stay before moving on to our next stop. In December, Grand Island was very cold with lots of snow and ice. After we had landed there, we were taken to the office to be told that we would have to provide our own security guard until takeoff the next morning. Since there were 10 crewmembers, we were split up into pairs. Each pair had to patrol for two hours. One person to patrol the outside of our plane for one hour as one stayed inside the plane. I drew the short stick so I had to do the outside first. We were not issued winter flying clothes so as you can imagine, it was very cold patrolling outside of our ship.

When the first hour was up, I came to the door to complete my second hour inside, Larry complained bitterly about how cold it was inside the aircraft. I did not say to him that it seemed much warmer inside, than it was where he was going. Since our shift was done in the next hour, we would be through for the night. We were taken to the mess hall for hot coffee, cocoa or you could have something to eat. There were temporary cots set up in the mess hall, should anyone care to take a nap, before our early-morning takeoff.

The night went by without any problem, as all six crew completed their guard duty without any incident or trouble. So at 7:30 am all fed and watered, we were ready for our next adventure. We will find out where we are going this morning, Military secrecy prevails as always.

Presque Isle, Maine

Our next stop is Presque Isle Maine; we would be taking off that morning at about 10:00am. Our engineer had a special request; he asks Lieut. Young if it was possible for us to deviate from our flight plan to fly over his hometown, Coffeyville, Kansas.

When most of us had our furlough, to go home to visit family before our flight to Britain, the distance was too far for Sgt. Koon to visit his folks. Our pilot asked headquarters for permission to deviate from our flight plan to Presque Isle Maine, to accommodate our engineer. This request was thankfully granted for one pass over Sgt Koon's home much to the relief of all our crew. When we arrived we made a slow pass over the chicken farm, where we could see his folks. Sgt. Koon asked for a low pass so he could wave to his folks. As we flew over, the prop wash from the plane lifted the chickens up into the air, blowing them over the fence. Later on we found out that the family had to chase chickens all over the farm to try and catch them. His mother said later that the foxes had a lot of the chickens.

We were back in our flight plan almost immediately to continue on our way to Presque Isle. When we got out of our aircraft the other crews were all there to greet us, they tell us that we are all invited to a pre-New Year's party at a local gymnasium at 7:30 PM. dancing and snacks are promised as were soft drinks. The next morning at breakfast we all decided that we had had a very good time, with no hangovers. After breakfast, the enlisted men were asked to report down to hangar number six to receive a subsistence allowance. That meant to us that it was "payday", evidently the good feeling it gave us may have cause the inevitable snowball fight on the way back to the mess. While aiming a huge snowball at Sgt. Sujowski, I slipped on the ice and fell backwards, hitting my head on the tarmac. It stung a bit but it didn't hurt me at all. Two Air Force nurses came by asking if I was injured, I assured them that I was not. They insisted I go with them up to the hospital to have my head injury looked at. It seems there is a rule in the Air Force that anyone who is on flying status suffering any trauma to the head; must be hospitalized for at least five days for observation. The surgeon in charge decided that I should be observed for the five days even if my trauma was minor. The next morning my whole crew came down to visit me quite early, which caused me to wonder why they were up so early, we had three more days to stay here.

Lieut. Young sat on the foot of my bed to tell me he had news, they had received clearance to take off at 8:00 am for the next stop on the trip. I was overjoyed asking him to tell the orderly to bring my clothes. I was then told the devastating news; I would not be flying off with them as I still had three days of my trauma observation to complete. Of course,

I ranted, raved and swore that I felt 100% healthy; there was no reason because of a little bump on my head that I couldn't fly off with them now. It didn't matter how hard I tried, I could not go with my fellow crewmembers, until my five days were up. The good news was that I could possibly be flying out in a couple of days or so, to catch up to my friends in Britain, this satisfied me. Actually three days past then even though I cleared my five day detention, there was no aircraft leaving for Europe at this time. Two more days passed, still no ride. On December 30th I was told that I was going to a hotel in New York City by the name of "Henry Hudson".

It was close to LaGuardia airport in case a ride for me should become available, I would be nearby. Two more days passed then, I received a phone call telling me that I would be picked up shortly to be taken to the airport as there was a space for me, on a plane that was leaving for England. I joyfully went down to the office of the hotel to tell them I would be checking out shortly, as I have my ride to the airport. The clerk said "Just a minute he will get your bill", I replied "Send it to the Air Force they would pay". The clerk said that I had to pay the bill; I should collect the $31.84 from the Air Force, I paid and went unhappily on my way to LaGuardia Airport.

LaGuardia Airport

A short while after takeoff it was announced that we would be stopping briefly in a town called Stephenville, Newfoundland. After landing we were told the reason we were stopping was there was a huge storm brewing which was right in our flight path. We would be staying here for a few hours until the storm cleared and it would be safe to fly on. As time went on it seemed that the storm was not going to clear the area very quickly, so it was decided that we would stay overnight, then take off the next morning. The officers were taken to the bachelor officer quarters, while the crew from the aircraft and I were given a bed in the barracks, I was told that we would be taking off again at 8:30am in the morning. Next morning we were all waiting to board the aircraft again. I was last to get on but the pilot stopped me at the door, he was sorry but he couldn't take me any further because, this was the outer limits of the continental United States. Beyond here we are entering a foreign country and without proper credentials, I'm not authorized to take you any further. I found out later from headquarters that I would be detained here until they found out what to do with me. It wasn't very long before they found out that they could take me on to my destination, but the plane had already left the area. Luck was with me as the plane had to turn back, because of another storm brewing somewhere further out in the Atlantic. I thought it gave me another chance to continue my journey to where my crewmates were waiting for me. The next morning I was there early on the airfield then after everyone was boarded a crew member came to the door he said to get on, I quickly did.

Glasgow Scotland

On the plane we were told that we would be making a quick stop at Glasgow Airport as several of the passengers were going to continue their journey by train. I was then informed by the aircrew that I would be one of the passengers that had to continue my trip that way. The officers were going in one direction I was going in a different direction. Arriving at the train depot the stationmaster asked me where in England I was going. I told him that I was not sure where the 452nd Bomb Group was located. The stationmaster related that we still had a long train ride ahead, but maybe we would stop at an American military post, where I could find out where I had to go. As I had one hour and a half until my train came in I became bored, I was told if I ventured out of the station to be very careful. The City was under extreme blackout conditions, so traffic on the street would be very dangerous. Glasgow at that time was one of the main shipbuilding areas in Scotland, which made it a prime target for bombing by the Luftwaffe. Inside the station there were a few dim lights, which would be extinguished at the first sound of the air raid siren.

Outside in the street there was not a light to be seen anywhere. Then as I stood on the curb side I noticed across the street a light flashed in a building when someone went in or out of the front door, so I thought that it must be a coffee shop. I dashed across the street as fast as I could and ran into what we call in our country, a picket fence, which startled me but I was across the street safely. As I slowly moved along the fence, (because it was so dark) using my hands to feel where I was going, when I felt something soft and round. It was then that a woman's voice said "You must be a Yank", which startled me as I did not realise anyone was standing in my path. The lady asked if she could help me get some place, I said yes the coffee shop. Once we arrived there I asked why she said that I must be a Yank, she replied because all you Americans love to squeeze things. I asked her if she would care to have a cup of coffee with me, but she said that she was on her way back to work with still a ways to go, so she didn't want to be late. She said thank you very much for the offer, then disappeared into the darkness. The man at the coffee shop said that he would help me back across the street, when I was ready to return to the train station. After I had refreshed myself with a coffee and a cookie that's what he did, so I got back to the station safely.

The train was on time, as I boarded the attendant told me that any lighted car was okay for me to enter, but not to disturb the blackout blinds. When the train started up I thought to myself that after all this time and difficulty I was now near to home base. The train moved out of Glasgow then across Scotland to Edinburgh, here it headed south on the East coast line crossing the English border at Berwick. From here the train would travel the length of England, before heading east toward Norwich in East Anglia the new home of the Mighty Eighth. Because of the war this journey would last for most of the night.

Deopham Green

Arriving at the local train station I was collected by a driver in a Jeep; looking at his roadmap he said we don't have to go very far. This road map was an essential piece of equipment in Britain; to confuse the Germans in the event of an invasion, all the road signs had been removed from the highways. He also informed me that an officer had called the Field, to say that they were bringing a Sgt. Silva over to them. But someone told him that they were not aware that I was coming. This made me very apprehensive as we got closer to the field. What kind of reception would I get? When we arrived at the main gate the driver showed his credentials and then asked for directions to the 728 Squadron Headquarters. We had to travel across two airways to get to the other side of the field. When we arrived I got out of the Jeep, thanked the driver then went up the steps to the front door of the office. It was some time before anyone asked if they could help me. I told the Sgt. my name and serial number telling him that I was Lieut. Young's radio operator; I had just got in from Presque Isle Maine. He said that they had heard about my travel and the Major would be here shortly to talk to me. The officer when he arrived started our talk by informing me that I had been replaced as radio operator of Lieut. Young's crew. He asked me for my orders; I told him I didn't have any. He asked me to check my pockets; there in my back pocket neatly folded were my orders. How they got there I have no idea. After reading my orders, we found that I was supposed to go to Salt Lake City, Utah for reassignment. I had made it to England but, I was not supposed to be there! The Major said he had been in touch with Headquarters, he had told them he would like to keep me.

As a new arrival in Britain I had to learn the local R/T procedures before I could fly on a mission. This allowed me some time to take in the British countryside and the people. I have never seen so much greenery, there was the grass, the tree's, the hedgerows, it was all simply stunning. The County of Norfolk itself where we are based is very flat, which makes it ideal for operating airfields. But again the lack of any lighting when the sun goes down is a nightmare. You have to memorize every buildings location on the field which I learned the hard way. One night I stepped out of the Mess then started to walk down a gravel path to our quarters when I came to a sudden halt. It was so dark I had no idea which way to turn to get there, fortunately someone else came out just behind me so I ask directions. From then on I studied the location of everywhere I was liable to visit in the dark.

Now there are the British people; considering they have been at war for nearly four years, I am surprised at how cheerful they are. They see our U.S. uniforms then go out of their way to speak to us. Our boys have made themselves popular with the local children by handing out candy or chocolate bars which are almost nonexistent in the U.K. Despite the war, life seems to be carrying on much as normal. Though to be honest, with the food rationing in Britain all of the kids looked scrawny, as though they could do with a good feed. I start to realise how tough things have been for the British people over the last few years.

There are dances being held in village halls which our boys are making full use of. A couple of days later the base Bus was taking anyone who wants to go to a local dance, eight or nine guys are making the trip. When we arrive there is a small Band playing with locals already on the dance floor. Then at the next break the orchestra leader explains to the American visitors, the location of the air raid shelters. We start to dance, then about an hour later the building is shaken by a nearby explosion, followed by the hall being plunged into darkness. When the lights come back on the Yanks find they are the only ones left standing in the hall. Slowly the locals begin to return, then as the band strikes up dancing continues, by the end of the night we have had a great time. On the bus back to our base the boys are talking about how calmly the local had taken the explosion. I suppose it's something they have had to get used to over the years.

Back on our base we employed gardeners, to keep the grounds tidy around the officer's quarters. One morning one of these guys asks if I would be interested in buying a bottle of Old Irish Whisky. "Yes please I said" and part with $40 for it. My idea is on those chilly nights, I would have a little nip to keep out the cold. However, the first night after lights out, I carefully attempt to ease the cork out of the bottle. The first loud squeak from the cork as I try to remove it brings the lights on; everyone in our hut has a glass in his hand. My bottle lasts about five minutes. Next day I approach the gardener but alas he has no more Whisky, but he sells me a three speed bicycle for £5 about $20, At least I have some transport of my own. Then comes a bit of good news there was a crew that needed a radio operator to continue flying missions. Before that could happen, I have to relate to the officers on the base; how I had managed to get from Presque Isle Maine to Great Britain. The officer then wanted to know how I knew Lieut Young; I told him I had trained with him and the rest of his crew. He then informed me that pending a talk with Lieut. Cook I would become his radio operator. There would also be further questioning about my unauthorised travel from the U.S. to Britain which I promised to do. But for me the foremost thing on my mind, was to meet Lieut. Cook's crew then tell them how happy I would be to become a member of the "Passionate Witch".

After my conversation with Lieut. Cook and his crew, they decided that they would very much like to have me as a radio operator. Cook informed the office of their decision, but he was told they were waiting for word from stateside on whether I could stay or be shipped back to the U.S. They would have the decision in a day or so, only if that was favourable would I be staying in Britain. I could be a good choice as a radio operator for Lieut. Cook's crew. Later that evening I was visited by Lieut. Young, he told me that he was sorry to lose me as a crew member, but sometimes things are beyond an individual's control. He asked me if I would care to make a mission with them tomorrow. I informed him that I was waiting for word from stateside, so I wasn't sure that I could go on a mission. Lieut. Young informed me that he had asked permission from headquarters for me to go with them as a gunner, to replace the one that was ill with the flu for this one trip. When permission was granted I was very pleased, as a successful trip would be one mission in my favour, I was already six trips behind my new crew of "Passionate Witch". So now I had to wait until we hear from stateside about my situation. The very next day the office was told that I could stay in Britain to become Lieut. Cook's radio operator. Now, happily I move my gear from where I was staying to the barracks where my new crewmates are, so now begins the getting to know each other.

Operational Squadron, "RAF Elsham Wolds" 05/02/44.
Standing on the top, of the Lincolnshire Wolds, Elsham is the highest airfield, in One Group, it could also be one of the coldest places, on earth Jack remembers. Built to the standard three runways 'A' formation, the main runway 14-32 is 2000 yards long (1800m). The alternative runways are 08-26 at 1600 yards long (1440m) with 02-20 at 1400 yards long (1260m). This airfield was one of some twenty that were built to include an arrester gear system, similar to that used on aircraft carriers. Some aerodromes had this gear fitted at each end of the three runways, though at Elsham it was only on the eastern end of the main runway. The system consisted of two cables about 100ft apart (30m), stretched across the runway threshold and supported in such a way as to keep the cables clear of the surface. These cables were attached to hydraulic cylinders in pits at the side of the runway to bring aircraft to a progressive but rapid stop.

However, this required Lancaster's and Halifax's to be fitted with arrestor hooks capable of stopping a 40,000 lb bomber from 100 MPH.

As hooks were never fitted to these aircraft this device was not brought into service on the base. Elsham Wolds was No13 Base Station for One group with its two satellite fields at Kirmington and North Killingholme. Other fields at Hingham and Hemswell would be added in 1944.

We are assigned to 103 Squadron which has a long and distinguished history, going back to the RFC during the First World War. It served in France during that period then; it was there again at the outbreak of hostilities in World War Two, flying the Fairey Battle. The Squadron Badge is a Black Swan with the Latin Motto "NOLI ME TANGERE" which translates into English as 'Touch Me Not'. We share the base with a second unit, 576 Squadron which was formed from 'C' Flight of 103 Squadron in late 1943. Their emblem is a Merlin Falcon with a Serpent in its talons. Its Latin Motto is "CARPE DIEM" which is loosely translated as 'Seize the Opportunity' but the literal translation is more accurately 'Seize the Day'

We arrived by train on 5th February 1944 at Barnetby-le-Wold station to the south of Elsham, with an uphill walk of about two miles to the main gate. Fortunately, transport was provided in the form of a small RAF truck. Our arrival as a crew at the base raised no interest at all amongst the battle hardened residents. No welcoming banner is stretched across the camp main entrance; we were just another sprog crew with a lot to learn. There was a settling in period, while we learn to find our way round our new station. We had to be checked out, by the base medics plus the dentist, who promptly changed our fillings for new ones. These fillings had been changed, by the dentist at the HCU, when we arrived there, twelve weeks ago; but I suppose they have to justify their job.

We are straight back in the air again, with two cross country flights every day, then one day and one night cross country trips. On the 11th February we finished off with a night time 'Bulls Eye' (spoof raid) to Newcastle on Tyne to check our progress. Night time cross country flying is to instill confidence in each member of the crew, that the other members are good at their jobs. The pilot has to keep the aircraft in the air while dodging incoming fighters with the gunner's providing protection. Our navigator has to be able to find his way around the countryside with accuracy in any weather with the Wireless operator maintaining contact with the base. Our Bulls Eye starts out from Elsham, then inland toward the Pennines before heading north. To us it's a practice run, but down on the ground we could be an intruder who will be fired on. Heading back toward the coast we have three main rivers to contend with. There is the Tyne, the Wear then the Tees, each of which have heavy industry along their banks. This means there are Anti-Aircraft defences plus the barrage balloons.

The local air defences airfields along the coast may be aware of our presence, but the rest won't be. As I stand in the astrodome, around us the sky is dark but below us the Tyne is a silver snake winding toward the sea. There are no lights to show any habitation, or signs of life. Heading south, we cross the River Wear, then onto the Durham coalfields. Ahead is the river Tees our next.

We are now crossing into Six Group territories airfields. The Canadians have their own group starting with Goospool airfield on the river Tees down to Linton on Ouse near York. The air will be thick with their Halifax's and Lancaster's heading to Germany so we have to be wary. Below we see the Tees winding toward the sea, there is a large yellow glow in the distance. At first it looks like a fire, until we realise it's the glow from the steelworks Blast furnaces. We see similar sights at Scunthorpe when they are tapping the Iron furnaces; it's the only sign of life in the darkness. We now pass back into the darkness of the North Yorkshire Moors before heading inland to avoid Hull with its air defences. Within a short time, I have to return to my office, to make contact with Elsham ground control, for permission to land. Our own base aircraft; are all well on their way to Germany, so there is no delay in entering the circuit. On the ground the Control Tower want to have the runway lights on for as short a time as possible. We taxi back to our dispersal, before a quick dash to the mess for a jar or two, wondering what is in store for tomorrow.

Then next morning to our surprise, ten days after arriving at Elsham, we were given six days leave so I choose to go home to Carlisle. Arthur our flight engineer lives in Penrith to the south of Carlisle, so we travelled home together on the train. It's a long haul, first we travel from Barnetby le Wold station to Doncaster then, we wait for the connection to Newcastle on Tyne. Here there is another long wait for the milk train to Carlisle. The final leg is a bus to Harraby with my only thought, a cup of char then my comfy bed. Arriving home I find my bed occupied by Uncle Jim Robinson my mum's brother, which means I have to sleep on a camp bed. Jim was the black sheep of my mum's family; he was in Carlisle for a six week appearance at one of the local theatres. He with his stage partner a Scot, did a Flannigan and Allen type singing act, they were both very good singers. As a relative, I was allowed into the theatre, to see the show for free then, meet the other artists back stage. It was quite an experience for me; I was treated very well especially by the chorus girls in the show, because I was in uniform. My grandfather, on mum's side was Irish from Portadown, a strict Catholic who considered his son Jim's stage career a family disgrace. Grandfather also worked on the railway as a guard and whenever I saw him, he was reading his bible, but he was nobody's fool.

Mathew & Ellen Spark   Cousin Lillian Thomas & Jack

Jack & Dennis Langhorne camping   Jack in Alston 1939 aged 17

Thomas in Pilot Training   Lillian in the Wrens

Jack in Training in Blackpool   Dennis Langhorne in the RAF

Jack at Wireless Operators Training Course Blackpool 1941

Jack Back Row 2nd from Right Corporal Adams Centre with White Belt

Yatesbury DH Dominie Wireless Training Aircraft

No.18 Air Gunnery Course Stormy Down No.6 Group July 1944
Jack Back Row 1st Left Reg Tailby Front Row 1st Left

Crew of M-Mother at Elsham Wolds on the Morning of the Berlin Raid
L/Right Spark, Walker, Barker, Richardson, Browning, Smart, Thomas

Belleville Scott Field Radio School Spring 1943 USAAF Postcard

Typical of the type of Aircraft that was in use at RANDOLPH FIELD Texas
George would have had Gunnery Training in this type of aircraft in 1943

Brownings Crew
Ken Smart, Bob Thomas, Ron Walker, Arthur Richardson
Jack Spark, Fred Brownings, Norman Barker

George's original B17 training crew "Star Eyes"
Back l/r - Sherman Farr, Edward Wodicka, Charles Clark, Charles Young
front l/r - Robert Andrews, Fredrick Buckingham, Joseph Sujkowski, George Silva, Kenton Anderson, Lawrence Koon

Original Passionate Witch Crew
Dick Thayer, Hubert Roughton, Gerald Poplett, Carl Blichmann, John McLaughlin
Robert Cook, Ronald Casey, Jogh Rowland, John Oswalt

Reginald J Tailby 625 Squadron   Ronald (Bob) Thomas RAF

Silva Family Bobby George Dad Hercules & Brother Herk

Lancaster M Mother in a final Embrace with the B17 Passionate Witch

B17 Passionate Witch & Lancaster M Mother Dunsfold 25th March 1944

Richard Thayer

George Silva portrait by Harold Rhoden

George Silva's poems written while in Stalag 17b

Gerald Poplett

George Silvaon furlow before embarkation

Fremont Granade
High School Photo

Carl Blichmann with a neighbour

Final moments of the Passionate Witch 2 over Chateaudum March 28th 44

equipment were pulled by oxen or cows. Have even seen a cow and a horse teamed up. Do you recognize the back porches of 31, 30 and 29? No one should fail to recognize 36A's porch. It finally ended up completely dismantled. Remember when we moved into the "new air force camp" in November 1943 and the boys

Ben Phelper's Stalag 17B photo of George Sila's Hut 31

P/O Fl/Eng
Unknown

Fl/Of Pilot
Unknown

P/O Pilot
Joe Munsch

Sq/Ld Pilot
John Marshall

Fl/Lt/Pilot
Carey

Fl/Of Pilot
Unknown

P/O Fl/Eng
Uknown

Fl/Sgt W/Op
Unknown

Fl/Sgt Fl/Eng
Unknown

Fl/Sgt Fl/Eng
Jock ???

Fl/Sgt Fl/Eng
Sid Gunn

Fl/Sgt Fl/Eng
Jack Spark

Fl/Sgt W/Op

Sandtoft 1667 O.T.U. 'D' Instructors Flight August 1944

So, when in the company of granddad, you had to remember not to blaspheme, or talk about your exploits with the ladies. It's nice to be home but mum is not happy to here I am now on an operational Squadron, "Don't be doing anything rash" she comments. I can only assure her I will be careful as I tuck into some of her home cooking and a brew of tea; normality if only for a short while.

On the 21st February, Jack is back on the Squadron, still preparing to join the offensive against Germany. From his training days, Jack remembers the international distress signal is the firing of a RED Very cartridge, because of this he begins collecting Reds. This was the cause of much amusement, with the rest of the crew, who would pull his leg about it unmercifully. Because the Canadians were officers, we did not socialise with them on the Base, so we took every opportunity to gather together in a pub somewhere. Here we would talk of our respective families plus their home towns. Ron Walker and Norman Barker found they had a lot in common with Jack. Living in Toronto they had the great lakes, with the mountains to the North, there was good fishing and hunting to enjoy. Jack talked about his love of fishing, though the Lake Districts lakes were not on the same scale as Lake Ontario.

Norman revealed he was an artist before the war, so I spent some time talking to him about my brother's talent for water colour painting. We swopped stories of our parents, which revealed they had the same fears, about our part in the war. The more we sat talking, the more it became obvious that although we came from different countries, deep down we were the same in so many ways. Our crew's first trip into Scunthorpe's Oswald pub was a revelation; we started out downstairs downing a few beers, before ending upstairs in the lounge. Sitting taking in the vista of young ladies, we were surprised by the appearance of seven burly airmen. They promptly introduced themselves as the Elsham Wolds welcoming committee; we stood to shake hands with them. As we did so, they calmly took hold of our ties with one hand then, cut them off below the knot with scissors held in the other. Everyone in the room started to laugh then, we joined in accepting we had been had good and proper.

Fred Brownings our Flt/Sgt Pilot, was originally from Brighton, here he ran his own electrical business before the war, at aged thirty one he quickly became known as Dad by the crew. Being a bit more mature, he was a man who would voice any complaint he or his crew had. This earned him a reputation, as a bolshie troublemaker, by the top brass. Because of this, any promotion prospects were blocked, even when it was ordained, that all pilots would be commissioned Fred was overlooked. Jack always believed the brass thought if our crew got the chop, then they would not need to make Fred an officer.

Poor weather during late February and early March saw snow covering the airfield, there had been no operational flying for days. I remember waking up one morning in bed feeling so cold but having to come to terms with the fact, I was going to have to get up. Having shaved washed then dressed, we were informed the C.O. wants all personnel including aircrew, to clear the main runway. One runway; 2000 yards long, 50 yards wide, 12 inches deep in snow. (1800M by 45M, 30cm thick). Shovelling snow for a few hours you forget the cold, my only thoughts was for the wind direction, if it changed, all this effort would be in vain. Although there was no operational flying taking place, training continued apace during this period. Our next flight, from the station, took place on the 1st March 44 when we took Lancaster 'N' Nuts, for an hour air test. That same night, 103 Squadron, took part in a raid on Stuttgart, which fortunately resulted in no loss of aircraft, from the base. The following night we were back in the air again, for a three hour cross country in the same aircraft. It's Friday the 3rd March; we take 'M' Mother for a bombing practice run then a four hour, cross country flight. We are being brought up to speed for operational flying very quick. Bad weather brings flying to a halt for three days, before we take 'N' nuts up for an air test plus another cross country flight.

Our crew are now ready to start operational flying, but before they can begin, Fred has to fly a second Dickey trip with an experienced crew. This will give him the opportunity to take part in and see the effects of an operational raid, without the responsibility of being the skipper. The rest of his crew are there to see him off, then before dawn they are there awaiting his return, as the fire truck and blood wagon take up their positions. Aircraft appear then fly overhead to continue to other airfields, others turn into the circuit to land, some with visible damage or an engine feathered. Slowly the dispersals begin to fill with Lancaster's coming back from last night raid, but Fred's aircraft is not amongst them, our crew are anxious. Two hours pass, Jack begins to think the worst, they would not be the first crew to lose a pilot, on a second Dickey trip. Then a message from the Ops room, informs them that Fred's aircraft running short of fuel, has landed away, they will be back the next morning.

Stuttgart Raid

We did not fly that day, but the next night 15th March we were briefed, to attack Stuttgart, our first operational trip. On the morning after breakfast, we trouped up to our dispersal to check 'M' for mother. Every crew member was responsible for checking out his equipment prior to the raid, then report any problems to the ground crew.

This would give them a chance to rectify any defects before takeoff. The day started normally, but I quickly noticed, that by mid-day, the phone boxes on the base were empty they had been sealed. Fred Brownings was informed of the afternoon briefing and to have all of his crew in attendance in the relevant Op's room. At the appointed time each of our crew reported to his designated Op's room. I reported to the wireless operator's group, sitting in one of the chairs in the room waiting to see what would happen. We did not wait long before Flight Lieutenant Stewart DFC entered the room, we all snapped to attention. Sit down gentleman came the order, everyone lights a cigarette, the air filling with smoke. At this point the target was revealed "Stuttgart". I was interested by the reaction of the old hands to this target but they seemed fairly relaxed.

But at this stage I was unsure as to whether this was a good sign, or a bad one. Then it was onto the business at hand, all the relevant signals info was given out and noted. After the briefing we sat as a crew, discussing this first raid, to make sure we were clear, about our collective responsibility. When we were happy with our roles, we all trooped of to the mess, for our meal before the raid, which we ate in relative silence. Later we gathered, to kit up in the locker room, here we would go through each other's pockets, to remove all incriminating trivia. Any bus or picture house tickets that could identify our base location were removed as was any money, to be kept safe for our return. We then put on our flying suits, boots and heated suit for the gunners, the final call was to draw our parachutes. Here we would indulge in nervous banter, with the WAAF's, "If the chute doesn't work bring it back, we will give you another". Then it was outside to the transport trucks for the short ride to our dispersal. All crews have rituals they perform, or mascots to carry to bring them good luck, Fred's team is no different. Watering the tail wheel before takeoff was popular, wearing a special scarf or the carrying of a toy, given by a family member is another. Jack's only concession to this is a St Christopher ring he wears; before he boards the Lancaster he rubs the ring on the skin of the aircraft, to protect it. Accepting his crew's belief, in these things, Fred makes it clear there is to be no external decoration of the Lancaster. While we are having that last smoke before takeoff, Fred is walking round the aircraft talking to the ground crew 'Chief'. There would be discussions, about what had been done to the aircraft, since its last raid, covering the engines and airframe. When he was happy Fred was expected to sign a form 700 accepting the aircraft, as fit for the operation we were about to do.

Standing below the fueled and bombed up aircraft we are acutely aware, this is our first operational trip, we had never taken off in a fully loaded condition before. Just standing there, looking at the four thousand pound cookie and the boxes of incendiaries, hanging in that enormous, bomb bay it's incredible. We have tried to extract from Fred, his impressions of his second dickey trip, to prepare us for what is to happen. His comment is, you have to experience it yourselves to fully understand, so we wait in anticipation. The Op is on, we board Lancaster 'M' for Mother with a mixture of fear, excitement and a hope we will achieve what we have been trained to do. Fear is a complex thing it is the fear of failure, the fear of not being able to cope, letting the rest of the crew down, but not dying. This is something that happens to other crews not ours. Once aboard we are too busy with our own duties to think of anything, other than the moment at hand. Fred and Arthur, my fellow Cumbrian flight engineer are starting the engines with the help of the ground crew. In front of me, Ron the navigator is laying out his maps, checking our route to the target. Behind me down the fuselage Ken Smart the mid upper and Bob Thomas the rear gunner are checking their weapons, getting comfortable. Though when it's minus forty centigrade, up at twenty thousand feet, how someone can be comfortable is a puzzle. Up in the nose of the aircraft, Norman Barker, our bomb aimer is checking the bomb release sequence on his switches, while I am busy with my radio sets.

Then it's time to go; our aircraft rolls out of the dispersal onto the perimeter track, slipping in behind another passing Lancaster. As we make our way to the take off point Fred is keeping a safe distance from the aircraft in front. There have previously been collisions, between aircraft as they taxi, he does not want to become another one of them. The rear gunner of the aircraft we are following is also keeping a careful watch on us, ready to abandon his turret if the need arises. With a full load, the Lancaster is slow to respond to the throttles; we have to negotiate a number of turns on the way to the take off point.

Fred is being watchful to keep the aircraft in the center of the Peri track; if we drop a wheel into the soft earth, we will get bogged down. This will bring all the aircraft behind us to standstill; we will be very unpopular with everyone, especially the Ground Chief. It would be his ground crew that would have to extract any aircraft from that situation, after the armourers had unloading the bombs. Looking out of my window on the port side of the fuselage, I see we have finally arrived at the end of the runway, ready for takeoff. Waiting by the runway are a small group of ground staff including WAAF's, standing by the control van, to wave everyone off. Then a green light from the controller gives Fred the all clear, we are on our way. The engines are run up to full power against the brakes, when they are released we gather speed slowly. Rumbling down the tarmac I feel the tail lift, but Fred holds the aircraft down, until the end of the runway.

Lifting the aircraft over the perimeter fence at the last minute, the ground drops away sharply into the valley below; I make a note of the take-off time as 19:05. As the main wheels retract the airspeed increases, we climb away from the snow covered ground. We now start circling the airfield below us to gain height. Ron's voice over the intercom, gives Fred the heading for the first turning point, 'Reading'. This route has to be followed accurately.

If we deviate to the East, the London Anti-Aircraft batteries will let us know, there will also be the inevitable barrage balloons. From Reading we head toward the coast at 'Selsey Bill', our next turning point. Fred all the time is keeping the aircraft climbing, to reach our bombing altitude. At Selsey Bill we head south over the channel, to cross the French coast at Le-Havre. Here everything changes, none of the straight and level flight, of the training cross country trips. Fred keeps the aircraft on the move, side slipping to port then using the speed built up, to regain the height lost. Now we nose down to lose height, building up speed again then stick back to climb back to altitude. Then we side slip to starboard, before climbing back to where we started from. Ducking and diving like this, Fred hopes to put off any night fighter, looking for an easy prey.

Our flight path now runs to the South of Paris, toward Dijon when, "Fighter corkscrew port" calls Bob Thomas from the rear turret. Down we go but the fighter passes by without opening fire, so we did not draw attention to ourselves by firing on it. Had the fighter seen us we could not tell, but he did not return. Corkscrewing is a fierce manoeuvre, coming unannounced like that it catches everyone out. Only the pilot is always strapped in to his seat, the rest of us have lap straps. So, when I am taking star shots or helping to watch for fighters, I have to grab the nearest thing to hand then hang on, for grim death. Maps, writing pads, pencils, navigational instruments fly around the cockpit as well as people if they are not quick to respond. This encounter brings the crew, to a new level of concentration; we have a long way to go so this is a bad start. Fortunately for us we fly on without any further incident. Ron now gives Fred a course change flying north east to avoid crossing into Switzerland. We are headed into Germany, then another course change, turning due north to attack Stuttgart. Over the target the flak was something of a shock, never having experienced it before. The sound of the shrapnel rattling on the aircraft skin, makes you realise the next burst, could penetrate the thin aluminium surface. Our target is covered by cloud this makes the marking very ragged. So, Norman our bomb aimer puts our load, into the middle of the marker flares and the growing fires. Now it's straight and level, until the bombing photo is taken, though I doubt it will show much of value.

Once the photo flash fires, Fred puts the nose down; we head for home hoping not to attract any more attention on the way. The return trip is quiet, crossing the coast we see searchlights and flak, but at a distance. Someone is on the receiving end, thankfully not us this time. But our trip has one more twist, even as we approach Elsham Wold; Jack receives a signal to divert to Lindholme near Doncaster. This is because our base, has become fog bound making it inaccessible. Finally, back on the ground Fred quickly dampened any elation we felt; "They won't all be that easy" he said; "The flak you saw tonight was light, with the searchlights almost non-existent". After eight and a half hours in the air we are billeted, where space can be found for us to bed down. Next morning we are up early, ready for a return to our home base, in case there is an Op on. Last night's raid on Stuttgart involved 863 aircraft of bomber command, 19 of which were from 103 Squadron. Out of the total, 43 aircraft were lost to fighters or flak. Allowing for aircrew taken P.O.W plus some evaders, the night's raid cost the lives of over 220 young airmen. This shocking total brought home to our crew what to expect, we have twenty nine more trips to do. Fortunately, this time none the aircraft lost on the raid; were from either of the two Squadrons on our base.

There are no operations posted for the next night, so it's a trip into Scunthorpe for the crew. The Oswald pub, on the long high street has become the main watering hole, for Elsham's aircrew. They will also be able to hear the news, good or bad from the other stations in the area. The chat amongst experienced crews often turns to tough sorties they have experienced; inevitably the talk is of Hamburg or Berlin. We as sprog's are eager to learn from these time-served men, hoping to find how to survive our tour. They can only tell of fighting their way to the target and then back again, depending on the route that has been chosen. Then while you are over the target, the flak is as intense as anywhere, only the Ruhr Valley is more concentrated. Here in the pub, they will also relax with the local girls, to forget the stresses of the war. When we had refuelled ourselves at the bar, there was the attraction of the local dance halls. But from what I can recall dancing was very limited, there would be a small band pounding out a tune on a raised stage. Out on the dance floor, there was not a square inch of space anywhere, everyone just seem to shuffle round in an anti-clock wise direction to the music. Smoke fills the air as the heat from the number of people on the floor turns the place into a sauna. We were rowdy and very noisy, but we considered we were entitled, there is a quotation "Eat, Drink and be Merry for Tomorrow we Die". This could have been written especially for Bomber Crews.

One night in Scunthorpe, I recall we were in the Oswald tanking up, before heading to a local dance. There seems to be hundreds in the pub that night when an airman called to us, "Come on boys can't keep the popsies waiting". We all laughed and called back, "Save me a good looking one". Ok came the reply "But don't leave it too late, you don't want to die a virgin do you"; how right he was.

Frankfurt

March 18th just three short days have passed, we are on the board for our second trip Frankfurt. We are assigned to the third wave of the attack, because we are a sprog crew and are allotted 'M' mother again. The first aircraft was airborne at 18:40 with the Squadron contributing eighteen Lancaster's to the total of some eight hundred and fifty bombers. Our route from Elsham was south to Orfordness, then South East over the North Sea, to cross the French coast near Dunkerque. We cross into Belgium without incident, making use of the scattered cloud to avoid being spotted by fighters. Our route now changes heading to a point between Cologne and Frankfurt, then the final turn toward Frankfurt. Approaching the target, the glow of the fires started by the main force, are clearly visible with the new flares confirmed this as the aiming point. The defences are heavy there is a lot of searchlights and the flak, thick but scattered, Ron quickly drops our load into the growing fires then we beat it for home. Just as we are staring to relax a little, Ken our mid upper reports a night fighter to starboard, flying parallel to our course. Both gunners take turns to watch this aircraft, but keep a wary eye open for a partner. Night fighters can sometimes work in pairs, with one of them acting as a distraction, while the other sneaks in to attack. When after a minute or so, it turns to starboard and flies away from us, we heave a sigh of relief. Fred eases our Lancaster to port then drops our height, changing position just in case, we had been seen and the fighter comes back. Crossing swords with a night fighter, is not something we want if it can be avoided, they all carry 20mm canon, these bullets explode on impact. This scatters red hot shrapnel around the inside of the aircraft, shredding equipment or people. These canons also have a range advantage, the fighters can fly out of range of our 303 machine guns knocking lumps out of us with these canon shells with impunity. Fortunately it does not return; we fly on toward Mannheim, Saarbrucken then the last leg to Calais. As we cross into the Channel, Ron gives Fred our last course change for Elsham. The final run over Suffolk and Norfolk is without incident though we have to remember this is US Air force territory. As we taxi back to our dispersal it's another trip completed, an even quieter one than the previous. Bomber command losses for the night totalled 22 aircraft but once again our squadron loses no aircraft. Though, two crews have landed away; Fl/Officer Moore crash lands in Sussex due to engine troubles with Fl/officer Johnson putting his disabled aircraft down at Manston.

The wireless operator's position, in a Lancaster is the hot seat, in more ways than one. Heating for the aircraft cockpit is provided by both inner engines, the air enters just above my knees under the wireless operator's table. On the starboard side of the fuselage, the other heating vent blows directly at my position. While the crew in the cockpit are wearing thick jumpers, scarves and gloves, I am wearing trousers and battledress top. The cry "Turn that heating up" is a frequent one from the skipper or the flight engineer, as we fly toward the target and I swelter in the heat.

I often wondered, would I have survived a bail out from twenty thousand feet, dressed as lightly as I was. Last night's operation had been split into a number of separate raids; one was a diversion to Heligoland for sea mining. Another was an attack on an explosives factory in France. In addition, Mosquito bombers attacked a number of German cities, to create confusion amongst the fighter defences. The total number of aircraft involved in the night's raid was 1046, with a loss of 10 Lancaster's and 12 Halifax's. This resulted in the loss of 98 airmen, with the rest becoming POW's, though some would manage to evade capture.

US Air Force Into Combat with the Passionate Witch

The new crew I am a member of fly an aircraft called the 'Passionate Witch", named after a book of the same name. The female star of the book is a white witch who uses her powers to look after her man; our crew are hoping to empower the B17 with the same good fortune. At first, I wondered about the Radio operator I was replacing. It transpires he had flown a few trips already, but could not get past the French coast before becoming violently airsick, in the end he was transferred to a ground job. The new 10 man crew of the B17F that I am joining comprises.

Pilot 1st/Lt Robert M Cook from Hollywood California originally, Monroe Washington
Co Pilot 2nd/Lt Ronald J Casey from Pontiac Michigan
Bombardier Nose Gunner John A Rowland from Bynum Montana
Navigator Cheek Gunner Lt John Oswalt from River Forest Illinois
Radio Operator Gunner George A Silva from Mendocino California
Engineer Top Turret Gunner Tech Sgt Gerald H Poplett from Peoria Illinois
Ball Turret Gunner Assist Radio Man Staff Sgt Carl H Blichmann from Dubuque Iowa
Left Waist Gunner Sgt Hubert C Roughton from Sandersville Georgi
Right Waist Gunner Staff Sgt Richard L Thayer from Hope Indiana
Tail Gunner Sgt John C McLaughlin from Hadden Heights New Jersey

From the Diary of Richard Thayer, copies provided by his granddaughter Jessica Thayer Kidwell.

Monday 25th December 1943 our crew have completed 25 Months of training, we are now travelling by train to a Port of

Embarkation. We have not been informed where yet, but the direction of travel is east so it looks like England is the favourite. Sure enough we travel through Chicago with its bright lights flashing by the train windows onward toward the East Coast. The hours go by as we pass over highways with the lights of cars moving below us or the street light of a small town as we pass through it. Then we are told to get ready to disembark from the train. Our final destination is Camp Shanks to the north of New York; this will be our holding point before being allocated a ship, it's now Wednesday 27th December. After five long days, we celebrate New Year's Day in the camp; our only news is we have been allocated a Ship tomorrow. Next morning after breakfast we prepare to leave for the harbour in New York. Transport arrives, we are on our way to the dock, alongside is the biggest Liner I have ever seen the 'Queen Elizabeth'. By five o'clock in the afternoon of the 2nd January we are all aboard, it is rumoured there are eighteen thousand of us on the ship. At 6:00pm we slip away from the dock side to head down river for the open sea. On board the ship every available space has a bed in it; we are informed that there will be a strict rota for access to the deck & fresh air. Below decks all the portholes a blacked out, then on deck there are no lights at all, this is to ensure we are not visible from the sea. By midnight we are out to sea which is quite calm, when we are on deck the stars are brilliant with the only visible light the white foam of the ships wake.

One of crew tells us we are travelling at 30 knots (about 40 mph) while we can, but we may have to slow down as there is a storm brewing ahead of us. Sure enough the following day 4th January the sea starts to become rough, but the ship's crew say this is only the start, expect it to get much worse. Next day we are in the teeth of the storm which is causing havoc among the service men on board. Many of them are being violently sea sick everywhere is in a mess. Fortunately, the following day Thursday we are out of the storm with the ship back up to full speed. After two more days we are in sight of Ireland, though we are sailing to Scotland's river Clyde. The ship anchors in the river with boats ferrying all of the servicemen ashore.

The last part of our journey will be by rail to Norfolk at the other end of the country. At this point the young Americans begin to realise they have entered a war zone. As they travel on the train through Scotland into England, they immediately notice the complete lack of lighting in the streets everywhere is in total darkness. Even the railway carriage windows are fitted with blinds which we have to leave down as German intruders are about. Eventually Richard Thayer and the rest of his crew arrive at Attleboro station, with the last two miles courtesy of the US Air Force transport. Once on camp we start to settle in, then one day I travel 36 miles away to another field where I meet up with a buddy Carl Hogan. I have not seen him for a few years; he tells me he has completed twenty three missions so is sweating on completing his last two to finish. As I listen to his experiences I am shaken, this is one rough theatre, reality of what is in store strikes home. The weather is also an eye opener; the morning started out sunny, but as we set out back to our base the fog comes down. By the time we arrive back at Deopham Green you could almost cut it with a knife. Richard Thayer and his crew would complete a number of missions before George Silva joined them, his first mission would be on 20th February 1944.

February 44 Tutow

Sunday the 20th February, George Silva is on his first mission with 2nd Lt. Young and his old crew as an air gunner, there are over one thousand bombers taking part in today's raid. Our targets are Tutow or surrounding area targets, unfortunately we will have no fighter escort. At the briefing we are advised to only start our engines at the last minute, we will be at the extreme range of our aircraft. After takeoff we assemble into our formation over the North Sea, before climbing to eleven thousand feet. We are aided in forming up by the coloured flares the formation leaders are firing, all the skipper has to do is find the correct colour flare then follow it. Our altitude has been chosen to conserve our precious gas for the return trip. Standing in my Gunnery station, I have to just keep vigilant for enemy fighters. As Denmark appeared ahead of us so did the fighters, FW190's came streaming in to attack our formation. But they were not having an easy time we are giving them a hot reception with our 50 Caliber. This battle continued until we were well out into the Baltic, we have lost at least two aircraft. We are now on our way to Poland; we start to climb to our bombing altitude of seventeen thousand feet. Below us the cloud is gathering and by the time we reach the target, it's completely obscured by cloud.

The formation leader now makes the decision to head back northwest to attack our alternative target, which is Rostock on the German coast of the Baltic. But the cloud does not stop the fighters from coming back again; the air is thick with Ju88's and Me110's. They come in waves sweeping through our formations; our gunners have their hands full fending them off. The noise inside the aircraft when all the gunners are firing at the incoming fighters has to be experienced to be believed, it completely drowns out the sound of the engines. As we approach the Heinkel Marine Shipyards the German fighters are still hitting us, but they break away as soon as the flack starts. From a distance flack just appears as small clumps of black smoke, but as we enter the barrage our aircraft is buffeted by the exploding shells. This is followed by the rattle of shrapnel against the airframe. If it's really close there is a load bang as it hits, and even worse when it penetrates the skin of the aircraft. But now we are on the run up to the target, then as soon we drop our bombs, we head out into the Baltic heading back toward Denmark. The fighters now re-engage us, with our gunners hammering away at them with our 50 Cal.

But as we fly out into the Baltic, the fighters seem not inclined to follow out over the sea. There is a short respite, then the Fw190's return to make our lives miserable as we fly back over Denmark. Finally,we reach the North Sea and relative safety. We can now drop down to a lower altitude to conserve what gas we have, but it's still going to be a close run thing to reach our base. We finally touch down at the end of a ten and a half hour mission, some aircraft are coming to a stop they do not have enough gas to reach their hard standings. This mission has resulted in the loss of six aircraft with one landing in Sweden and the crew being interned. There is also thirty seven aircraft suffering damage, requiring repair work before they can fly again.

February 44 Rostock

We have had four days of rest, some of our guys have been Skeet shooting, the top Brass encourages it as it helps keep the gunners accuracy up to the mark. The rest of the boys will organize a game of baseball or sit around playing cards. Dick Thayer loved to play Poker and he was very good at it or lucky, however you look at card games. Over the weeks he amassed a large pot of money which he sent back home to his parents. This would allow them to buy a family farm, hopefully for Dick to come back to after the war.

Next day I am told to report to 2ndLt. Miller, he is a man short so I have to replace him on this mission. In the briefing room we find the target is Rostock in Germany. The 3rd Air Division we are part of will take three hundred and fifty aircraft to bomb the Submarine shipyards plus the Aircraft plants at Poznan. Our take off is early, then we start forming up over the North Sea at ten thousand feet to save gas.

As we are only going to Rostock our gas is not critical, but it's always good to know we have some in reserve. Approaching Denmark, we climb to seventeen thousand feet as we prepare for the inevitable fighters. Sure enough the top turret gunner spots them as they come at us diving through our formations in waves. But they are not having it all their own way; our gunners answer the attacks with a barrage of 50 Caliber from all the aircraft in the formation. All around us there are enemy fighters going down smoking or in flames, they are paying a heavy price. Then as we approach Rostock, the flack starts to lay down a barrage in front of us, the fighters shy away. The flack is not very concentrated as we start onto the bomb run. As our aircraft surges upwards we know our bombs are released, we start to turn for the flight home. Back over

Denmark the fighters return, but there does not seem as many. Our tail gunner reports some of our B17's falling back out of the formation. We can only hope they make it home, or at least to Sweden. Back on the base we have five aircraft missing, this means there are fifty of our boys lost or P.O.W.s in Germany. The ground crews are going to be busy, over fifty of our planes have been damaged they will need to be repaired. Later it transpired there was a mix up over the target with an accidental release by the pathfinder aircraft causing 60 aircraft to release their bombs early. This was quickly rectified with the rest of the formations hitting the target as planned. We spend the afternoon quietly on the base then hit the sack early; it's been a long day.

25th February 44 Regensburg

Finally, I have transferred to 2Lt. Cooks crew on the 25th February, then at 03:30hrs we are up to prepare for the mission planned for today. In the briefing the tape on the map runs across Germany to Regensburg. Our 3rd Air Division are putting up a combined total of 290 B17's. This mission will be a two pronged attack; the 15th Air Force in Italy would hit the Regensburg plants an hour before we arrived. Their arrival over the target would also draw the fighter defences away from our group we hope. As we lift off the runway at Deopham Green the sky was clear and the sun shines brightly. Our group starts to gather into our protective formation as we climb to twenty thousand feet over the English Channel.

We are to cross the French coast to the North of Le Harve, but we must be south of this track as a barrage of flak greets our arrival. The accuracy is beyond belief, it must be Radar guided as within seconds it's all around us. Some aircraft in our group suffer hits, they are turning back toward England with engines trailing smoke some have visible damage. The Witch has been bounced around by the flak, we can hear the shrapnel crash against the airframe but we are still flying.

Soon we are out of range of the guns on the ground and head for the target. The skipper's voice on the intercom asks for everyone to look out for our fighter escort which is due to joins us. We fly on for another half hour but still no fighter cover arrives. Then our gunners call out fighters circling our formations, but they're not ours it's a gaggle of Me 109 and Ju88 with help from a few Fw 190's. The whole German air force seems to be on our case. They then fly off ahead of us, to begin a frontal attack sweeping through our formations.

During these head on assaults only Gerald Poplett in the top turret, John Rowland in the nose position and Herbie Blichmann in the ball turret can see the approaching fighters. The waist gunners Richard Thayer and Hubert Roughton can only shoot at the fighters attacking other aircraft in our formation. They in turn can see the fighters attacking our plane, so they give supporting fire to us.

When the fighters run out of ammo, they could be seen diving toward the ground to land at nearby airfields, there they will re-arm take on gas before coming back. Then at midday we could see ahead a rising column of smoke from the 15th Air Forces attack on Regensburg. There was a cheer from our gunners as they report P38 Lightning's swooping on the German fighters. Our escort has finally arrived; there has clearly been a mix up with the timing. We can now concentrate on dropping our bombs on the target with less hassle, so we make sure they are on the nose. As we turn for home we are joined by stragglers from other formations seeking protection by linking up with us. Behind us there is an even greater column of smoke rising to over twenty thousand feet from Regensburg. As we fly back toward the coast our gunners report a P38 flying alongside one of the bomber formations. He has an engine out with the propeller feathered so he will fly home with us rather than risk it alone, wise man.

Back at Deopham Green we are absolutely dog tired, we have flown two long trips back to back, it's beginning to take its toll. The trip to Regensburg has resulted in the loss of twelve aircraft. One has ditched in the English Channel, but the crew were saved by the air sea rescue launches of the RAF. Four airmen in returning aircraft were found to have died at their posts, with another twelve wounded, they were transferred to hospital. After debriefing we head off for a meal, then a comfy bed for a long sleep.

The day after the Regensburg raid the sky over most of Great Britain was covered with dense clouds that made flying very hazardous so we were stood down for at least three days with no flying. My buddy Don and I decided that since we were not going to be confined to the base that we would take a bus to the little town of Hingham which was about 3 miles southwest of our airbase.

When we arrived there, we decided that we would get a transfer to go on to Norwich. The main attraction in Norwich was the castle and a museum that had many suits of armour. There were signs in the building that said "Please do not touch anything." My friend Don did not heed these signs; he wanted to see what the armour felt like. Just as he touched one suit of armour it fell over, sending it tumbled down the stairs with pieces flying all over. The ladies in charge of the building were very distressed; they asked that we leave the building so they could put armour back together again. Outside we thought about what we could do now. I remembered that it was Friday and on every Friday the Air Force would provide a bus down to Norwich taking anyone who wanted to go, to a dance. Then it would bring them back to the base after the dance was over, so that is what we decided to do. Heading for the dance hall we saw across the street too large horses attached to a carriage. When I got across the street the horses were standing there with bags over their heads, I asked a man why the horses were standing there with bags over their heads; he laughed and said "They're having their lunch". He explained that they put their oats plus a cut up apple in the bag then at lunch time he slipped the bags over the horse's heads. He wanted to know if I wanted to take a ride in one of the carriages. I asked what do I have to do to drive the horses, he said they're so well trained that all I had to do was say "Giddy up", they would start to go on a prearranged route around the park stopping on the other side so you could get out to get an ice cream. You can eat your ice cream there then; they would come back to the starting place. Whenever you wanted them to stop all you had to do was say "Whoa".

Nearby on a bench was a young lady sitting by herself so I wandered over to ask if she wanted to take a ride with me in the carriage. She said, "My goodness no! If my friends saw me ride in that Princess Elizabeth style carriage, they would laugh and make fun of me". I told her that I would have to ride around by myself. At this she changed her mind saying perhaps she would go around the park with me. I stopped the horse as I had been told, got out and bought us both an ice cream cone. When we had eaten the ice creams the horse duly set off to return to the start point. Here I asked her if she would be going to the dance. She said no because she was in charge of the local anti-aircraft battery, so would not be able to leave her post for the next three weeks. I asked if we could meet at the dance hall in three weeks. She thought that would be all right as several of her teammates often attended the dances. She told me her name was "Marguerite" then since it was time for the bus to leave for the base, we had to say goodbye. When we arrived back at the base from Norwich we found that a red alert was on.

A red alert meant that there could possibly be an early-morning mission; we should get as much shut eye as possible. The 3rd March was another early-morning mission, Jesus it started with a wake-up call about 05:00am. Breakfast at 06:00am followed by briefing for all officers and enlisted personnel. It was then we were told where we were going as well as the route we were taking to get there. We would however return by a different route to get back as safely as possible. The target was a ball bearing factory in north western Berlin; the flight would be a round trip of nine hours. We were told that we could expect heavy anti-aircraft fire, plus the usual fighters waiting for us in and around the target area. We were notified that cloud cover was very dense for our takeoff, continuing up to about 5000 feet. After takeoff we circle in cloud as we climb, but with other fields being as close as three miles, there were other aircraft doing the same very close by. This meant we had to keep our circle very tight, to avoid a possible collision. Sadly, these types of accidents did happen and being close to the ground the chance of surviving was almost nonexistent. Thankfully we emerged from the cloud without a problem; it was something to see hundreds of bombers, popping out of the clouds into the clear blue sky. In order to make sure that all planes that were participating in this mission were up out of the clouds, we circled around the area until everyone was accounted for. We then started to get into our formations.

We now flew on to meet all the other aircraft that would be coming from different areas of East Anglia, to take part in this all out bombing raid on Berlin. As we neared our target area it was strange that anti-aircraft fire was almost nonexistent, fighter planes were also very difficult to find. Then just before the bombardier announced that we were on the bomb run, all hell broke loose. Fighter planes appeared from everywhere attacked our formation then when they cleared, anti-aircraft fire took over. There was damage being suffered by our planes as we fought off many German fighters. We were very successful on our bombing run and were able to fight off the hordes of enemy aircraft that came after us. We received a lot of damage to our plane but thankfully no one was injured, so we were able to land back at home with no physical injuries but a lot of damage especially along our fuselage. In about four days all the damage was repaired by our very able ground crew, we were once again airworthy. For a few days we did no flying, nonetheless we were still confined to the base. Basketball or baseball took up a lot of our time while we were waiting for the next mission.

Monday 6th March 44 Berlin

Today we assemble in the briefing room to hear our fate, when they pull back the curtain the RED tape runs all the way to Berlin again. There is a collective groan running round the room but the mission briefing starts oblivious to it. We are taking 730 heavy bombers to Berlin and the surrounding areas. The First Air Divisions 248 aircraft will go to Berlin, while the Second Air Division will target Genshagen with 226 aircraft. Finally, our Third Air Division are contributing 242 aircraft to attack Templin, Verden, Kalkeberge, Potsdam, Oranienburg or Wittenberg. Our take off is timed to allow all aircraft to assemble over the North Sea in the required order. The First Division are in the air earliest with our Third division right behind them, only then will the Second Division take to the sky. We first assemble into our own formations then look to join with the First Division formations ahead of us. Somewhere behind us the Second Division are doing the same to become our air armada on its way to Germany. Very soon we are crossing the Dutch coast as Bob Cook our skipper asks everyone to watch for our 800 strong fighter escorts assigned to support our mission. By the time we reach the German border we are still without our fighters.

Unbeknown to us the Germans have played a diversionary tactic by assembling a fighter force of their own to attack our escort as they cross into Holland. This leaves our bomber force without protection as the Zuider Zee slips past below us, we cross into Germany. Suddenly the air is full of reports of approaching Me109 and Fw190's; they are circling before coming head on through our formations. George Silva leaves his radio to man the machine gun above his station to provide additional defensive firepower. This head on attack is an unnerving experience, the closing speed of the fighters with our bombers is over 500 miles per hour. They stream through our formations firing their canon and machine guns throughout this brief encounter. One of the main dangers of this head on attack is collision. As they sweep toward us, they reach a   point when they have to pass below the bomber they are attacking, or pass over it. If they rise over us Gerald Popplet in the top turret is waiting to rake the underside of the fighter as it flashes by. Similarly, if they pass below us Herbie Blichmann in the ball turret is waiting to give them a hot reception. An even bigger danger is, if a bomber deviates from level flight, then an impact is a real possibility.

When a collision does take place, nobody sees it. They only hear the explosion created by a fighter hitting a bomber with half full gas tanks and a full bomb load. This can cause a shock wave large enough to damage or destroy other bombers in the formation around it quite easily. Fortunately, we escape that possibility on this occasion. As we continue to Berlin the fighters disappear back to their airfields to re-arm and refuel, they will return to attack us on the way home. We now have to contend with the flack. Ahead is our lead aircraft with its H2X equipment, this allows it to see the ground outlines through cloud to ensure our bombing is accurate. When the flack starts this aircraft is surrounded by it, one engine catches fire but there must be other problems, it is losing height rapidly. Then unbelievably it explodes right in front of our formation, a bright flash even in the daylight is followed by a black cloud. There are no parachutes seen to fall from the wreckage, though later we find four of the twelve man crew were taken prisoner. The rest sadly perished in the explosion. Our bombardier is now advising our pilot of the target ahead, directing the Passionate Witch on the bomb run. Heavy flack was still bursting around us, with the sound of shrapnel rattling against the hull, very disquieting. The wait as the Bombardier searches for a target of significance seems like an eternity, then the upward surge of the Witch shows the bombs have gone.

Our formation now starts to turn for home while maintaining our contact with the other formations in the group. Passing out of range of the flack we find our fighters have joined up with us. But they will only be able to stay for part of the way home as their earlier dogfights had used up their gas supply. But now the German fighters are back, coming in from behind our bombers. John McLaughlin spots them approaching, he engages them from his tail gun position. One Fw-190 crosses in front of him and receives a long burst from his twin 50 caliber guns, the fighter immediately catches fire to spiral out of sight toward the ground. Our fighters catch up with the last of them, so we are given a respite. We are half way to Holland when our fighters wish us good luck, we are on our own again, they promptly dive away to do hit and run attacks on any airfield they find on the way home. As we reach Holland the German fighters return, diving through our formations from ten o'clock high with our gunners hitting back with everything they have. We are taking casualties as aircraft are falling out of formation, but the fighters are paying a price for their daring. Our gunners are calling out hits, with fighters falling away trailing smoke or flames. Our tail gunner John McLaughlin is having a field day shooting down another German fighter as it swings in to attack a B17 in our formation. The rest are flying away back to their bases to lick their wounds and count their losses. The remains of our formations are crossing the Dutch coast to the safety of the North Sea to reach our bases. Back at Deopham Green the scale of the damage is revealed, the raid has resulted in the loss of sixty nine aircraft in total. This is a loss rate of 9.5%, with over two hundred aircrew paying the ultimate price in this fight for freedom, the rest were taken prisoner. We in the Third Division have lost thirty four planes with one hundred and twenty damaged. The Germans on the other hand, have lost over one hundred and seventy fighters either damaged or destroyed. While the aircraft can be replaced the Luftwaffe are running out of experienced fighter pilots to take the place of those lost.

The Eighth Air Force would later credit John McLaughlin with the honour of being the first bombing gunner to shoot down an enemy fighter over Berlin.

9th March 44 Berlin Thursday.

Its 3:30am, we are called from our beds to head down to the mess hall for breakfast. Then it's off to collect our flying kit, parachutes, heated suits, oxygen masks and flak jackets before heading into the briefing room. When I first joined my new crew, I was offered a choice of parachute type either a back pack or a chest pack, I picked the chest type as I would be able to lean back in my seat. Unfortunately, this became a nuisance when I lean forward to send or receive signals, so I normally unclipped it to store it under my desk. This would prove to be an unfortunate move on my part at a later date. We have had a three day break, but any recuperation disappears in the briefing; as the curtain is drawn back It's the big city again. All three divisions are involved so there will be 526 aircraft taking part comprising B24's and B17's. Our fighter escort will be an 800 strong mixture of P-38 Lightning's, P-47 Thunderbolts plus P-51 Mustangs. Today the First and Third air divisions will bomb Berlin, with the Second air division targeting Hanover, Brunswick and Nienburg. We have been warned that cloud cover could be thick over the target so radar equipped pathfinder aircraft will be used to identify targets to be bombed. The crew of the Passionate Witch are climbing aboard; each member now goes through his own personnel check routines before takeoff.

George is checking the radio as the ground crew are preparing to fire up the engines when the mission is given the OK. As we sit waiting the silence of the English countryside is broken by the sounds of birds calling from the trees. Then the GO flare arcs across the sky, the mission is on and our skipper starts up the engines. All round the base aircraft are firing up their engines, the noise levels rise dramatically. This causes the birds to rise from the tree's to fly away from the Base, hopefully they will fly away. A bird strike on takeoff is the last thing we need, losing an engine at this time could spell disaster with a full gas and bomb load. Bob Cook our pilot is now looking to leave the hard standing to join the queue of aircraft waiting to takeoff from Deopham Green. All too soon we are on the end of the runway ready for the off. There is a sequel from the brakes as the Witch comes to a halt on the end of the runway. When Bob receives the signal to go, the engines are brought up to full power before he releases the brakes. At first the Witch is slow to pick up speed, but then the acceleration becomes noticeable, as the tail wheel lifts we are really moving fast. Before the end of the runway, we are lifting clear of Deopham's airfield.

This is a critical time, if we have an engine failure now Bob will have his hands full keeping us airborne. But the four Wright Cyclones just keep roaring away, as we climb to follow the rest of our formation out over the North Sea. Cloud has started to gather ahead as we approach the Dutch coast.

We are now flying at over twelve thousand feet; we are level with the top of the cloud. Then as our fighters arrive, they spread out, looking for any German fighters who may show up. Soon we are over Germany approaching Berlin when there are calls of fighters approaching. It's strange but there are only about six Me 109's who turn to attack the formations, but our fighters are onto them before they can get near. The Germans put up a short combat, but with our fighter boys queuing up to shoot at them they disappear into the cloud for safety. They do not reappear, which pleases the bomber crews but frustrates our fighter pilots, they were looking for a fight. The first black puffs, indicating flack ahead of us sees our fighters swing away, leaving us to our bomb runs. One thing is for certain cloud or no cloud the flak gunners can always give us a rough ride, their Radar can see where we are and at what height we are flying. Ahead of our formation the pathfinders are having problems with their H2X equipment, they are struggling to find the target. Eventually they release their bombs, we follow suit adding ours onto the city of Berlin. The Germans are getting a taste of the medicine they have been handing out over the years. Our flight back to England was uneventful, our fighters flying around us while keeping an eye open for any German opposition that might dare show their faces. We arrive back at Deopham Green to find three of our planes are missing, though two crews are picked up by the Air Sea Rescue boats. This means ten of our boys are now POW's in German Camps. Even though we are all tired we have to report for debriefing, the intelligence people want a report on everything. What was the weather conditions like during the mission, how much flak had we encountered? How many fighters we saw, how many are we claiming to have shot down and how many of our bombers we saw shot down. We have lost quite a few planes today and a lot of good men are not coming home.

Bad weather gives us break from combat, we have time for a little R and R. One of my buddies Max and I are on the way to Norwich to a dance with an overnight stay in the City. We board the local bus settling down on the long back seat. We are both a little tired, the bus is not very warm, in no time at all we both nod off to sleep. The driver wakes us up at the terminus with the bad news this is the end of the line, he will return in the morning at 7:30am to go back to Norwich. We both call into the local Pub but apart from a pint of beer there are no rooms available. Apparently, the British army have brought some of its troops back from the Middle East so they have commandeered a lot of the accommodation in the area. One of the locals suggest calling at the police station, they will put us up in a cell for the night in an emergency. On the way we ask another man for directions, when we explain why he offers to put us up overnight. The lady of the house is amazingly relaxed, about letting two strangers stay in her home, I cannot believe it. There is a single bed upstairs which is the daughters who is away at school. Max gets this single bed; I pick the sofa in the front room because there is a fire lit. Next morning, we are served a cup of tea with a few cookies for which she apologises, food is in short supply. We both thank them for their kindness; we promise to return with some goodies from the base. Max makes a note of their names along with the address. Well two days later, Max's crew fail to return from a mission and I became a POW not long after. I still think about that lovely couple, I hope they did not think we had deliberately forgotten them.

16th March 44 Augsburg Thursday

Today I am about to do my seventh mission, it's been a few days since our last trip to Berlin; in the briefing we are being tasked to bomb Augsburg to the North West of Munich. We will be joining with the First Division to provide a force of five hundred B17's to bomb factories or airfields in the area. There will also be an escort of eight hundred and fifty fighters, comprising P-38's, P-47's and P-51's all looking to give the Germans Hell. Our route from Deopham across the North Sea is uneventful, but once we cross into France and Germany the Luftwaffe fighters arrive in force. Our fighters pounce on them straight away, but there is still enough of them to get through attacking our formations. Aboard the Passionate Witch everyone who can man a gun is defending our formation from the Me109's and Fw190's. Doing everything possible, they can only watch damaged B17's falling out of the formations, they will not be coming home with us. Then as we approach Augsburg the German fighters veer away with our boys in chase, they will be harried all the way back to their airfields. We now have to contend with the flack from the defences on the ground. Our third division drop their bombs on the markers laid down by the pathfinders, but cloud is becoming a problem. About twenty of the last bombers over Augsburg cannot see the target markers, so they divert to attack Ulm as a target of opportunity. Our return journey back to the coast is fairly quiet; our fighter escort must be keeping the German fighters busy elsewhere.

When we arrive back to Deopham Green we find just how costly the mission has been, we have lost thirteen aircraft. Later we are informed that four damaged aircraft have landed safely in Switzerland with twenty eight airmen now being interred for the rest of the war. One of our bombers has gone down in the drink as the British say; they have been saved by the RAF air sea rescue launches.

Dick Thayer with the rest of the crew now has a couple of days leave. With his pals Red and Wally, he heads into Norwich, what a quaint old world town it is. Much to our surprise two British Officers introduce themselves, they promptly give us a guided tour of the City. They show us round the narrow winding lanes with their cute little shops selling everything from shoes, clothing or groceries. But the Cathedral was amazing with its stained glass windows; it just takes your breath away. Next morning after breakfast we continue our exploration, then after lunch we take in a stage show. Later we had tea and cakes in a little old world cafe, before catching the bus back to camp. Unfortunately, this bus stops at a terminus about three miles from the base so we have to walk the rest of the way in the rain.

Frankfurt 20[h] March

Frankfurt is again on the receiving end of this concentrated air assault, when on the 20th March the American Air force makes a daylight raid on the City. George is on his eighth mission since arriving with the 452nd Bomber group at Deopham Green in Norfolk. With his crew George prepares for this Frankfurt mission. Climbing away from the airfield the B17's circle to gain height, then begin gathering into the box formation essential for their defence. Setting out for the target across the English Channel the high winds and the varied cloud is causing the Fortresses problems. The risk of midair collision, in the turbulent conditions, force the aircraft formation further apart, thereby reducing their defensive strength. Each box formation had also drifted apart causing problems for the escort fighters who had to scurry between them trying to provide cover. Approaching the target, we turn onto the bomb run, to be greeted by a barrage of flak which is thankfully poorly aimed. That wonderful feeling of our B17 lifting upward as the bomb load was released raised our spirits as we turned for home. Drifting in and out of the now heavy cloud we became separated from the rest of the group. Then as we skirted Paris, this protective cloud cover deserted us, we felt completely naked flying through the clear sky. Our vigilant gunners were the first to spot the approaching fighters, a group of about eight Me109's and FW190's as they quickly swooped on us. The fighters with their heavier armament opened fire first; our B17 shudders under the onslaught. One of the Witches engines has been damaged, the propeller spins to a standstill reducing our speed. Their attack was quickly answered by the rattle of the Witches gunners hitting back. Up in the cockpit Bob Cook is listening to the gunners calling out the direction of the attacks as they began. This allowed him to turn our aircraft in response, to reduce the time the fighters could bring their guns to bear on us. Such is the ferocity of the battle that as one fighter attacks from the ten o-clock direction. Bob Cook and Ron Casey in response turn toward the oncoming foe which the bombardier John Rowland engages with the nose guns.

The fighter pilot is so shocked by this aggressive tactic; he veers away from the bomber rather than risk a head on collision. One of the first passes by the other fighter's results in both waist gunners being hit by an exploding 20mm canon shell. Hubert Roughton suffered serious injuries as he was thrown across the fuselage by the impact, but the chest parachute and his flak jacket he was wearing saves his life. Our Co-pilot Ron Casey has arrived from the cockpit, he starts to attend to Hubert's injuries, there were wounds to both of his legs; his right shoulder and arm are badly broken. His crew mate Dick Thayer is bleeding from a facial injury, he has also been hit in both legs during the attack which are also bleeding badly, but he continues to man both guns as the battle continued. When he finds no-one to engage with the left waist gun, he moves to the right waist gun to continue the battle, he is fighting like a man possessed.

We were not totally defenceless as one pass results in the top turret gunner Sgt Popplet sending a FW-190 down in flames. Then the Navigator John Osswalt who has now manned a gun position fired on a second FW-190, which just blew up on the run in to attack us. Sitting in his radio compartment, George Silva was transmitting SOS messages, asking for any friendly fighters in the area to come to our aid. As he continued to transmit, there was an explosion close to his head he instinctively ducks, to find a glowing piece of shrapnel embedded in his table. This attack raked the Passionate Witch from end to end wounding the tail gunner John McLaughlin in his back. Then mercifully everything went dark as our pilot finds a bank of cloud to hide in, the attacks stopped.

Moving back along the fuselage, George releases the ball turret gunner Carl Blichmann to assist the injured waist gunners, allowing our Co-Pilot to return to the cockpit. John McLaughlin has to leave his tail gun position as a fire breaks out in one of the ammunition boxes which put us all at risk from an explosion. Fortunately, he manages to extinguish the fire before it gets out of hand, then he returns to his tail gun position. Standing there I could not believe the number of holes in the aircraft, air was screaming in through them, as was the cold. Moving back to my radio position, our Navigator John Osswalt was giving the pilot a new heading for home, as we descended to very low level. Hugging the ground, we hope to use our camouflage to hide our presence from the air. Moving into the nose section, George joined the Bombardier John Rowland, who was manning the nose gun, so I manned the cheek guns. As the French country side flashed beneath us, I marvelled at the speed of the Witch considering we were running on three engines. Then we settle down to looking for targets of opportunity; a radio station we spotted was promptly raked with bullets, a flak battery received the same treatment. A train running on a rail track was given a good hosing of 50 cal as we flashed by, as was a Tug boat on a river. There were other occasions when we passed over workers in the fields who waved as we exchanged victory signs with them.

Whether they saw our returned greeting's I am not sure. Any sign of movement was evaluated then fired on if military, a gun battery we approached opened fire as we machine gunned them. Their return fire punched a hole through the empty bomb bay removing the walkway to the rear of the aircraft. Then when the coast appeared we thought we were safe, but a coastal battery opened fire on us. Huge plumes of water erupted in front of us; I thought the Witch was coming to a stop as we hit them.

But as we came out the other side, we were still airborne. As we flew out of range of the gun battery the decision to lighten the aircraft was taken so guns, ammo, flak jackets all went over the side into the Channel. Everything that was not bolted down went overboard to keep the Witch in the air. Crossing the English south coast near Hastings, we headed for the nearest airfield, a Canadian field at Dunsfold. While the crew take up crash positions, the skipper lowered the undercarriage, but the lack of hydraulics, meant we were without brakes. The landing was smooth; we just rolled down the runway out of control, coming to rest after we left the concrete, drifting onto the grass infield. As we climbed from the aircraft, the base personnel arrived to begin removing our injured crew for attention, as we all exchanged words of relief at our survival. I remember Sgt Roughton being carried away on a stretcher he called to Lt Cook our skipper. "When I am better I want to come back to the crew", "You Bet' was Bob's reply. Then as Hubert Roughton, Richard Thayer and John McLaughlin were taken away to hospital, the rest of the crew walked slowly round the Passionate Witch, staring at the extent of the damage. There did not seem to be an undamaged panel on the whole aircraft, how had it kept flying. We could only stand thinking how or if, a repair crew could bring her back into flying condition again.

A few days later back at Deopham Green, George Silva began wondering, would he have been better off with his original crew. His answer came sooner than he expected, when the B17 named "Star Eyes" Piloted by Charles Young with the rest of George's original crew, flew on a raid to Germany. Over Rodenbeck they were attacked by fighters, their aircraft explodes into a ball of fire which turned into a large black cloud. From this cloud fall's the four engines with other large pieces of debris trailing black smoke down to the earth. What was left hanging in the sky, looked like a huge grotesque airborne jellyfish, waiting to snare other aircraft with its tendrils. George's original crew were as follows.

Pilot 2nd/Lt Charles C Young Jr
Co-Pilot 2nd/Lt Charles W Clark
Nav 2nd/Lt Edward S Wodicka
Bombardier 2nd/Lt Sherman H Farr
Engineer T/Sgt Lawrence A Koon
Radioman S/Sgt Charles L Saul (George's replacement)
Waist Gunner T/Sgt Frederick Buckingham
Waist Gunner Sgt Kenton H Anderson
B. T. Gunner S/Sgt Robert A Andrews
Tail Gunner Sgt Joseph O Sujkowski

From the ten man crew, only three survived to land on German soil; Edward Wodicka was uninjured but Frederick Buckingham only sprained his ankle on landing. The engineer, Lawrence Koon suffered a broken back; he was in severe pain from internal injuries. He was quickly taken to the hospital at Oldenburg on the 28th March 44. There despite the effort of the medical staff at this hospital, he died from his injuries on the 15th July 1944. This shocking news of the loss of the crew he trained with, brought home to George there would be no safe options, not in this war. All of his thoughts though are of the young men he trained with who will not be returning home to their families and the pain this will cause.

Frankfurt

Back at RAF Elsham Wold's, Jack Spark is getting ready for his next operational trip it's the 22nd March 1944. Walking into the briefing for our third trip, we find its Frankfurt again, at first, I wondered if there had been a mistake, has the name not been changed. That illusion lasted only seconds, when the Section commander confirmed, we were going back to finish the job we started. There was the usual patter about the importance of this target for the war effort, so we have to concentrate on our accuracy. Climbing into the aircraft, we prepare for takeoff thinking about how this trip can be different from the last one, it's the same target. Take off time was 18:40, after circling over the base to gain altitude; we set out for our first turning point Mablethorpe. From there it's East across the North Sea, to a point off the Dutch coast; over the sea we are watchful for enemy aircraft. Our bombers are on the way to Germany; their aircraft are coming the other way, to attack Britain.

So, it's not unknown for a confrontation, to come out of nowhere and with a closing speed of 500 mph, it can be over in seconds. Crossing the Dutch coast, we turn for Osnabruck in Germany; the route has been chosen, to make it difficult for the defences to determine the final target. Approaching Osnabruck, we have Bremen to the North, Berlin ahead with Dusseldorf to the West. When we reach the City we turn to the South, heading for our real target Frankfurt, as the searchlights rise to probe the sky for us. Our gunners report night fighters, attacking bombers to our rear, so we gratefully accept the cover offered by light cloud. Running up to the target, the pathfinder flares are already falling as Norman our bomb aimer prepares, to direct Fred onto the aiming point. The flak is much more concentrated than our last trip, but the searchlights seem to be more prolific than before. Despite this barrage we manage to drop our bombs without suffering any damage. Then BANG!, BANG!, the shock as the flack hits has to be experienced to be believed. Fred swings our Lancaster to starboard then dives to throw off the aim of the anti-aircraft gunners.

As things go quiet, he asks are there any injuries, thankfully there are none, but the aircraft has suffered damage somewhere. Arthur our flight engineer is watching his fuel gauges for any leaks, we seem to be ok. The mid upper gunner Ken Smart, is rotating his turret looking for damage, the only thing he reports are marks on the port outer wing section. Leaving the target area, Ron our Navigator gives Fred a heading for our next turning point, Mannheim. We are on our way home, but the gunners are reporting more fighter activity. There is tracer flashing in the dark sky some distance away, giving evidence to the duels still being played out in the thin air.

From Mannheim we cross Belgium, Northern France, then over the North Sea to cross the coast near Ipswich. We are back over England almost home, only Norfolk and Lincolnshire to cover to reach Elsham. Joining the circuit Jack announces our presence; he is answered by the voice of the ground controller. It is a brief conversation, but reassuring as we wait to be given instructions to land. Flying in the circuit there is still danger, we must always be vigilant. Night Fighters often arrive over bases like ours, knowing tired crews will relax, thinking they are home safe and sound. Aircraft can be attacked as they touch down, with the rest waiting to land thrown into chaos, as the runway lights are extinguished. Once on the ground, Fred walks round our aircraft, there is damage to the port wing with holes in the lower surface through to the upper surface. The ground crew are looking to repair the holes as we get rid of our flying gear, then it's into the debriefing room, to talk to the Intelligence officer. He wants to know everything; nothing seems to be too trivial. Were you attacked by fighters, did you see any bombers shot down, how concentrated was the flack, or searchlights.

When he was finished we all trooped into the mess, for breakfast, our bacon and egg treat. In the mess, we sit talking to Jerry Chase's crew, Fred trained with Jerry and as both our crews started at Elsham together we had become friends. During the breakfast, it comes out, that one of the aircraft attacked, by the night fighter's was Jerry's crew. They had put up a ferocious defence, with both gunners, claiming a possible FW 190 destroyed in the encounter.

We lost one aircraft from 103 Squadron on the raid, when the Lancaster of Flt/Sgt McInerney (RAAF), explodes over Rodelheim he is the only survivor. One of his crew, Sgt D. J. Findley aged 18 becomes one of the youngest airmen to be killed, in Bomber Command during 1944.

The Crew of Lancaster III	ND329	PM-A
F/S	L.J. McInerney RAAF	POW	
Sgt	S.A. Lewis	RAF	Kia
W/O	N.J. Trewavas	RNZAF	Kia

Sgt	W.A. Munday	RAF	Kia
Sgt	S.W. Tolley	RAF	Kia
Sgt	D.J. Findlay	RAF	Kia
Sgt	N. Graham	RAF	Kia

There were 816 aircraft, taking part in last night raid on Frankfurt, with a diversion to Kiel to try and confuse the German defences. Total losses for the night were 26 Lancaster's plus 7 Halifax's, 184 young airmen have paid the ultimate price in the fight for freedom, with 47 taken pow or evading.

Passionate Witch #2

March 23, 1944 an officer from the 452nd headquarters came into our Hut, he tells us we are to meet our officers out near the landing field. When we met up with them, they were looking at the sky toward the north, as we watched we observed an aircraft coming in for a landing. As it got closer to the landing field, we saw that it was a new B-17G. It was all silvery then as it landed; the officer told us that this was our replacement aircraft, which caused a lot of excitement among our crew. After the plane came to a stop in the parking area, we all hastily got to our crew positions. I went immediately to my radio position, marvelling at all the new equipment. After lunch we returned to our new plane to take it for a ride around the countryside for about an hour, we all agreed that it was a great plane. The rest of the day was spent at each position, making sure that all was in working order. After we were all out of the plane, the ground crew taxied her off to the paint shop, where it would have to be painted with our logo of Passionate Witch #2.

Jack Spark Berlin 24th March 44.

It's a fine morning, Jack and his crew are up, ready to face the day when someone produces a camera suggesting we take a crew photo. We have not taken one so far and cameras are not really allowed, but we troop off to stand in front of M Mother. Here one of the ground crew takes our group photo under the nose of our Lancaster, before Bob has a photo taken in front of his rear turret. The ground crew are filling our aircraft's tanks to the maximum, so it's going to be a long trip; the rumours are it could be Hamburg or Berlin. Later operations are confirmed for tonight, but we have to wait for the briefing to know where too.

As we start to file into the Op's room, the people in front of us could be heard muttering and grumbling. Its Berlin was the word filtering back to those waiting to enter, a feeling of uncertainty swept over me. We had all listened to the old hands, talking about the Big City with its fearsome defences; we know it is going to be a rough trip. The last time the Squadron flew to Berlin, was the 15th February, just as we were going home on our first leave. Our route tonight is to Denmark, into the Baltic to a point North of Berlin before heading south to the Capital, then returning across Germany, Holland to return home. The Met officer has given a projected weather report for the raid, which included a North Westerly wind, with a speed of 60mph (96Kph). Our crew were also informed, that we had been chosen, to gather actual wind speed figures then relay them back, to Bomber command Head Quarters. Fred is told that we were to be one of the first aircraft to take off, we are one of sixty aircraft to back up the pathfinder force. This means we have to be there, when the flares go down, to bomb the target area, helping to illuminate it, for the following aircraft. After the briefing, we collect our kit then wait for the transport, to our dispersal. Standing there is, M Mother waiting for us, with the ground crew fussing round her nervously, putting the final touches to their aircraft. Working in the open all the time, ground crews are resourceful people, to the extent that they have built a wooden hut from scrap timber to shelter in. It is in the lee of this hut that we stand, out of the freshening wind, waiting for them to hand over the aircraft.

Our crew are standing together, but no words are exchanged between us, we are acutely aware that this is the 'Big City' we are off to. There is also an ominous feeling among the crew; this is to be our biggest test; we are headed on a 'Trip into Hell'. Finally the ground crew hand over the Lancaster, we climb aboard take off time was 18:30.

We start to climb to altitude on a triangular route, before heading for Mablethorpe the first turning point. Here Ron the Navigator gives Fred a heading for the Danish coast with an E.T.A. I busy myself listening for signals from H.Q. every fifteen minutes. As we approach the coast Ron and I realise there is something wrong, we are much earlier that predicted plus we are south of our track. We should have crossed the coast at Romo but we are over the North Friesland Islands.

I confirm our position as Ron calculates the wind speeds, "It's almost 120mph (192Kph) Jack" exclaims Ron, double the expected figure. After doing the calculations again, Ron gives me the figures to transmit back to Bomber Command H.Q. "This is going to have serious consequences for the bomber stream, especially the new crew's" comment's Ron. Over the intercom, he talks to Fred, about the time problem the winds are causing; we are going to have to zigzag, on the Baltic leg to use up the time. Over Denmark I take up my position in the astrodome, to provide extra eyes watching for night fighters. Looking back down the fuselage, I can see Ken Smarts turret slowly turning, checking for any movement that will betray the presence of a fighter. Up in the nose, Norman Barker our bomb aimer is also manning the front turret, helping to look for fighters. We must spot them first if we are to survive tonight; there is no chance of us competing with their heavier armament. Looking at my watch it's time to return to my radio; when Bob in the rear turret calls "Fighter Corkscrew Starboard". Grabbing hold of anything to hand, I know what is to happen; Fred stands the Lancaster on its Starboard wing tip as we plunge in a diving turn. As I hold my position in the astrodome, I watch the tracer from the Ju88 flash through the night sky, but thankfully it scores no hits on our aircraft. The Corkscrew manoeuvre we have just performed is the standard procedure, for fending off night fighters. During an attack from a fighter the gunners have to allow a deflection for the high speed pass the enemy aircraft makes. However, during the corkscrew, the bomber turns into the fighter's path so the mid upper gunner, now looks straight up at the fighter. This gives him a perfect bead on the incoming aircraft. After the war it came to light that during an attack, the night fighter pilots most fear the mid upper gunners position, because of this. As we resume our course, I return to my radio to receive a message from H.Q., they confirmed the severe gale force winds we had found. They had at first refused to accept the wind speed we passed to them, continuing to transmit a 60mph figure. But as other aircraft confirmed our higher figure, they eventually accepted our figure as correct.

This led to the raid becoming known as "The Night of the Big Wind". I pass the message to Ron, who nods in agreement; he has already started a zigzag course to avoid arriving at the target too early.

Though this information is not well received by Arthur our flight engineer, the wind on our run home from the target will be a head wind. This will use up our fuel more quickly than expected so this additional zigzagging will reduce our precious reserves. By now though, we are out in the Baltic to the North of Berlin, Ron finally gives Fred the new course for the target. It's a short half hour run from the Baltic to Berlin with the tension building. Starting our bomb run we are still early but there are already fires ahead of us, then all hell breaks loose, searchlights appear and we are coned by them. The unbelievable brightness, is something I have never experienced before, my radio position is normally illuminated by a very small light. But now I can see every rivet on the inside of the fuselage, I can even see the paint is badly chipped in places. Then this surreal image changes as the flak arrives, our aircraft plunges as Fred dives to break free from the searchlight. The noise of the air screaming over the airframe is terrific; I began to wonder how much more our Lancaster can take. Then Fred starts to hauls back on the column; as we level out the searchlights loose contact with us. We are also now over the target so Fred opens the bomb doors and Norman drops our load into the middle of the fires. Our aircraft is now in a very dangerous position, above us are 800 aircraft dropping their bombs down onto us. Fred loses no time in turning away from the target; we escape into the darkness of the surrounding countryside. Clawing back the height we have lost I stand in the astrodome, off to starboard the searchlights are still waving back and forth. Then I see them lock onto another target, though it's a German night fighter that's about to get the treatment as the flak starts to burst around him. But as I watch he fires a Red and White star flare, the effect is instant the searchlights are extinguished, the flak ceases. I make a mental note of this, to report back at our debriefing as I go back to my radio. Climbing away from Berlin, Fred calls on the intercom to ask if we should go home alone, or circle to rejoin the bomber stream, before heading home. Arthur comments that this will use up fuel we can ill afford, we all agree to continue alone risking the night fighters. We drone on through the darkness when Bob calls enemy aircraft dead astern "Corkscrew Port Go", Fred flings the Lancaster violently to port. His response was so fierce, that I was thrown to the floor on the starboard side, as the first burst of canon fire rips through the fuselage. My radio station takes a direct hit as hot shrapnel flies about me; I wait for the seemingly never ending assault to pass. Lying on the floor behind the wings main spar, I prayed this strong frame would offer me some protection from the attack. Unlike my grandfather, I was never a deeply religious man, but I remember laying there terrified. At the top of my voice, I am singing the hymn "Oh God our Help in Ages Past" trying to make sense, of the madness taking place about me. Then in an instant it stops, now as Fred levels out our aircraft I start to get to my feet, then it starts all over again. Ken Smart our mid upper gunner is hammering away at the incoming FW190 as Fred corkscrews the Lancaster to Starboard to throw it off. Grasping the step in front of the main spar, I watch flashes as sparks fly around the wing and fuselage on the port side. Fred is throwing the Lancaster all over the sky try to get the fighter of our backs, when the firing stops again. Then one more time the FW190 returns to rake our battered Lancaster, before disappearing into the darkness, as quickly as it appeared. The fighter has either expended its ammunition, or has lost us in the darkness as he did not return.

The steady beat of our four Merlin's, brings back some normality to the chaos of the last few minutes, as I cautiously checked my equipment. The ground to air set was a total wreck; the intercom is also u/s so we could not communicate with each other. Looking from my window, there is a huge hole in the Port wing, with a large section of the skin missing one of the fuel tanks clearly visible. The only good thing was, we are not on fire, as this really would have brought the fighters down like Vultures to finish us off. Ron's head appeared round his curtain with a written note from the Skipper, 'Check the rest of the crew then get the intercom working'. I could see there was nothing wrong with the intercom set, there must be a break in the circuit somewhere aft. Uncoupling my main oxygen line, I clipped on a ten minute bottle then with my torch I set off to check on the crew. Climbing over the main spar I could not believe the amount of damage, the fuselage was riddled with holes, the cold of the air coming in was intense. The sight of Ken Smarts legs, hanging loose from the mid upper turret hits me, I feared the worse. Reaching out I touched one of his legs as I shine my torch into his turret, his thumbs up sign came as a great relief. His gun turret's hydraulics are out of action, he was operating it by hand, his footrest had been shot away in the fighters first pass.

My ten minute set was nearly exhausted, I have to go back to collect three more bottles before continuing to the rear turret. Easing past Ken's position while trying not to put a foot into one of the gaping holes, I neared Bob's turret. As I shone the torch on the inside, the sight that confronted me, made me retch violently. Bob had taken the full brunt, of the first attack and the sight of what a 20mm canon does to the human body, will stay with me for the rest of my life. I had never experienced a death in battle, or any death for that matter it was horrific. I tried to open the doors of the rear turret to remove Bob's body, but they were buckled, totally jammed shut, so I had to leave him where he was. Turning away from the rear turret, I found the extreme cold of the air, blasting into my face brought relief from the horrors I had just seen.

Then in front of me I could see the damage to the intercom wiring I set about fixing it, while holding the torch under my arm. The wiring of the Lancaster was colour coded which helped me in identifying the torn cable of the intercom. Affecting any repair, however crude, is all that's required of me, I must bring the communication system back to life. As I returned to my radio station, the voice of the skipper already talking to the crew greeted me, as I plugged my headset in. I conveyed the death of Bob to the crew plus the extent of the damage, which they received in silence, though the sadness could be almost felt in that silence. The skipper's voice explained that the damage was causing the aircraft to climb violently. He was only able to retain control, by jamming his knees behind the control column to push it forward. There was no means of correcting this with the trimmers; such was the damage to the flying control surfaces. This renders us virtually defenceless with such limited manoeuvrability, though we have no alternative but to continue, into the night. Up in the cockpit, Norman the bomb aimer is helping to hold the control column forward, to give Fred some relief and time to massage his aching legs. Then just as we thought things could not get worse, the searchlights hit us again. We are miles off course, somewhere over the Ruhr, the flack starts to burst around us. Completely at its mercy, Fred ordered "Clip on chutes" as I reach for mine to find it in shreds. Then the intensity of the light brought a flash back, of the night fighter caught in its own searchlights. I plunged into my bag of flares to retrieve a triple red and white star flare, without asking I fired them off into the sky.

The effect was instantaneous, the searchlight went out, the flack stopped firing; we flew on into the darkness. Fred's voice comes on the intercom asking me what I had done; I recounted the night fighter firing off flares, to escape the searchlights. Our crew now start to hope we had seen the end to the attacks; mercifully we did not encounter any more trouble.

Ron our Nav is now asking me to try for a radio fix, because we had been blown so far of course, he was unsure as to our location. After a short delay, I obtained the fix, Ron's plots show we were out in the Channel off the French coast but headed out into the Atlantic. He immediately gives Fred a new heading, he slowly brings the sluggish Lancaster ever so carefully round onto it; we are on our way home. Crossing the English South coast we head for the nearest airfield. But unbeknown to us the Luftwaffe had heavily bombed London and the South that night, so everything was in total darkness. As we have no means of communicating with the ground, I decide to stand in the astrodome looking out over the featureless blackness below. Then in the distance, I saw a flashing pundit light, the Morse code signal was DD, the first and last letters of the airfield name. Checking my code book it showed it was Dunsfold, in Surrey, I inform the skipper. Fred starts a wide circle around the light as I begin firing off the Red Flares I had so carefully hoarded over the weeks. After firing off about a dozen or so, someone on the ground takes a chance on our being a friendly they switched the runway lights on. Immediately Fred gave the crew a final chance to use their parachutes, rather than risk the crash landing. Jack kept the knowledge of his wrecked chute to himself. Fortunately, the crew all voted to stay with the skipper and bring Bob's body home. We did not need a second invitation to land so Fred as quickly as was possible brought our crippled Lancaster round to start our landing run. The crew had moved to our crash positions behind the main spar ready to evacuate the aircraft after landing. As we approached the runway Fred lowered the undercarriage, he starts to line up for landing. Without flaps to slow our airspeed plus the limited directional control over the aircraft Fred had to juggle with the throttles to reduce the airspeed. If it drops too low, we would fall out of the sky, but too high then we may run out of runway if the brakes are not working. Fred brings the Lancaster lower and lower, as we slip over the boundary fence we only just make the threshold of the runway. For the very first time, Fred greases the Lancaster in for the best landing he ever made. At first, we did not realise we were down, until we heard the rumble of the wheels on the runway. But then as the load settled the damaged port tyre disintegrated, our Lancaster slews off the runway.

As we crossed into the darkness of the grass infield, we wait for our aircraft, to come to a halt. When it does, it was to the sound of grinding tortured metal, the Lancaster rearing nose up as it stopped. For a few seconds, the crew sat in silence until the overpowering smell of Hundred Octane aviation fuel, brings them back to reality. Grabbing the escape hatch over his head, Jack climbs onto the fuselage then down onto the wing. Slipping off the trailing edge of the wing, Jack falls into the darkness below; as he hits the ground, a searing pain runs up his spine. He rolled onto the ground in agony, but the smell of fuel drives him back to his feet, he staggered away from the wreckage. The sight of a fire engine and ambulance approaching brought Jack to his knees as the medics rushed to offer him assistance. Sitting on the ground, he could see in the lights of the fire engine, the strange sight of their Lancaster perched on top of a B17 Flying Fortress. Then the medics helped him into the ambulance, to be taken away with the rest of crew to the station's sick quarters. Here our injuries were seen too, while one of the nurses served up steaming mugs of coffee, well laced with rum. As we were being treated the station medical officers staff returned to our aircraft and recover Bob's body from the rear turret.

They later confirmed he had died instantly in that first attack by the night fighter. This brought little comfort to us as a crew, but our feelings were of little concern to the officers, we are ordered to report for debriefing. After debriefing by the Intelligence Officer, we were taken to a billet to rest. Lying there in the darkness totally exhausted, sleep should have come easily after our seven and a half hour nightmare, but it did not. The events of that night; were still going round and round in my head, like a never ending film that I could not seem to stop. Memories of Bob at his prayers in the billet returned, I kept asking how could this good living young man die so violently, where is the fairness. I just laid there smoking cigarette after cigarette, as were the rest of the crew, but not a word was exchanged between us. Now as the dawn was breaking, having not slept I got to my feet and walked out of the billet onto the airfield. I had only gone a few steps when I was aware of Fred's presence beside me; we walked in silence together, each with our own thoughts. The fresh morning air was wonderful; the sound of the dawn chorus almost unreal, as the morning sun warmed our faces.

I could just not take it in, only hours earlier we had been fighting for our lives, in the skies over Germany. Back in the billet we are told to wash and shave, get some breakfast, then report to the C.O's office for further instructions. When we arrived there we were handed travel warrants back to Elsham Wold's. To our question about the fate of Bob

Thomas, we're informed his body would be taken to his home town of Chippenham in Wiltshire. There he would be buried with full military honours at some time in the future, but we had to report back to our base as soon as possible.

Ronald (BOB) Thomas was born in Chippenham Wiltshire in 1924 to Herbert and Emily Thomas. He first attended the local Junior School before winning a place at Chippenham Secondary School. Here he excelled at all sports, but gained his colour's playing Hockey at the school. On completion of his education, he started work at the Westinghouse Company Works in Chippenham. The company manufactured signalling and braking systems for the Railway Industry in Britain. Ronald started work in the Testing Department, but six months after his seventeenth birthday he volunteered for the Royal Air Force. He was immediately sent to Southern Rhodesia for training: here his training would not be interrupted by the nightly bombing raids in Britain. After training in Africa, he returned to England where he was promoted to Sergeant, before being sent to join an Operational Training Unit at Sleap in Shropshire for crew selection. Finally, he and his crew were allocated to a front line Lancaster Bomber station at RAF Elsham Wolds in Lincolnshire they arrived on the 2nd February 1944. The first raid they would take part in was on the 15th March 1944.

Sadly, he would complete only four more night missions to Germany before he made the ultimate sacrifice only ten days later; he was just 20 years old.

Before leaving, we all went back to M Mother to see the damage; she looked a sorry sight standing there, still on top of the B17. From the ground in daylight the damage was worse than we imagined. Fred examined the flying controls, he muttered about why there was so little response in the air. As we approached the tail of the Lancaster, we saw Bob's turret for the first time, it was totally wrecked, almost unrecognisable. The B17 Fortress we hit had taken the full brunt of the impact; its fuselage was broken in half behind the wing. Its Starboard outer wing had been snapped off; the outer engine had been torn from its mountings. It would not fly again, later it would be broken up for usable parts. (It is a strange coincidence that this damage to the starboard wing would be repeated in the Passionate Witch 2 at a later date). As I stood looking at the B17, I spotted the painting on the nose, "Passionate Witch". It was then that I realised, however different compared to the Lancaster, it was another crew's pride and joy, but now it was time to go. We are transported by truck, to the local railway station to catch a train to Waterloo Station in London, carrying all our flying gear including parachutes. Crossing London on the tube to Kings Cross, we meet with a lot of strange looks from locals on their way to work. There were also a few rude remarks, from a group of Navy boys offering us direction to an airfield. Boarding the train to Doncaster we hoped to get our heads down for a while, but the train was already packed, so we slept on the floor in the corridor. Climbing down from the train at Doncaster, very stiff and weary we had to wait for our connection to Barnetby le Wold. When it arrived, we were thankful to find an empty carriage; we slept all the way home. Back at Elsham, we spent just one night on the base before being given six days leave.

As I travelled back to Carlisle and home, the events of the previous night, are still playing back in my head. Then when I arrived home, I have to conceal the horrors of the raid from my Mum; I distract her with talk of my bad back, caused by a fall. Later in the evening Dad asks me to accompany him to his allotment, while he watered his vegetable patch. Here he asks, "What's going on lad"; he is not taken in by my story and quizzes me about what really has happened. As I relate the facts to him, the look of horror on his face, shows how little, ordinary people know, of what is actually taking place in this war. Afterwards I felt a certain amount of relief, having shared the story with my father, but insisted he does not burden mum with it.

The Raid that night involved over 1000 aircraft of Bomber Command but only 811 of these were assigned to bomb Berlin.

Our losses totalled 72 aircraft, 44 Lancaster's and 28 Halifax's, 382 young men would not be coming home again. Many of these losses took place over the Ruhr, due to aircraft being blown off course by the exceptionally high winds. Many years later, Ron Walker our Navigator and I would discuss the high winds of that night, after the discovery of the Jet Streams after the war.

At Elsham Wolds we lost only one aircraft when Squadron Leader Bickers aircraft of 103 Squadron failed to return. He becomes one of the youngest, Flight Commanders to be killed; he was 21 years old and was already on his second tour of Operations.

The Crew of Lancaster 1		ME665 PM-C	
S/L	K.G. Bickers DFC	RAF	Kia
F/S	J. Wadsworth	RAF	Kia
F/O	C.J. Plummer DFC	RAF	Kia
F/O	P.A.C. Bell	RAF	Kia
F/S	L.J. Comer	RAF	Kia
F/S	D. Cannon	RAF	Kia
F/O	N. Tombs	RAF	Kia

His aircraft was on the way home from the target, when it plunged into the ground and exploded, there were no survivors. Our Lancaster 'M

- Mother' was later recovered from Dunsfold, to be repaired to fly again with 57 Squadron at East Kirkby. Then almost one year later on the 2nd March 1945, it is involved in a mid-air collision, with a Lancaster of 207 Squadron, both crews were lost. The aircraft was on a fighter affiliation exercise.

US Air Force Passionate Witch 2 Missions

Higham, a small village northwest of 452nd air base supports three pubs, two coffee shops a two lane bowling alley, a small hotel plus a three-bedroom rooming house owned by Mrs Higgins (Iggy). She lived on the premises in a downstairs apartment. Her rooms were adjacent to the center of town so were in great demand. If you wanted to stay overnight, Iggy had a very strict rule anyone desiring a room must call to reserve the room by three pm the previous day. Only one occupant was allowed in a room. For some unknown reason to me, I became Mrs. Higgins favourite boarder. My name is George, which she pronounced "Geeeorge". This was one place I would use whenever I was in the area.

Friday 24th March 44, Dick Thayer recalls being in the Canadian Hospital with John McLaughlin and Hubert Roughton after the Dunsfold crash. We are all being well looked after by some very pretty nurses. Hubert is improving but it looks as though he will be going home for treatment, he will not return to combat flying. The following day John and I are transferred to an American Hospital, we were sad to be saying goodbye to those lovely Canadian nurses though. Here the American Doctors say we should both be fit to return to combat flying in a couple of days. I am thinking about my crew, who are on a mission today, I can only hope they get back ok. Must say I am dreading the next mission; it's going to take more that luck or good gunnery to get us through.

26th March 44 Sunday. Cherbourg.

We have three new crew mates; Sgt Fremont Granade is taking over the right waist gunner position replacing Hubert Roughton who was badly injured on the Frankfurt raid. Hubert would not fly again he would be returned back to the States. Sgt Clark is our new left waist gunner and S/Sgt Jack Browne is our new tail gunner, until Dick Thayer and John Mclaughlin recover from their injuries.

Cherbourg is the target for today which means it will be a relatively short trip most of it over the English Channel. First and Second Air Division will be providing a force of 428 heavy bombers to attack V1 weapon launch sites in the Pas-de-Calais area. Our Third Air Division will be sending 145 B17's to attack similar weapons launch sites in the Cherbourg peninsular area. To accompany us will be 266 P47's from the 8th Air Force fighter groups, these V1 weapons we are to bomb have become a real problem lately.

They are a small pilotless aircraft with a one ton high explosive warhead; the Germans launch them from small sloping ramps in forested areas toward London. The Ram Jet engine has just enough fuel to reach London, when it stops it plunges to earth without any specific target in mind. Some of our guys have seen them on weekend passes to the English capitol. They say they sound like a large truck with a faulty muffler but when the sound stops everyone in the street looks up to see where it will fall. When it does the explosion is tremendous, the ground really shakes. Then the locals just go about their business again as though nothing has happened, how strange this war has affected people.

We take off then fly toward the North Sea to gather into our formations before heading into the English Channel toward the target. Our fighter escorts are patrolling the Normandy coastline looking for the Luftwaffe fighters, but they are thin on the ground or should that be thin in the air. German airfield locations in this area are well known, so some of our escorts go looking for the Luftwaffe in their lairs. We continue down the Channel to attack the target from the sea. We will cross the Peninsular in one pass dropping our bombs on the launch sites. As we approach the target the ground batteries put up a carpet of flack in our path. It's not as concentrated as we have previously encountered but its accurate, some aircraft are taking hits. Then it's all over as we drop our bombs on the markers then head for the sea. In no time at all we are back over the sea, we are turning to head back up the Channel for home. The Passionate Witch has taken hits from the anti-aircraft fire but it's nothing serious, Bob our skipper calls for a crew check, everyone reports in they are no injuries. Landing back at Deopham Green, thankfully we find we have no casualties or any aircraft losses though over sixty planes have been damaged. That makes it a good mission in my book.

27th March 44, Monday. Bordeaux

We have two new crew mates; Sgt Clark is being replaced by Harold Cook (no relation to the skipper Bob) and he will be manning the left waist gunner's position. Then Sgt Steve Zajac is replacing S/Sgt Jack Browne as our tail gunner. Another day another target, this time it's more German airfields in France; it will bring my mission total to ten. Our Third Air Division is tasked with three main targets; the first is Cayeux on the Normandy coast between Calais and Dieppe. The second target is Chartres south west of Paris then we will continue toward the Bay of Biscay for the third target Merginac to the west of Bordeaux. Yesterday's trip to Cherbourg was six hours but this one will be another long haul of ten hours. Our job will be made easier with the help of the 960 fighters that will be our escort on the mission. This force will be made up of P-38 Lightning's, P-47 Thunderbolts and P-51 Mustangs. Not all of these will be assigned to our protection; the P-51's will precede us to jump the German airfields strafing anything and everything in sight. Hopefully they will also give the anti-aircraft gun emplacements their attention too. Our 3rd Air Division is providing 256 B-17's made up of aircraft from the 94BG, 95BG, 100BG, 385BG, 388BG, 390BG, 447BG and our 452BG. The total force of the Three Divisions taking part in this mission totals 720 aircraft which includes B-17's and B-24's.

George and his crew are sitting in the Passionate Witch waiting for the GO signal that will indicate the mission is on. "This is the time when we are all tense, wishing we could just get on with the mission. I am sure all the guys in the other aircraft are feeling just the same, then the flare gives us the OK and it's all go". Engines are firing up, ground crews are moving starter units out of our path, Bob is inching the Witch onto the perimeter track, heading for the runway threshold. Takeoff is uneventful and we climb to start forming up into our defensive groups. The first part of the mission is straight forward a short run down the East coast of England then a quick dash over the channel to France. Part of our group will attack Cayeux, the rest now continue toward the next target Chartres South West of Paris. Here the last part of the group breaks away to our final target Merginac, west of Bordeaux.

At each location the flak batteries are giving us a hard time, though at least it keeps the Luftwaffe fighters away from us. Our gunners are reporting lots of our planes taking damage from the flack but there are no aircraft dropping out of formation. We finally reach Merginac and start giving the Germans a taste of their own medicine, though the anti-aircraft batteries are fighting back. Our boys are being hit, I am sure there will be casualties in some of the aircraft. It's a great feeling when the Witch bounds upward with the release of bomb load. But now we have to face the long run back across France. Even though we no longer represent a threat, those manning the ground flack positions are still shooting at us at every opportunity. Once out into the English Channel, things start to quieten down and we are so pleased when our airfield comes into view.

Back on the base we start to take stock of our losses, two aircraft are unaccounted for, we also have over fifty planes with damage and the repair crews are going to be busy. Sadly, in the returning planes, there are eleven fatalities among the crew members, with two wounded being removed to hospital. The loss of these airmen comes as a shock; we have suffered worse damage on other missions but received fewer casualties. There seems to be no rhyme or reason to this war.

We start the day with good news; Dick Thayer will be back in his usual place as a waist gunner alongside Fremont Granade. At the same time John Mclaughlin reclaims his tail gunner's position both men having been declared fit to return to combat. They have both been back on the base for only one day, but Dick Thayer has been playing Poker again. Having seen the damage to Hubert Roughton's chest parachute on the Frankfurt mission he gambols to wins a back parachute from someone in a hand of Poker.

28th March 1944 Chateaudun

It's the 28th March 1944, George Silva and his crewmates at Deopham Green airfield are preparing for another raid with the U.S. 8th Air Force. Today is to be another personal mission, we are hitting back at a Luftwaffe airfield at Chateaudun in France. The airfield with its bomber and fighter units would be a threat to the forthcoming Normandy invasion, which at the time they are unaware of. As they climbed aboard the B17G, "Passionate Witch 2" the crew was talking of another Milk Run, as we would have fighter cover all the way for protection. Sliding into formation, we cross the English Channel with a clear blue sky; the bright sunlight floods the interior of the bomber. Then below them, the water gives way to the checker work of fields of the French countryside. But danger in not far away as George Silva prepares for the known flak positions on the way to the target. When they appear the radio operators on each bomber, starts to dispense Chaff through the chutes, to confuse the radar controlled anti-aircraft batteries. This thin film strip, metal coated on one side was of a specific length, to coincide with the frequency of the radar controlled guns. On the ground it would cause maximum disruption to the aim of the AA Batteries.

I am not sure about this use of chaff for daylight missions, the flack gunners are not firing at individual aircraft so the chaff does not help. In fact, it only helps to confirm our altitude to set their shells to explode at. It will not hide us from the fighters who can see us clearly. If this had been a night mission where the fighters could not see us, the chaff would stop the ground radar from guiding the fighters on to an individual aircraft. All they would see would be a cloud on their screens with no individual aircraft being identifiable. But ahead of us the anti-aircraft gunners laying down a carpet of flak set to our altitude, we still have to fly through this barrage. Our gunners were already calling out aircraft being hit by flak, losing height they are dropping out of other formations. Down in the nose of the 'Witch' John Rowland the bombardier was getting ready for the run up to the target. He was keeping an eye on the lead bomber, who would initiate the attack, while at the same time watching the approaching carpet of flak.

Back in my radio operators position I was pushing bundles of chaff down the tube like a crazy man. My chest parachute pack was also there on the floor, so I moved it under my radio table out of the way. Entering the cloud of Flak, an exploding shell smashes the nose of our

104

aircraft. In an instance, an icy blast of air sweeps through the fuselage. Our skipper's calls to the Bombardier John Rowland and the Navigator John Osswalt went un-answered; they were either injured, dead or lost overboard. As the crew listened to the damage report from the Pilot and the possible loss of the crew members the aircraft suffered an even greater blow. Another anti-aircraft shell hits between the Starboard engines, the whole outer wing with the outer engine is ripped off. I remember says George, "Looking out of the window to see a large hole appear in the wing which quickly folds upwards before tearing off completely". The now exposed ruptured fuel tanks turn into a roaring fire as the Witch turns on its back, to start its final spiral to the ground. Sitting in his radio compartment, George was thrown across the fuselage; he watches as his parachute floats away from him. As the spin increases, he is pinned there against the hull, but with a final lunge he grabs hold of the chute. Clipping it on he found he was now unable to move at all, he watched through a window as the world rotates ever faster. Sky replaced ground repeatedly in the window, as the B17 plunged toward the earth; he now starts to contemplate his own death.

At the same time Dick Thayer, trapped by the rotation forces begins thinking how his parents would react to news of his death. Determined to avoid this, he used all his strength to claw his way to an escape hatch, then launch's himself out into the cold air. As he did the Passionate Witch disintegrates in front of him, he has to delay pulling the ripcord until he was clear of the burning debris. This would mean he would drift with the wind, to land a long way from the other survivors. Unknown to George at that time, a crew member of another B17 was taking photographs of the Passionate Witch, as she spun toward the ground. In his own mind George started to say goodbye to his family back home. He was beginning to black out with the centrifugal force, when another explosion shakes the aircraft.

Unable to withstand the forces involved, the Witch sheds the starboard wing. One side of the fuselage is torn away catapulting George clear of the doomed B17. The next thing George remembers was the cold blast of air in his face with the bright Sun shining in his eyes. Not knowing how close he was to the ground he pulled the ripcord immediately, the harness tightened as the chute opened, a cry of relief leaves his lips. For a while he watched the falling bomber, hoping to see other chutes leaving it, but knowing there was very little chance by now. Looking down at the countryside below him, he thought he saw large raindrops falling past, but there were no clouds. In horror he realised it was bombs not rain, falling from the aircraft overhead then, from his memory he recalled a John Wayne movie. The hero a paratrooper pulled on the shroud lines to manoeuvre his chute away from danger. As I tugged on my parachute lines, I only succeeded in partly collapsing the chute and being plummeted toward the ground at a great speed. Quickly he released his grasp on the lines, thank God the chute reformed, George now saw he was falling toward a German gun emplacement. As I hit the ground, I slid into a shell crater and used the time before the soldiers arrived to damage my chute panels with a knife to make it unusable. The Germans arrived shouting "Rous" at me which I took to mean get moving, they then took me prisoner. When I had removed my harness, I saw that our tail gunner, John McLaughlin was lying injured not far away, being attended to. In a gesture of compassion, the Germans allowed me to sit with him bringing a friendly face, to what may be his last moments. His injuries were horrific, a broken leg and arm were compounded by internal damage, as he was coughing up blood. He was asking for a cigarette which I lit for him as we exchanged a few words. I wanted to stay until an ambulance arrived but the Germans pulled me away; they want me to accompany them for interrogation. So I have to leave John, hopefully he will be taken to a hospital quickly. Dick Thayer having jumped from the aircraft had delayed opening his chute, he has landed a long way from the other crew but eventually he is taken for interrogation past the injured John McLaughlin. Despite the protests of his guards, he goes to comfort his injured crew mate. When John see's Dick Thayer he again asks for another cigarette, which Dick lights for him before he is bundled away to the local military headquarters.

Robert Cook sitting in the cockpit had been knocked unconscious when the Witch shed its wing, then as the aircraft breaks up and the cockpit tears apart, the blast of cold air brings him around just in time to bale out. His decent is short and as the ground approaches the German soldiers are standing waiting to take him prisoner. There was an initial questioning by the local military, before he was transported to Paris for further interrogated. When this was completed, he was taken to somewhere in Germany, where he was questioned over several weeks. The German officers here spoke excellent English; they also had a surprising amount of information about our Base and the group he was from. He was kept in a dark cell without windows for the whole of that period. Finally, when they had completed their interrogation he was transferred by train to Stalag Luft 1 at Bart-Vogelsang, in Prussia. Arriving at the local railroad station he and the rest of prisoners from the train had to march to the camp under the watchful eyes of the German guards. Here in the South Barracks, Robert would spend the rest of the war, though as he settled in his health was already starting to become a problem.

For a time, George Silva thought he was the only survivor, only later would he find the skipper, Robert Cook and Dick Thayer were also prisoners. Dick would later join George at Stalag 17b. Sadly the rest of our crew did not manage to escape from the aircraft, these brave young men have made the ultimate sacrifice, they were.

Co Pilot 2nd/Lt Ronald J Casey from Pontiac Michigan
Bombardier Nose Gunner John A Rowland
from Bynum Montana
Navigator Cheek Gunner Lt John F Osswalt
from River Forrest Illinois
Engineer Top Turret Gunner Tech Sgt Gerald H Poplett
from Peoria Illinois
Ball Turret Gunner/Radio Man Staff Sgt Carl H Blichmann
from Dubuque Iowa
Left Waist Gunner Sgt Fremont Granade Illinois
Tail Gunner Sgt John C McLaughlin
from Hadden Heights New Jersey.

The loss of the Passionate Witch 2 and with it the lives of seven young men is a tragedy for the surviving crewmembers, the 452nd Bomb Group and its crews. But more than this it is a tragedy for the seven families involved. To that end I think it is fitting that these families are remembered.

Ronald James Casey was born on the 24th January 1917 to Robert and Grace Casey in Pontiac, Oakland, Michigan. He had two older brothers, Howard aged 16 and Robert aged 23. By 1940 Ronald had attended College, but he was only able to complete his first year, sadly his father had passed away and he needed to work to support his widowed mother. He started in a car production plant working on the line earning $1500 a year. On the 7th December 1941 his career in the car industry was brought to an end with the Japanese attack on Pearl Harbour. By the 5th February 1942 he had enlisted for training at Fort Custer, Michigan. After being processed by the system he was transferred to the air force where he trained as a B17 co-pilot. He was assigned to the 728BS/452BG at Deopham Green in 1944. Here he completed a number of missions over Germany suffering badly at the hands of the Luftwaffe on a raid to Frankfurt on the 20th March 44. Then on the 28th March 44 he and his crew were tasked to attack a German airfield at Chateaudun, France. Sadly, their aircraft the "Passionate Witch" would fall victim to anti-aircraft fire. Ronald was unable to leave the aircraft and died with five of his crewmates in the crash, he was just 27 years old.

John Albert Rowland was born on 22nd June 1916 in Bynum, Teton County, Montana. This small farming town had a population of only a few dozen people in 1940 with a one room School a Post office a Church and a General store. It was here he lived with his parents, Homer Orin and Della J Rowland on the family farm, with his sister Julia Rowland 3 years his junior. The highest educational grade he achieved was High School 4th year. The census of 1940 shown he worked 52 weeks of that year and receiver nothing in pay, probably a normal situation on a family farm at that time. With the start of the War he enlisted in the Air Force and trained as a Bombardier/Air gunner. This would entail learning the complexities associated with using a Bomb Sight. There were allowances to be made for wind speed and direction, aircrafts speed and altitude, all of this had to be set into the bomb sights controls. Without this information the bombs would not hit where they were intended. With the completion of his training, he travelled with his crew to the East coast of America to embark on a ship for Great Britain. His final destination was the 452nd Bomb Group at Deopham Green in Norfolk. They were immediately thrown into the battle against Germany and they completed a number of missions before George Silva joined then as their new Radio man. Together they would fly only five more missions with the "Passionate Witch" before it was destroyed in an accident at Dunsfold Airfield in Surrey. A new aircraft was then allocated to them, which they christened "Passionate Witch 2". Sadly, they would fly only three missions with this new aircraft before they came to grief. They were on the approach to the target at Chateaudun when John's position in the nose of the aircraft received a direct hit from an anti aircraft shell. Whether he survived this explosion or was killed in the ensuing crash is not known. Eventually he was returned to his family and interred in the local cemetery in Bynum he was 28 years old.

John F Osswalt was born in Brooklyn New York in 1923 his sibling Alice was also born in Brooklyn, on 21st October 1930. Their parents were Oscar & Alice Myldred Osswalt, sadly Oscar passed away in 1932. After the attack on Pearl Harbour in 1941, war was declared and John F Osswalt enlisted into the Air Force where he trained as a Navigator. When his training was complete, he found himself travelling to England's East coast county of Norfolk to become a part of the 452nd Bomb Group. Here he joined the crew of the "Passionate Witch" under the command of Robert M Cook. Together they would complete and survive a number of missions over Germany, until that fateful day on the 28th March 1944 over Chateaudun, France. On the run up to the target an anti-aircraft shell exploded in the nose of their B17g. John Osswalt failed to answer calls from his skipper and was presumed killed. Whether he had survived injured is not known as the "Passionate Witch" crashed with John and five other crew members still in the aircraft. Eventually the news of John's death reached his mother and sister in New York, John F Osswalt was just 21 years old. It was a devastating blow for the pair of them. Some years later his sister Alice would enter and graduate from Vassar College in 1951, then in 1952 she married W Lansing Reed in New York. Sadly, only one year later her mother Alice Myldred Osswalt passed away. Alice never forgot her brother naming her son John after him.

TSgt Gerald H Poplett was killed in action on 28th March 1944, his loss leaves behind a grieving wife Jane (Hatfield) Poplett and their only daughter Miss Roberta Jayne Poplett. His parents were Wilbur and Kate Poplett of Peoria, Illinois. Gerald was born on 13th November in 1920, where he attended Peoria High School. It was here he would graduate in 1939. After graduation he began working at the Le Tourneau Co. in Peoria before his enlistment in the Air Force on 20th June 1942. Here he trained as a Top turret gunner/Engineer before being assigned to Norfolk in England with the 452nd BG. At Deopham Green he became a member of the crew of the "Passionate Witch" B17 Flying Fortress Bomber. Here with his crew he would face the might of the Luftwaffe over Germany over the coming months. On many occasions he would be called on to defend his aircraft and would acquit himself with distinction. During his service there he was awarded a Purple Heart Medal, Crew Wings, Air Medal with Two Oak Leaf Clusters, European Campaign Medal with 2 Battle Stars, Army Good Conduct Medal and the WW II Victory Medal.

Carl Herbie Blichmann's loss on the 28th March 1944 brought tragedy to his widowed mother Mrs Elsie Blichmann for the second time. Only a month earlier she had been informed her second oldest son Sergeant C.C. Blichmann of the United States Army had been killed in action in Italy on 26th January. The text of the War Department wire concerning the second casualty was as follows: "The Secretary of War desires to express his deep regret that your son, Staff Sergeant Carl H. Blichmann, has been reported missing in action since 28 March in the European area". It was Signed Dunlop, acting adjutant general.   S-Sgt. Blichmann enlisted in the Army Air Forces on Oct. 28, 1942. Early training at Goodfellow Field, Texas preceded his attending mechanics school at Gulfport Field, Mississippi. From Gulfport air base, he was sent to gunnery school in Las Vegas, Nevada, after which he was transferred to Seattle, Washington. When his training was complete, he was shipped out to Norfolk, England to join the 452nd Bomb Group at Deopham Green. It was here he joined the crew of a B17 Flying Fortress bomber named the "Passionate Witch" as their Ball Turret gunner. In this position he would give a good account of himself defending his crew mates on many missions over Germany. Sadly it would be the anti-aircraft gunners on the ground who would seal his fate over Chateaudun, France.

Fremont Granade   Elwood Myer was born on 14th August 1915, the son of Alfred Meyer. His mother passed away when he was young, and his father remarried Carrie Granade. She brought her son Fremont, born on 13th September 1922 in St Louis, from a previous marriage along with his two sisters, to the family. Elwood was one of three sons of Alfred Meyer. Elwood and Fremont both enlisted early in the war, Elwood, was the first on 29th December 1941, only three weeks after the attack on Pearl Harbour. Fremont followed him on 4th November 1942. Both enlisted in the U.S. Army Air Corps and would train as air gunners. Fremont was engaged to his girlfriend Rose Ella Kfelscher prior to his enlistment. Fremont was sent for training, first to Amarillo Texas then to Las Vegas Nevada, Salt Lake City Utah, finally Delhardt back in Texas. Elwood would serve in the Pacific with the 43rd Bomb Group while Fremont Granade was allocated to the 452nd Bomb Group at Deopham Green in England. Sadly, on the 1st or 2nd of July 1943 Elwood was killed flying with the 64th Bomb Group in a B-26 medium bomber. Then just nine months later Fremont Granade would also make the ultimate sacrifice in the sky over Chateaudun, France. In this short space of time Alfred Meyer and Carrie Granade have both lost two of their sons, a tragedy of unimaginable proportions. Fremont leaves behind his fiancée, Miss Rose Ella Kfelscher, two sisters and two step brothers.

John C McLaughlin was born in Pennsylvania in 1924, the son of Mr. and Mrs. Henry J. McLaughlin and the youngest of their three children which included Jane and Edward. The family moved to New Jersey where he attended Haddon Heights High School for 2 years, graduating in 1940. He then started work in the Philadelphia Navy Yard for almost 2 years, before enlisted in the Air Force on 12th February 1942. Here he qualified for flight duty and was sent to Kingman Army Air Field in Kingman, Arizona for aerial gunnery training. On completion of the course, he was promoted to Sergeant and sent to Salt Lake City, Utah for further training. After that, he shipped out to England and assigned to the 452nd Bomb Group operating from Deopham Green, England. At the end of 1943 he began combat missions with the 728th Bomb Squadron; here in March 1944 he became the first gunner to shoot down an enemy aircraft over Berlin. He was also credited with shooting down a second aircraft on the same mission. Word of Staff Sergeant McLaughlin's death came in August 1944. Surviving him were his parents, Mr. and Mrs. Henry J. McLaughlin of Haddon Heights New Jersey, and a brother Edward J McLaughlin who was serving overseas in the Navy.

These stories sadly would be repeated many times all over the country until the end of the War. Thousands of ordinary young men would perform extraordinary deeds in all of the armed forces, Hero's all.

It was these sort of sacrifice's that I have read off that prompted
me to write the following poem about all these young men & the
price they paid for our freedom

The Cold Blue

The Cold, Cold Blue
Fighting a war for me & you
From the plains & the mountains
They answered the call
City boys & farmers one & all
To fight the war in Europe's sky
A bloody cruel battle ever so high
At 35 thousand feet its 40 below
But there's sweat on my brow is all I know
Those that were there will say it was so
It's a fearful place but still we went
Fighters attacking, Fighters to defend
Let's hope one day it will come to an end
Till then we fight on facing the flak
Please lord help bring us all back
But if we should fall remember our deeds
Bring peace to our loved ones & see to their needs
Then in the future commemorate what we did
And speak of us often when you teach our kids
Remember a soldier was once heard to say
For your tomorrow, We gave our today
AD Crawford

Walking with his captors George is suddenly stopped, the guard's
motion for me to remove the cigarettes from my pocket. They then tore
the packet open to divide the cigarettes between them. I made a note that
they didn't offer me one. We kept walking across the field until we came
to what looked like a small storage shack, here I sat on the steps while
both soldiers after looking around, sat down to light up a cigarette each,
making sure their rifles were still pointed at me. After they smoked the
cigarette, they motioned for me to go into the little building. I noticed that
there was no furniture or windows, the one door into the hut had a big
chain attached to it on the outside.

By this time, it was late afternoon, the sunshine began to fade so
they indicated I should sit on the floor then, they walked out. I could hear
them chain the door, soon complete silence took over. I must have slept

111

some, stretched out on the floor, because when I woke up it was dark, I was also very cold. There was no light showing round the door frame so I curled up, trying to stay as warm as I could until the morning. At daybreak I heard voices outside the shack, someone opened the door, I saw soldiers with two prisoners. One was a British airman; the other was an American, so now there were three of us. The German soldiers told us not to talk to each other; one of them took us one at a time around the back of the shack in case we had to relieve ourselves. Our guards then decided it was time to march on. Finally, we came to a railroad crossing here we were told to sit down. Soon a train came along, the soldier stopped it from passing us as there was no station. Everyone that was on the train car was moved from one side to the other by the soldiers. They then motioned us come in and sit on the empty side. Then the train took off, but after a short while I noticed something that looked very familiar to me as I had read about it at home in books with some pictures. It was the Eiffel Tower; we were on the outskirts of Paris. At the next station we were taken of the train then, up to a second floor balcony, here we stood so people who were coming in out of the station could look at us. Some showed compassions, others did not. We stood there for at least 45min before we were led back down to the street, here we were told to march not on the sidewalk, but on the street. This was very dangerous because of the rapid moving automobiles in this city in the afternoon. We were marched through the city to another little train station, here one of the guards that spoke a bit of English told us that we were to get in the car then sit in the back which we did. We had barely sat down when one passenger sitting up near the front got up, he raised his fist then yelled in German something that made the guard go up to talk to him. When he got back, he said the man told him that he wouldn't ride in the car with "American Gangsters". We had to get off to wait for another train. One came along shortly, so we got back on to sit in the back. There was a ruckus from the front, the guard went up to talk with the train manager, when he came back, he said the men would not ride in the car with "American Gangsters", unless they stood up. So, we had to stand, a lady sitting near where I was standing asked are you Americans? I said yes, she then said she was also American, but had come over a couple years ago to collect her mother and her father to take them back to Boston with her. She said since arriving she was not able to go back to the US either alone or with her family. She told me that we were being taken up to a detention area which as far as she knew, anyone that came back from their noted that they were treated well.

When we got there, we were separated by nationality. I was put in a cell by myself with a bucket for sanitary purposes, a burlap sack filled with some straw that served as a bed on the floor. Early the next morning a guard came by with a cart of food, he said would I please sign this paper.

I told them that whatever it was I did not want to read it nor was I going to sign it. So they took the food cart away, later that afternoon I was served a cup of coffee with a piece of bread.

The guard told me that, tomorrow morning I would be going on a long trip to a great place called Stalag 17B near Kremms in Austria. Here there were hundreds of my fellow American flyers, who were enjoying themselves. After we left that day we walked a mile or so, before we came to a huge railroad yard. I was separated from the group then taken to a railroad car, here I was told to go in and take a seat. I did that but found to my surprise that I was sitting among French speaking people. A conductor from the train came by; he said that I should stay on the train until we reach Krems. He told me that as it was quite a long journey, but food would be provided at least once during the trip. Sometime during the night, we had to change from a passenger train to a boxcar. There were at least 20 other people in that car with me, they were all prisoners being taken to different prison camps.

We stopped at a siding somewhere along the line where all of us were given a small bowl of soup, a piece of bread with a drink of water. Sometime after daylight the train stopped, all the passengers were taken off except me. I was in this huge car all on my own, the conductor said that we had just a short way to go; the next stop would be Krems.

Stalag 17b Krems, Austria

When we arrived, I found myself in a huge railway station. We stopped near an office; here I was given a bowl of soup, a piece of bread plus a cup of coffee. After this breakfast I was taken to a men's restroom where I could wash and use the facilities. Two young German soldiers waiting for me at the door they told me they were going to be my escorts for the long walk to Stalag 17B. They said that this would probably be my home, for the duration of the hostilities between our countries.

One of the guards who understood English said that since it was a long walk, they would set their pace to mine. After walking for nearly an hour we all sat down for a brief rest, one of the guards carried a thermos of cold water. After both had had a drink, they offered me a drink from the cup which I was very thankful for and told him so. After walking another hour or so we arrived at a small building outside of the huge camp. I was told to go in then remove my clothes; I was led into another room where they used electric clippers to cut my hair off. I was told that my clothes were being deloused or as they put it "Cleaned".

I then walked through a doorway where a guard sat on a stool with a wand in his hand to examine our privates before we went into a shower. Through the doorway there was a bar of soap in a dish, as you stepped through the door you grabbed the bar as the water came on. The water was warm; the only thing was that is only stayed on just a few moments so if you had not been able to rinse you had to leave the shower anyway. I was then handed a piece of cloth that served as a towel, I dried as well as I could, before we were lead outside. All our clothes were stacked on the ground after they were deloused. It was very difficult to find the clothes, that you had on when you took them off, I was fortunate to get my own clothes, except my shoes were gone. I had been wearing boots that were lined. When I asked about them, I was told that the boots were gone; I should try to find a pair of shoes that fit among those that were left. Again, I was lucky to find a pair of shoes that fit very well, which was fortunate because I had them for the next year and five months I was in the camp.

Stalag 17B is small and basic, originally designed to hold some 250 Kriegsgefangen (prisoner of war). Eventually it will hold four thousand five hundred. This long German word is quickly shortened by the inmates who call themselves "Kriegies". My new home in this village will be Hut 31a. Here for the first time, I also find incarcerated in Stalag 17B our waist gunner Dick Thayer. Back home Dick had been awarded the Silver Star, the Bronze Star and a Purple Heart. All of these would have to be accepted by his father on Dick's behalf, there was also a recommendation for a Medal of Honour for his conduct during the Frankfurt mission. Sadly, because he was a P.O.W. he would not be able to complete the necessary interview required for this medal. We walked up the company street where everyone gave me a smile or a thumbs-up gesture. We finally got to barracks numbers 31A, here I was told to go in, select the lower bunk of the fourth row, this I would share with the fellow that was already there waiting for me. The bunks were made of wood; they were four to a row, three tiers high. We were now told to go out to a pile of blankets, select one that would be our one and only blanket, so we should always keep care of it.

I selected one that looked like a quilted blanket that seem to me that it would be very warm, but when I got it back to my bunk to spread it out, I was dismayed to find that it was not a full blanket but about three quarters of a blanket. We had been told to select our blanket carefully, as we could not take it back to trade for another. But back I went immediately, I showed the corporal in charge, Mike Welt shook his head negatively he said, "Sorry no exchanging". Luckily again for me there was another fellow there, he said he thought it would be okay to exchange my quilt for this man's choice of another blanket which I did so I ended up with a nice full-length blanket, I felt very fortunate. Outside of the Camp the Germans run everything, inside we are allowed to appoint a Camp Commanding Officer and Barrack Officers. Another routine to get accustomed to was that lights were out at 9 pm. The latrines unfortunately were outside of our building, so if nature calls you had to get permission from the guard, to go out to the toilet safely. The rest of the time you could do anything as long as it was inside the barriers. At first the conditions in the camp were survivable, though they could never be called comfortable. Our food was mainly rutabagas (Vegetables) with a thin gruel soup; we were each given one scoop. As a treat we were occasionally given bread. "Bread is what they called it", in reality it had the shape of a loaf of bread, but that's where the similarity ended.

It was as hard as a piece of wood and the amount of sawdust used to make it, made it taste like wood. Being clean and tidy was always a struggle in the camp, we were allowed one bucket of hot water every day. What you did with it was up to the individual; for myself I used it to keep myself clean. There were others that did not; the resulting skin infection and related diseases were difficult to treat, with our limited medical facilities.

In the New Year things would get much worse, but thankfully we were totally unaware just how bad they would be. A week or so after I arrived in the camp several new prisoners were brought in, one of these was a fellow that was also a radio operator from my group. He told me that he taken a picture of our plane, as it spiralled down with its wing blown off and flames from one of the fuel cells. It was now an authentic Air Force photo. As radio operators from time to time we were asked to take pictures through the camera well, during the bombing run. Off course I had to wait until I got home to get a picture from the Air Force archives of my plane going down in flames. Mernie said, that there were only two planes on that mission that got into trouble one was ours, it was reported that no parachutes were seen leaving or around the stricken aircraft. Mernie loved to walk as I did, so we walked many miles around the track, as long as the good weather prevailed. We spent many hours together either in my bunk or his, putting things in our logbooks. I was not very apt at drawing a lot of things. I copied a lot from other fellows. I still have that logbook today. There was nothing for me to do until dinner time. So I decided to take a walk down the company street to visit a friend who had greeted me when I first arrived in the camp. He had invited me to come over to his bunk for a brew. A brew is what they call coffee so you didn't say have coffee you said have a brew. We set up in "Reds" bunk while we waited for the brew to steep. He showed me some of the pictures that had arrived from home, he also asked me if I smoked, I said yes I did until I became a prisoner then the guards took my cigarettes so, I had decided to quit smoking. My friend then offered me one of the cartons of cigarettes he had received from home he told me that if I didn't smoke, I could use them for trading.

Three weeks after I arrived at the camp another group of airmen arrived one of these was Ben Phelper, though I did not meet him. Ben had worked for Walt Disney before the war as an illustrator then after enlisting in the air force he became a ball turret gunner in the 385th BG. While he was a P.O.W. he used the contents of his Red Cross parcels to bribe one of the guards. He first obtained a camera, then film for it; he now proceeds to take photos of many areas of the camp. Each photo was meticulously recorded, with a detailed description, but he had to be very careful, if he had been spotted taking pictures using the camera he would have been in deep trouble. After the war he would create the classic books "Kriegie Memories" and "Shot Down". Part of the camp contained Russian POW's who were segregated from us by a barbed wire fence. The Germans and the Russians hated each other with a vengeance, born out of the conflicts like Stalingrad. There was savage fighting on the 'Eastern front' as the Germans called it, where the casualties were unbelievable. Losses by the Russians, both military and civilian, during the war amounted to over 27 million people. Conditions in the Russian camp were far worse than ours, they were deliberately starved so daily burials would be seen taking place. After the war it was estimated that from the 5.7 million Russian taken P.O.W, 3.5 million would die at the hands of their captors.

Standing near this compound one day a Russian soldier signalled to me asking for cigarettes. Our system was to show the Russians what you had to trade. The standard trade was your cigarettes for whatever he had. You then put the cigarettes in a sock along with a stone, then tossed it over the fence, to get it into the Russian compound. He would then put what he had to trade in the sock then throw it back. When the sock came back with my trade, there was a small potato plus two onions. I thought that I could cook that along with whatever we got for dinner tomorrow I would have a great meal. Here I met Harold Rhoden, (though at the time I recalled calling him, Gil Rhoden) he had been watching my trade with the Russian soldier. Harold immediately offered to draw my portrait, in exchange for the food I had traded. I was quite taken with the idea of having my portrait drawn so I readily agreed; it only took him a day or so to complete the picture. The final portrait had me better dressed than I was, he showed my hair much tidier than it was at the time, I was very pleased with the finished job. Harold told me to protect the pencil work by keeping it covered with tissue before loosely rolling it. The only tissue I could find was German toilet tissue, but is sufficed as I still have the picture and the toilet paper seventy years later. One day I was standing in the line waiting for my bowl of gruel, when the man at the head of the line turns away with his ration. "Fred?" I call out.

This rather drawn featured young man looks back. "George is that you". He waits while I draw my ration of soup then we both walk away to sit together and talk. T/Sgt Frederick Buckingham was one of the waist gunners in my original crew, he along with 2nd/Lt Edward S Wodicka were the only survivors of the B17 named 'Star Eyes'. We spent the rest of the afternoon catching up on what had happened to the both of us. Fred talked about the loss of Star Eyes. He recalls they were approaching the target; I was watching for fighters. Then the next thing I know I am falling through the air before grabbing the handle of my chute. I spent the next few days unable to hear very much at all but slowly my hearing returned. He had not seen the Navigator since the crash but was very pleased to see me. Over the next few days, we reorganise our billets to enable us to share the same Hut 31a. Wintertime came along and since we were near the mountains, we got a lot of snow sometimes up to 3 feet or more. Since there was no heat in the barracks during the coldest part of the day, we could only keep warm by walking around. In camp there were a few hidden crystal set radios, so we got a news broadcast about the war every night from BBC London. A runner was scheduled to come into each barracks to read the news, as long as lookouts were posted in case a guard should come along. Of course, radios were forbidden and would be confiscated. Time just rolled along, but the news we were receiving made us feel that home wasn't too far away "God bless America".

The spring of 44 gives way to the summer then, from one of the secret radios in the camp, we hear of the Normandy invasion. Moral in the camp was given a much needed boost, with the thought that we may be released someday. Then as the allies started their advance across France into Belgium, the quality and quantity of the food in the camp deteriorated. We suddenly realised that despite the good news, we were not going to be released sometime soon. Life in the camp could be very boring, so most people set about using their time here to do something creative. There were many things that we could do in the camp, to take up time that was very interesting. One that I decided to do was to participate in a six week course on practical electricity. The everyday class taught you from the beginning how to properly change a light bulb. We hear so many jokes about light bulbs. After a six-week course of everything you need to know about splicing electrical wires checking or changing fuses, including the wattage of each different size. I enjoyed the program very much, I really learned about everyday electricity and how to do things safely. After the course was over, we were given a written test, if you managed a pass you were given a diploma, which by the way I still have in my possession.

We could also participate in any of the sports that were available, basketball, baseball, soccer and boxing; alternatively, we could run or walk around the track. It was always enjoyable when the weather was good, to walk around the track as a group, while talking about almost anything. I spent some time secretly digging a tunnel under our camp that went nowhere in particular, just to harass the "moles" as we called the people that spent a lot of their time looking for them. I was very fortunate as I was one of the tunnel starters, so I didn't have to go very far into the tunnel. I remember there was a choral group, other guys formed a theatre group and they would put on shows at Christmas or other occasions to keep our spirits up. Simple things of life were in very short supply, pencils and writing paper were worth more than gold. Fortunately, the Red Cross managed to include these, in the parcels they would bring into the camp for us. This would allow those with a creative streak to write poetry often about fallen comrades or the privations of the camp. Others kept a diary or log book of their life in the camp. I remember doodling or writing short rhymes, one related to our shoot down. On a regular basis, the Jerries would do a head count, or roll call of each barrack block which occasionally would lead to fun. We were all lined up in rows of forty men four deep, the guard would then walk along counting us off. But as he got further away, four men from the second group behind us would step forward, to join the front row. As the guard started counting this second row four men from the third would step forward to join the second row. This would result in a shortfall of eight men on his expected total, which he reported as escapees. However, when his superior arrived to conducted a recount, nobody moved so the resulting total would be correct. The officer would bawl the soldier out as an idiot, for wasting his time and not being able to count properly. We would repeat this trick at random for our amusement much to the annoyance of the guards.

One morning we were lazing about the compound, when the sound of an approaching aircraft caught our attention. Much to our surprise, a bright yellow U.S. P-38 Lightning appeared over the camp carrying German Swastika's on the wings. It must have been a captured aircraft the Luftwaffe were testing to evaluate its strengths or weaknesses. Realising he was over our camp the pilot decided to put on a show for us.

In quick succession he rolled or looped the P-38 then, he did two low passes over our heads, as we stood in silence. After the second pass he pulled the aircraft up into a tight loop to come back over the camp, but at this point he must have over reached its limits. As he exited the loop in a dive, we could see he was too low; the P38 plunged into the hillside in a ball of fire. In unison the whole camp let out a cheer, which went down badly with the Jerry guards. We were quickly rounded up at gun point then, forced back into our barracks. Here we were kept, for showing disrespect to the Fatherland. As a punishment, our water and electric supply into the camp were turned off for three days.

Stalag Luft 1

In Stalag Luft 1 Robert Cook found a camp filled with British, Canadian and Australian as well as American Air Force officers. In total there was almost nine thousand prisoners spread over five compounds. The camp was a large one with the Baltic to the North and the railroad we arrived on running around the west & south side. Beyond the railroad to the south was an anti-aircraft battery with an airfield attached. Some of the British POW's had been in the camp since 1940 which had become well organised. There was a barber's, somewhere to have your clothes repaired; we even had a camp newspaper being published. Because of the support of the Red Cross and the YMCA we also had a large collection of books for prisoners to read. But despite this, things in the camp were grim, being close to the Baltic, when the wind blows in off the sea the temperature drops dramatically. Then being this far north the winter was very cold, made worse by the lack of heating or clothes to keep us warm. Because of the limited food and lack of any heating people started to suffer, their health was not helped by the lack of even basic medicines in the camp. One of those who health was deteriorating was Robert Cook; he lost a lot of weight and was suffering from malnutrition and scurvy.

Elsham Wolds

Returning to RAF Elsham Wolds on the 3rd April Jack meets up with the rest of his crew in the Mess. There they were informed that they had been allocated a new rear gunner; 'Bert Burrill' a collective groan went through them. Bert was already flying with another crew, but was not liked by them; he also had a poor record for coming back from leave. He was invariably one or two days late which this did not endear him to our crew, so soon after losing a good man, like young Bob Thomas. But we have to get on with the war and Fred will soon sort Bert out if we have any trouble. Out on the airfield is our replacement aircraft, its R Rodger so we give her the one over as Fred talks to the ground chief.

We start out by doing a night cross country together on the 8th April. But life has a cruel trick to play on us; we have to land at Dunsfold to stay the night. Next morning, we could not set off for Elsham Wold's quick enough. On the way home Fred voices his unease about this new Lancaster, but it's nothing he can quite put his finger on, as yet.

Danzig Bay 9th April 44, Sunday

In the Ops room, we are one of nine aircraft on the board to do a gardening trip, to Danzig Bay in the Baltic. Gardening is a euphemism for dropping sea mines in the enemies shipping lanes. Standing out on the dispersal, we start to board the Lancaster; Bert is the first to do so. As he is helped up the ladder he turns to the rest of the crew; "I know what you lads have heard about me". "But, don't you worry about the Ar*e end of this aircraft, that's my job, you just do yours". Some days later it transpires that all Bert's problems were down to his lack of faith in his previous crew and their lax attitude to operational flying. His belief that he would not survive with that crew, was borne out when they fail to return from a raid, a few weeks later. Jack always held the view that Bert was specially gifted in his night vision; he could see night fighters long before anyone else in the crew. This endeared him to his new crew, who quickly forgot his previous history, which he never repeated. Usually, mines will be dropped by parachute from low level, but this time ours will be dropped from 15000 ft. (4500M). Take off was late at 21.10 hours, we head out over the North Sea toward Denmark. Fred is muttering to Arthur Richardson our flight engineer as he tweaks the mixture and throttles, something is not right. Despite the best efforts of Fred the Lancaster just does not want to climb. By the time we reach the enemy coast, we have only reached 18000 ft which looks like our limit. Crossing Denmark Fred turns toward the Baltic with Jack is in his usual position, the astrodome. Ken Smart our mid upper reports tracer from an aircraft in the distance with fire being return from another aircraft.

It's probably a bomber but we are too far away to see what sort. Approaching the target area, there are searchlights sweeping the sky from the coastal batteries. But we are coming in from the sea as Norman our Bomb Aimer sows our mines without interference. Then Fred turns back into the Baltic to starts the long trip home. There is a little flack as we cross Denmark, but it is not close so it could be aimed at another group in the area also on a mining trip.

As we cross into the North Sea there is a feeling of relief, but not relaxation as Fred drops our Lancaster to a lower level. Crossing the coast of Lincolnshire, Jack calls up the tower at Elsham, we are relieved to be given clearance to land, without any delay. Before we leave the dispersal, Fred is already talking to the ground crew, voicing the fact that there was a lack of power from the engines. The inevitable debriefing after this long flight is a pain, as the intelligence officer wants to know everything. After debriefing, we tuck into our bacon and eggs to the sounds of other aircraft landing back from the night's operation. This trip at nine and a half hours has been one of the longest we have to do, so we are all tired out.

In the morning we find that we have lost a 103 Squadron Lancaster, when P/O Nimmo and his crew fail to return.

The Crew of Lancaster III	ND420	PM-G
P/O J.A.H. Nimmo	RAAF	Kia
Sgt J.M. Roberts	RAF	Kia
F/S T.W. Bradley	RAAF	Kia

F/S	J. Bernaldo	RAAF	Kia
P/O	A.T. Thornton	RAAF	Kia
F/S	J. Smith	RAAF	POW
F/S	K.F. Clohessy	RAAF	POW

Aulnoye. 10th April Monday

We have a lay in bed before reporting for breakfast, then we find ops are on again for tonight. Fred is off to our dispersal with Arthur to see what the ground crew have done, to improve the performance of our aircraft. On his return he reports the Bowser is not filling up our aircraft fuel tanks, but the bomb load is higher, so it must be a short trip. In the Ops room the target is Aulnoye in France, we are to bomb railway stockyards and rail installations. There is also an edict from on high that all raids into France, will now only count as 1/3 of an operation. A ripple of disapproval runs through the room, this information is not well received by the aircrew. We have completed five trips so far, with twenty five still to go. If this decision is carried out, we could end up having to do seventy five Ops into France to complete our tour, an ominous thought. Standing waiting for takeoff we pace about the dispersal; cigarettes are smoked nonstop then at 23:00 hours we are ready to go. We contribute twelve aircraft to the total force of 132 Lancaster's for the raid. Hauling R Rodger into the air Fred starts to climb to operational altitude as we run down the country before crossing the channel. The ground crew have spent a long time working on our aircraft, but Fred is still not happy, it's better than it was but still not right. He is twiddling with the trimmers, the mixtures trying everything to get the Lancaster to fly better, but he is getting no improvement.

Our first two legs of the outward run are to Reading then Worthing on the South coast. By this time our altitude is well below twenty thousand feet. We crossed the Channel into France to the South of Le Harve, fortunately our bombing of Aulnoye is to be from ten thousand feet. There are a lot of searchlights ahead with fighter activity around Amiens. Aircraft are seen exchanging tracer with a number of bombers seen to be in trouble. When we arrive over Aulnoye we must be at the back of the bomber stream, because the target is already well alight. Fred voices his hope that we are the last to arrive, as he is concerned about the Lancaster's who may be above, dropping their bombs down onto us. Up in the nose Norman Barker our bomb aimer takes up his position and promptly drops our load into the centre of the fires.

Fred now waits for the target photo to be taken before getting us out of the area, back into the darkness of the surrounding countryside. Once the bomb load has gone, the aircraft starts to perform a lot better; it now climbs to over twenty thousand feet much to Fred's annoyance. We leave French airspace to re-cross the channel and retrace our route to Brighton, Reading then Elsham, I give thanks for another quite trip.

While we had a free run to and from the target the base suffered losses with both 103 and 576 Squadron each losing one aircraft. Out of the total of 132 Lancaster bombers and 15 Mosquito's of the Pathfinder force taking part in this raid we have lost 7 Lancasters.

Another forty nine young men have had to pay the price of fighting for a new world.

103 Squadron

The Crew of Lancaster III		JB732	PM-S
P/O	J.W. Armstrong RNZAF		Kia
Sgt	H.J. Beddis	RAF	POW
F/O	A.W. Draye	RAF	Evd
F/S	A.J. McCauley RAF		Evd
Sgt	L. Fisher	RAF	POW
F/O	M.F. Dillon	RNZAF	Kia
Sgt	R.P. Bowler	RAF	Kia

576 Squadron

The Crew of Lancaster I		LL830	UL-R2
F/L	F.S. Barnsdale	RAF	Kia
Sgt	J. Torode	RAF	Kia
WO2	A.G. Cambell	RCAF	Kia
Sgt	E.C. Edwards	RAF	Kia
Sgt	K.J. Willett	RAF	Kia
Sgt	C. Clamp	RAF	Kia
Sgt	G.M. Morris	RAF	Kia

Doing the Doncaster walk

It's a Sunday morning with the full day free; Fred is off to Doncaster to see a girl, he invites Jack along, as she has a friend. A trip to the cinema for the four of them, a few drinks afterwards then Fred disappears to take his girl home. His parting instruction to Jack is "22:30 Doncaster station for the last train, don't miss it". Arriving early at the station he is horrified to finds the train does not run on Sundays. Standing in the waiting room Jack ponders; has Fred already been and gone, do I wait to see if he turns up. By 22:30 he has his answer, no Fred. Setting out on foot Jack heads for Scunthorpe, hoping to hitch a lift from one of the trucks on the way to the steelworks. Three hours later, still a long way from Scunthorpe, hedgerows are starting to look like comfortable places to bed down.

Pausing for a breather, Jack is on the brink of falling asleep, when the sound of an approaching truck brings him back to life. His saviour is headed for the steelworks; the driver even goes out of his way, to drop him on the eastern edge of the town. Back on the road Jack is still 8 miles (13Km) from Elsham and by the time the airfield comes into view, the sun is getting ready to rise. Back in his billet, he finds Fred has not arrived, Jack falls into bed exhausted. One hour later Fred staggers into the room collapses on his bed to falls fast asleep. Lunch time comes round and Ops are scheduled for that night, but neither Fred nor Jack, are in a fit state to go anywhere. The crew finally decide to wake Fred from his sleep to give him the news about Op's. Realising he is still not in any condition to fly, he drags himself with Jack to see Doc Henderson, who promptly admits them both to the sick bay. The rest of the crew are stood down, just in case it may be something they may also have contracted. We are not the first crew whose bacon will be saved by this unconventional but well respected Medic. Doc Henderson is Elsham Wold's young medical officer who sees his duty, as more than just tending to injured aircrew, coming back from battle. He realised that these airmen are subject to mental as well as physical injury, it is his responsibility to see they are helped. To understand the stresses crews have to deal with, he decides to experience operational flying himself. Driving round the dispersals one night, talking to crews waiting to take off, he arrives at the last Lancaster. Dismissing his driver with a vow of secrecy, he climbs aboard this aircraft to seat himself on the rest bed until after takeoff. During the remainder of the flight, he positions himself beside the bomb aimer, to witness the horrors that crews endure each night. In total the Doc will fly some twenty operational trips, knowing that if caught, he will be in a lot of trouble. The experience he gains from these flights, he will use to help aircrew exhibiting signs of combat fatigue, often referred to as the 'Twitch'.

In his early days on the squadron Jack encounters this symptom at first hand when sitting in the mess. His attention is drawn to one airman, who displays involuntary movements, a slight repeated twist of the head coupled with a flicker in one eye. Turning to the nearest airman Jack asks about this behaviour, his answer, "Come back to ask after a few Op's". It is this sort of problem that Doc Henderson is hoping, to spot and take action, before it gets to this state. Sitting in an aircraft awaiting takeoff on an Op, crews could be given the message 'It's a scrub', there is a scramble to change then catch the bus into town. A Scrub can be because the weather over the target is poor or is expected to be bad locally for returning aircraft. The aircrew, furthest from their billets, could find by the time they are ready for town, they have missed the bus. To the rescue, comes who else but, Doc Henderson, his excuse was aircraft need air testing, the ambulance needs a run out. Cramming the unfortunate aircrews, into the back of the blood wagon, he would see they got to town for their night out. This is why the Doc is still talked about with such affection and regard.

Rouen. 18th April Tuesday R Ropey

Ops are on tonight but Fred is at our dispersal, talking to the ground crew chief trying to sort out the problems with 'R' Ropey. The ground crew are just as puzzled as Fred, "There are no major misalignments with the airframe the engines are also giving good power outputs". "So why won't she climb is Fred's question": the chief just shakes his head, "Maybe she's just a wrong-un". At the briefing Fred is still not happy about our aircraft, but has to concentrate on the next raid; Rouen's railway marshalling yards. Our bomb load is predominantly H.E. with our target only a short way into France from the English Channel. Therefore, it will be a short trip, hopefully a quite one of about five hours. There will be some 280 aircraft attacking the target our 103 Squadron are contributing eleven to this total.

Tonight, we are among the first to take off from Elsham at 22:00 hours to immediately head south to Newbury. Then it's a short run to Selsey Bill on the South coast. From here it's across the channel to the South of Le Harve. Crossing the coast our gunners are on their guard for night fighters. Ron our navigator gives Fred a heading for Rouen and in no time at all we are approaching the target. The sky is clear with the target flares clearly visible ahead of us; then as we make our run in, the flashes from exploding bombs are visible on the ground. We promptly add our load to the chaos taking place below us, before making a rapid exit from the target area. As we fly away from Rouen, Bert the rear gunner reports large explosions from the marshalling yards. Because we are so close to the coast we retrace our route back to the Channel then onto Brighton, Reading and home. It looks like this has been a successful raid; we encountered no opposition from fighters or flak. Landing back at Elsham Wolds, we are wishing all raids could be as easy as that one. Next day we find that there were no losses at all from the raid and the news is the marshalling yards had suffered severe damage.

Sitting in the Mess a bit skint, we are drinking on the cheap; I had brought out my banjo, we have had the usual sing song and drinking games. We have tried all the usual pranks to liven the evening up, but to no avail. Then Fred Brownings who has had a few by now stands up, in a very official tone announces, "Has anyone here seen a fart lit". Well "I am the President of the British Fart Lighters Association". There is silence then laughter after this proclamation, he follows it with the one rule for membership of the club. Any flame produced must be more than twelve inches long. For safety reasons, no attempt will be allowed in the naked condition, as a backfire could, cause serious injury. At first there is an air of scepticism over the whole thing, but later that evening Fred is ready for a demonstration. Calling for matches to be produced Fred lies back on a table then lift his legs in the air. As the lights are extinguished a match is ignited, Fred produces a flame that illuminates the room. A cheer runs round the assembled NCO's, who spend the rest of the evening, trying to become members of the Club

Cologne. 20th April Thursday R Ropey

We wake to find operations are on for tonight, Fred wastes no time in going out to our dispersal. Our ground crew know by his arrival that R Ropey is still not flying well. The engine fitters are rechecking the timing and fuel supply to find if there is any way they can fix this rogue aircraft. Fred is happy that the ground crew are working their socks off to find a solution, so he returns to the billet.

In the story of WW2 the efforts of these hard working men who serviced our aircraft is often forgotten. They would work in appalling conditions to ensure our planes were in tip top condition before a raid. Rain or Snow, they continued to work out in the open, I remember them working on Merlin engines with the cowlings removed. Laying full length over the wing and engine, they would make adjustments, while it was run up to full power. The only thing that prevented them, from being blown away by the slipstream, was a firm grip on the engine mountings. In the bad weather, they would wear the universal sleeveless leather jacket. This wind proof garment was the only protection they had; I think it was padded. After the war this jacket would be worn by every coal merchant in the country, on his rounds. When I saw them after the war, I was always reminded of our ground crew. Despite having perfectly good hangers, the Lancaster's were only taken inside, if they required major work to be done. On one occasion I was in one of the hangers watching a Lancaster being repaired, or should I say rebuilt. There had been an accident, the remains of two aircraft were being married together to create one good one from the remnants.

I remember there was a little white dog in the hanger, though nobody claimed ownership. It would run around the hanger following anyone and everyone. There was a rumour that quickly took root that if the dog refused to approach an aircrew man, that man was for the chop. It's my belief, this was a rumour spread by the ground crew chief, to stop aircrew bothering his boys at their work. Before each raid there was a sequence of events that took place, first the ground crew brought the aircraft to flying readiness. After this the armourers took over, they would deliver the bomb trolleys, with the nights load set up on them. The individual bombs would be winched up into the bomb bay then locked into position. When this was complete, they would remount the guns and fill the ammunition boxes, before running the belts through the tracks.

Finally, the tankers would arrive to put in the required fuel load then fill up the engine oil tanks. To complete the whole job the armourers would connect the bomb arming lines back to the airframe.

All of the ground crew would now sit back to pray the raid would still be on; if there was a scrub, then all their work would have to be undone. The bombs would have to be made safe then unloaded; the guns would be removed to be stored for the next raid. A lot of effort for the ground crews for little reward. Our Op tonight is Cologne; we are targeting the large industrial estates plus the numerous railway yards around the city. Our Squadron will put up fourteen Lancaster's for the raid. Out on the dispersal we are waiting for the off. Fred is talking to the ground crew who believe they have fixed R Ropey, but our skipper thinks they have their fingers crossed. After take-off we start the climb to altitude, Fred is happier that he was, but still complains Ropey is still not as good as old M for Mother. I have received a signal warning of intruders in our area, so I warn Fred and the gunners to keep watch. I log our take off at 23:30 as we head for Skegness, then across the Wash to Norfolk before heading out into the North Sea South of Lowestoft. Crossing the coast at Ostend we continue inland to Chatalet, before turning North East to Cologne. The weather is clear most of the way to the target which makes our gunners nervous. They much prefer it when the skipper can play hide and seek in the clouds, but they remain vigilant for night fighters. Our Lancaster has reached its bombing altitude but at the cost of airspeed, we are trailing the bomber force. To make things difficult for the radar controlled defences on the ground, we are dropping window which seems to be very effective. Arriving over the target late, there is a lot of cloud cover, but Cologne is well ablaze so we lose no time in adding to the inferno. Turning away from the target we head for home, when Bert calls "Corkscrew starboard", as a night fighter sweeps in to attack. Fred drops the Lancaster into a tight spiral turn toward the ground, as both gunners open fire on the incoming Me 109. Tracer streamed across our path into the port wing, when a cry of delight from the mid upper gunner indicates a result from the encounter. Ken gave the fighter a long burst as it passed overhead; he saw multiple hits along the fuselage with smoke or glycol streaming from the aircraft. The 109 was last seen diving away from us, he did not return. It was a short duel but the effect on moral was tremendous, we were all left with the feeling we could give as good as we got. Apart from this incident, I don't remember a lot of searchlight or flack on this raid, but maybe we are getting too used to it.

The return journey is routed over Holland, crossing the coast near Rotterdam without further incident and we land back at base in the early hours. In the debriefing Ken Smart claimed his Me109 but was only credited with a probable, much to his dismay. There were 380 aircraft on this raid, fortunately there were no losses on our base, but there are four aircraft missing from other Aerodromes. Friday 21ˢᵗ April, Fred did not visit the ground crew today; they would have their hands full, fixing the damage to the aircraft. He had also come to realise; this was as good as R Ropey was ever going to fly.

There is no Operation tonight so it's into Scunthorpe to celebrate Ken's fighter claim. Sitting in the bar at the Oswald, I get into conversation with Norman Barker our Bomb Aimer about Ken's Fighter shoot down. Norman starts to talk about Fred's roll in avoiding the incoming fighter. I did not realise how hard he had to work, during the corkscrew manoeuvre. Ron recounted the Berlin raid, "When we finally lost the fighter that night Fred was soaked in sweat, despite the fact it was minus 40 Deg". "I honestly believe Jack; we have the strongest dammed Pilot in the whole of the air force".

Dusseldorf. 22ⁿᵈ April Saturday. R Ropey

Dusseldorf is the target for tonight it's a short five hour trip, but it will be no milk run, it's the Ruhr which is well defended. Leaving our dispersal, we join the queue of thirty three aircraft from both Squadrons heading to the main runway. But something has gone wrong. One of the Lancaster's has left the runway with an engine on fire; we have to change to an alternative runway. This delays the take-off time for the rest of the aircraft; some will not get off at all. As Fred lifts our Lancaster off the runway, we can see others still on the ground; they will now be late over the target. Heading South to Norfolk we cross into the North Sea at Southwold then South to Dunkirk. We continue into France before turning East at Arras. Once again we are struggling to keep the airspeed up and the clear sky makes us a lone straggler, just what the fighters are looking for. Fred keeps our Lancaster moving about, hoping this will make it difficult for any ground controllers to track us. Our final turning point is Leige before running North to Dusseldorf. Approaching the target which is not hard to find, we could see the glow from miles away. Norman our bomb aimer drops our bombs into the center of the glow, then the agonising wait for the photo flash to go off before we dive away into the darkness. Again, there was little flack or many searchlights as we did our bombing run, though the gunners did report seeing fighters attacking bombers. We have a quiet run to Antwerp then Flushing before crossing the North Sea to home without incident, it was a relief to be home, we were thinking this has been another easy raid. When we land it comes as a shock to find other crews talking of the horrendous fighter activity into the target then out again. Next day we find that two of our Squadrons aircraft are missing, Fl/Of Birchall's aircraft was badly damaged by flack over the target. The crew were forced to bail out and have all been taken prisoner. Later it was found that Pl/Of Astbury's aircraft made it back home, but became lost over the North Yorkshire Wolds. Here it crashed into high ground near Thorp Hall, Rudston village, with the loss of the whole crew. Flight Lieutenant Allwood's aircraft was badly damaged in a scrap with a night fighter he had to put down at RAF Woodbridge. Pilot Officer Macdonald and Pilot Officer Chase were both attacked by night fighters but managed to return to base. Jack thought they had had a quiet trip; but from a total of 598 aircraft taking part in the raid, 31 are missing.

From the total of almost 4200 aircrew taking part last night, 133 have lost their lives, with 67 taken prisoner, 14 others would evade capture.

103 Squadron

The Crew of Lancaster ILL913　　　　PM-D

P/O	T.E. Astbury	RAF		Kia
Sgt	C. Whittle	RAF		Kia
F/S	D. Hopkins	RAF		Kia
Sgt	D.A.W. Leftley RAF		Kia	
Sgt	A. Jervis	RAF		Kia
Sgt	W.B. Graham	RAF		Kia
F/S	A. Hogg	RAAF		Kia

The Crew of Lancaster IME741 PM-G

F/O	J.W. Birchall	RAF	POW
Sgt	D.J. Hill	RAF	POW
F/S	D.T. Mitchell	RAF	POW
F/S	W. Meadows	RAF	POW
Sgt	T.W Wetton	RAF	POW
F/S	J. Hill DFM	RAF	POW
Sgt	B.J. Warren	RAF	POW

Greifswalder Bay, 23rd April Sunday R Ropey

Ops are off the board for tonight, but we are looking forward to a trip into Scunthorpe, with the rest of the Squadron. Sadly, it's not to be, we are designated as one of the crews listed for a gardening trip, we have drawn the short straw this time.

The target is Greifswalder Bay in the Baltic; we are to sow sea mines in the shipping lanes. Our aircraft is R Ropey again but Fred is not too unhappy; the weight of the mines is less than our normal bomb load so it should not be a problem. Our squadron provide four aircraft to the total force of 114 Bombers. Fred swings our Lancaster onto the runway then, waits for green light from the control van, before powering down the runway into the night. It's a short trip to Mablethorpe before crossing the North Sea; Fred is coaxing Ropey up to fifteen thousand feet, our drop height for the mines. As we approach Denmark, I leave my radio to stand in the astrodome, looking for fighters. This time we have an uneventful run into the Baltic, the fighters are thankfully busy somewhere else. Once over the sea, Ron is giving Fred a course change for the target, though there will be nothing to see when we arrive. Greifswalder Bay is a large semi-circle of land with an opening to the Baltic on the West. Our run in, is from the North tracking across the entrance to the bay but there are no fires or flares to guide us. The mines are dropped in sequence to straddle the shipping lanes hopefully to do their job in the next few days. Turning north we head back into the Baltic, before we reach Peenemunde, the flak batteries are thick on the ground there. We re-cross Denmark by a different route hoping to avoid any attention from the defences then; it's out over the North Sea and relative safety. Approaching the Lincolnshire coast cloud is gathering, by the time we reach Elsham Wolds the cloud base is down to two thousand feet and falling. This is a time to worry; waiting for clearance to land, we circle watchful for other aircraft in this poor visibility. We would not be the first to collide with another aircraft while circling in cloud, but eventually we enter the circuit. Fred gives us his usual triple bounce, as we trundle down the runway, before turning onto the Peri track to head for our dispersal. As we go through debriefing, I can see all four crews have returned from the gardening trip, it looks like we had another easy trip. Sadly, next day we find six aircraft from other airfields failed to return, though we don't know what targets they were attacking. Gardening is considered to be less dangerous than normal operations, but last night another thirty-one aircrew were lost.

After a number of weeks of operational flying, crews are given leave; most go home to their families. In the case of the aircrew from the commonwealth, the attraction of London with its night life makes it their destination. It's the 26th April we have six day leave; I am on my way to Carlisle. Sitting at home in the front room, Jack father tells him of his new greenhouse, which he had built and glazed a couple of weeks before. I remember he took me to see it; he was so pleased with it though I was shocked at how much it had cost. Though I can't recall what the actual figure was. Many men during the war years if not before, were out of necessity gardeners. Everyone in the street seemed to have an allotment, where they grew vegetables and some fruit which were in short supply, or expensive to buy during the war. These allotments were alive with men like my dad, busy fussing with the rows of plants they were growing. They stand around discussing treatments, for ailing plants while some of their sheds, were a home from home. Then a few nights later, Jerry arrived dropping a stick of bombs; one lands nearby, but does not explode. Dad returns home from work next day, to find an air raid warden, blocking access to the allotments. There are anxious hours waiting, for the bomb disposal squad, to disarm the bomb and save his greenhouse. We had a good laugh about it afterwards, but at the time it was far from funny. It was also nice to travel into Carlisle visiting my old haunts to resample the local brews. Although I did not get time to visit No.14 M.U. I did call in at Prices Tailors to talk with some of my old work mates.

Then ever so quickly, it's time to get back to the war, as my leave comes to an end. Arriving back on the base it's the 2nd May 44 sadly we find that the day we went on leave, the Squadron targeted Essen on the 26th April. In our absence P/O Shepherd's crew were allocated R-Ropey; tragically on the outward trip the Lancaster fell victim to the flak. Their aircraft crashed on the village of Stump to the west of Dusseldorf with the loss of the crew. As a group, we had mixed emotions about this loss; we would not miss the lame duck aircraft. It was just a shame it had to take a good crew with it and it could have been our crew.

Mailly-le-Camp 3rd May Wednesday U Uncle

The day started with a fine sunny morning, we all take a walk out to our dispersal, to check the equipment on our new aircraft. Ops are on so the ground crew are busy getting 'U' Uncle ready for tonight's raid. I spot Norman Barker our bomb aimer, is standing holding the starboard inner prop, having his photo taken. My mind went back to the last time we had photos taken; it was the morning of the Berlin raid. A cold shiver runs up my spine, but I quickly dismiss any notion it is unlucky; I even have my photo taken, stood by the rear turret. As we leave the dispersal, the armourers are delivering the bomb trolleys, Norman comments about the makeup of the bomb load. We are being loaded with one 4,000 Lbs Cookie, the rest being 500Lbs high explosives, there are no incendiaries in the load. In the afternoon we file into the briefing room to find somewhere to sit. When the cover was removed from the map board, there was an almost audible sigh of relief, it's a French trip.

A milk run, it was called, but would count as only one third of a trip; how wrong this would prove to be. Our target is Mailly le Camp a German army Panzer Tank depot; originally the camp had been a French one to the south of Reims. In the run up to D Day, these 21st Division Tanks were considered a threat to the invasion of Normandy, so must be destroyed. The raid had been split into two waves with Five Group opening the attack on one area of the camp. Then a few minutes later, One Group aircraft would complete the attack. At this point our attention was drawn to the proximity of the village adjoining the camp, it must be protected. It was important, that civilian casualties had at all costs, to be kept to an absolute minimum. The weather was expected to be clear with a full moon; our Squadron would be providing fourteen aircraft for the raid. After the briefing there was a relaxed air among the crews, the calm before the storm.

Sitting in the mess having our operation meal, we chatted together as though it was a cross country exercise, we were about to do. Later we walked back to the billets together to get dressed, before collecting our parachutes. Take off was 22:00 hours, as we climb into a clear sky with the moon shining brightly. Our route takes us down country to High Wycombe the first turning point; as I looked out of my small window, I was shocked at what I saw. Below us the country side was as clear as day, only the colours were muted with a bluish white hue. I also realised we would be clearly visible to every enemy fighter that was on patrol that night. Ron's voice on the intercom gives Fred our course for the French coast, brings me back from by visions. We crossed into France to the north of Dieppe then; it was a straight run to Challons Sur Marne south of Reims. Thirty miles from Challons, we found the red marker flare that the pathfinders had dropped to indicate we were on track; we are also on time. Approaching the holding point we could see the first wave aircraft still orbiting the yellow flares with a swarm of fighter among them wreaking havoc. As Fred joined the circuit the mayhem was obvious, both of our gunners started to report aircraft being shot down. All around us, bombers could be seen falling in flames, then exploding as they hit the ground. Fred's reaction was immediate "This is no place for the living, I am withdrawing to a safer location, Ron plot our diversion". At that he flew away from Challons toward the west, where we started to orbit. Fred calls, "Jack what instructions are you hearing on the radio". "Nothing came my reply, there seems to be some music interference on the frequency but I can't make out who is broadcasting. It could possibly be the Jerries". Even at this distance, we could still see the carnage taking place, as tracer arced between fighters and bombers. As we watched, Fred's voice came on the intercom "They are like Moths circling a candle", "Jack, go into the astrodome, Norman man the front turret". I remember listening to the radio; the air was thick with people asking why we were waiting, with the cries of aircrew in trouble. One man was screaming they were on fire and under attack, when a voice cut into his call. "Switch off your mike you are blocking the airwaves; If you are going to die, die like a man, in silence". This callous remark sent a shudder down my spine, but I knew deep down he was right. Fighters were streaming into the area, from the four airfields in the vicinity, they were decimating our bombers.

To my horror within a few minutes, I watch as three bombers are attacked by fighters and spiral to the ground on fire. Then at 00:20 hours, Fred reported aircraft from the first wave, flying south to start the attack on Mailly le Camp. At 00:32 hours I hear the master bomber, calling for the second wave to commence the attack, I inform Fred. Ron gives Fred a heading for the target as I feel the Lancaster turning toward Mailly. Lining up onto the bomb run, Fred hands over control to Norman Barker our bomb aimer, who has returned from the front gun turret. He quickly lines the Lancaster up on the target then drops our load, onto the RED marker flares. Once the photoflash fires we turn away from the growing inferno.

But as we turn Kan Smart the mid upper calls out a warning, we are crossing beneath another Lancaster with its bomb doors open. Thankfully the bombs fall to one side of us, but it just shows how easy it is, to become victim of the chaos. Heading for home a Lancaster passes us heading for the target only a mile away, suddenly it explodes in a ball of fire. In a split second the bright flash envelops the aircraft, when it fades the aircraft is no longer there. The fighting and dying is still going on, we are not free of it yet. Aircraft are joining the attack on the target from different directions with the danger of a head on collision. Bert Burrill's voice on the intercom calls, "Corkscrew starboard", as a FW-190 attacks from astern. It fires one long burst at us, which is returned by our gunners, then as quickly as he appears, we lose him. Flying on in the moonlight, Fred asks everyone to watch for fighters, so I step back into the astrodome. It seems as though the whole of the Luftwaffe is looking for us tonight, they are in a mean mood.

The return flight is done in an air of constant vigilance and trepidation; the last time we had it this bad was the Berlin trip, less than eight weeks ago. Our route back home is the long way; we head south from Mailly before turning west, passing to the South of Paris then on toward Chartres. Here we complete a long dog leg ending at Bayeux on the coast of France. All the time, we were watching for trouble, the gunners constantly quartering the sky with their turrets. We have had a mauling tonight at the hands of the Luftwaffe; which would be engraved on our memory, for a long, long time. Landing back at Elsham the mood at debriefing was agitated, the crews were angry, why were we kept circling the holding point for so long. The intelligence officer was swamped with questions; what caused the interference on the aircraft radios. The poor man had no answers for us; he could only note our complaints and report our observations, back to the Top Brass. This raid brought an end to the one third of an Op rule, which went some way to calming the anger over the debacle that was Mailly le Camp. Elsham Wolds lost four aircraft tonight, three from 103 Squadron one from 576 Squadron. Another 576 Squadron Lancaster piloted by P/O Reed, was badly damaged by a fighter over the target. He managed to bring the aircraft back to base, although the rear gunner Sgt Alf Hodson had been killed in the encounter with a JU88.

103 Squadron
The Crew of Lancaster IME673 PM-I

P/O	S.L. Rowe	RAAF	Kia
Sgt	J.H. Sallis	RAF	Kia
F/S	E.G. Housden	RAF	Kia
F/S	E.A. Metcalfe	RAF	Kia
Sgt	K.R. Warren	RAF	Kia
SGT	P.A. Staniland	RAF	Kia
SGT	D.J. Coldicott	RAF	Kia

The Crew of Lancaster III ND411 PM-J

P/O	J.E. Holden	RAF	Kia
Sgt	J.E. Moore	RAF	Kia
Sgt	T.W. Sykes	RAF	Kia
F/S	C.S. Gay	RAAF	Kia
Sgt	R.A. Wilson	RAF	Kia
Sgt	A.A. McCallum RCAF		Kia
Sgt	F.C. Hoxford	RCAF	Kia

The Crew of Lancaster III ND905 PM-B

S/L	H. Swanston	RAF	Kia
Sgt	D.A. Haddon	RAF	Kia
F/O	E.J. Dane	RAF	Kia
W/O	R.H. Boyd	RAAF	Kia
W/O	J.C. Smith	RAF	Kia
Sgt	G.F. Casey	RAF	Kia
Sgt	J.R. Rankin	RCAF	Kia

576 Squadron
The Crew of Lancaster IME586 UL-B2

P/O	R. Whalley DFC	RAF	Kia
Sgt	C. Vandevelde	RAF	POW
F/S	J.D. Ward	RAF	POW
Sgt	S.J. Barr	RAF	Kia
F/S	F. Burgess	RAF	Kia
Sgt	J. McCool	RAF	Kia
F/S	N.P. Reilly	RAF	Kia

The Crew of Lancaster IME703 UL-S2 written off

| Sgt | A.A.H. Hodson RAF | | Kia |

Out of the total of 340 aircraft taking part in the raid, we lost 42 last night, over 280 young men perished. They will miss the breakfast of bacon and eggs, they will not be in the pub tonight, they will join the ranks of those who will always be twenty one, or twenty or nineteen.

Whether it was in response to the chaos of last night's raid or the anger expressed by the crews I don't know. But we were all taken off Ops for three days.

Aubigne Racan 6th May Saturday U Uncle

It's now the 6th May we are open for business again, with a raid back into France, at Aubigne Racan to the south of Le Mans. The target is an ammunition dump; one group is putting up 51 aircraft to do the job. Our Squadron is only providing three aircraft for the raid with take-off at 00:28Hrs. The planned route is south to Reading then Shoreham before crossing the Channel to Caen. Fred Browning is a changed man, our new aircraft U uncle is wonderful, it's one of the new Lancaster's with the paddle blade props. It can climb to over twenty five thousand feet without any problem; Fred is like a kid with a new toy. Our route from Caen continued due south almost to Bordeaux then a sharp turn to the North West toward the target. The raid was uneventful; the weather was good without being as clear as it was for Mailly. One thing I do remember was the fireworks on the ground, as we dropped our bombs into the middle of the flares. There were explosion the like of which I had not seen before, so we must have been hitting the right spot. From Aubigne Racan we turned due east to Tours then North to Le Mans crossing the coast at Le Harve. We returned home without encountering any fighters, on landing we find all of our Squadron aircraft are back safely. Next day however there is bad news, our sister Squadron 576 has lost one aircraft last night.

Much later it transpires there was a second pilot aboard this aircraft; it's our base commander A/C Ronald Ivelaw-Chapman. Their Lancaster was shot down by a JU88 with Ivelaw-Chapman and Sgt Joe Ford the bomb aimer parachuting to safety they were the only two survivors from the aircraft. After spending a few weeks on the run, being helped by the French they were finally captured. We did not know it at the time, but Ivelaw-Chapman had been involved in the planning of the D Day Invasion. So when the top brass heard he had taken part in the raid, been shot down and captured, the balloon went up. Winston Churchill ordered that if Ievlaw-Chapman was in danger of being captured by the Germans he was to be killed. Fortunately, the Jerries despite interrogating him; did not realise just how important he was, they finally ended up sending him to a normal POW camp. How different things could have turned out.

576 Squadron
The Crew of Lancaster III	ND783	UL-C2
F/L J.M. Shearer	RNZAF	Kia

A/C	R. Ivelaw-Chapman	RAF	POW
Sgt	S.N.G. Drew	RAF	Kia
W/O	A.H. Biltoft	RAAF	Kia
Sgt	J.A. Ford	RAAF	Evd
Sgt	C.V. Fox	RAF	Kia
Sgt	J.W. McLeod	RAAF	Kia
Sgt	A.R. Jackson	RAAF	Kia

The Squire, his monocle and the chip shop.

The two Squadrons at Elsham Wolds had their fair share of characters; one of these airmen was nicknamed 'Squire' (Cunliffe). His appearance was enhanced, by the plain glass monocle, he wore at all times. He would stand in the bar, of any Pub in the area recounting tales of clashes with the Luftwaffe while the locals bought him drinks. He would talk of Flak thick enough to walk on, with fighters swarming like flies round a horse's tail. All the time he was shooting a line, he would be polishing the monocle. Locals knowing that he may be making up these stories; would still seek him out for more tales. One night, leaving the Bull pub in Brigg, Jack encounters the 'Squire' on his way back to the Drome. "Evening Jack" came the greeting, together they walked up the dark high street. "Do you fancy some fish and chips" he asks as the chippy comes into view, "Have you seen the size, of the queue" replies Jack. "We will miss the bus back to camp, if we wait to be served". "Queue; I never queue, I'm a war hero in this town, I always get served straight away". So into the fish shop he goes; waiting outside Jack can only discern shapes, through the steamed up windows. Suddenly the shapes merge then move toward the door, which is thrown open, the Squire sails through the air. He lands in a heap in the road as Jack rushes over. The Squire retrieves his monocle from the tarmac, carefully cleans it before replacing it in his eye. Looking up at Jack; "Ungrateful buggers" is all he says. While Scunthorpe was the favourite haunt of aircrews, Brig still had its attractions. The town was much closer, to Elsham Wolds than Scunthorpe so it could be reached by bike, though the ride back was always a bit of a challenge. In town there was a midweek dance plus a good supply of pubs, which always attracted a ready crowd of airmen. One of Brig's strangely named pubs was the "The Dying Gladiator" in Bigby St. which was quickly rechristened by aircrew as "The Dying Navigator". Above the front doors portico, stands a full size gold covered statue of a fatally wounded Gladiator. Perhaps the visiting aircrew regarded this macabre statue as a reminder, of their mortality. The Landlady Mrs Clark was a great friend to the young airmen, she would even let them sit in the bar eating bags of fish and chips, while they supped their beer. Though, woe betides any local who tried to do the same.

Fort Mardyck 9th May Tuesday U Uncle

I have looked at my log book and can see this raid was Mardyke a gun battery at Dunkerque so we were in the air for only 3hours. To be honest I have no recollection of this raid. From the squadron ORB I see take off was about 22:00 hours, our route was south to cross the coast at Orfordness. Then we would head South East toward Dunkerque. Our time over the target would have been very short before turning back into the channel to head home. Once again, the squadron had suffered no losses on this raid. Because there were no losses on this raid plus the short duration is why I cannot recall it, or my age.

Heligoland Bight 10th May Wednesday

The day starts bright and sunny, so we walk out to the dispersal to see what the gen is from the ground crew. When we arrive, the armourers are delivering bomb trolleys loaded with sea mines, so we know what we are doing tonight, but not where. As we march into the Ops room there are only six crews present, our target is revealed as Heligoland Bight.

This area of the North Sea is the entrance to the Elbe and Weser rivers, along with the huge Wilhelmshaven dock complex. Our job is to sow these busy shipping lanes with our vegetables, hopefully to sink a few ships. Our takeoff is 22:00 Hrs, we set off across the North Sea, with the trip expected to last about four hours. Approaching the target from the North at about twelve thousand feet, Jack is dropping window to confuse the ground controllers. Almost in response, a Flack ships put up a barrage to greet us, as Norman our bomb aimer takes up his position in the nose of the Lancaster. Tonight, however it will be Ron Walker, our Navigator who will be determining the release point from the H2S screen. There is none of the left, right, steady calls by Norman this time, only Ron's voice calling steady, steady, Drop Norman releases the mines as instructed. We then turn west to re-cross the North Sea, making sure to avoid Heligoland with its defences as we head for home. Back in debriefing we find all six crews have returned; they reported flack but no fighter contacts, all in all, another quiet trip.

Heligoland Bight 12th May Friday

Friday the 12th May we are scheduled for a fighter affiliation exercise in Z Zebra, we take off at 10:00Hrs then fly out to sea for the rendezvous. We have been airborne for about fifteen minutes when the weather closes in and I receive a message cancelling the exercise. Fred wastes no time in returning to base; as we taxi back to the dispersal, we pass our dispersal where our ground crew are preparing U Uncle. The armourers are also there with their bomb trolleys loaded with sea mines

136

once more. In the Ops room we are one of two aircraft assigned to mine the Heligoland Bight area again. Our take off time is 22:20Hrs with the other aircraft following fifteen minutes later. Talk about déjàvue the trip is a repeat of the Op two nights ago, we cross the North Sea, but for a change we run into the target area from the South. From twelve thousand feet we sow our mines using HS2, with the flack ships again giving us a twenty one gun salute. I am in my usual position in the astrodome, but we don't see or encountered any opposition from night fighters. The only sensation I have is of the Lancaster buoying upwards as our mines are released, before Fred banks away west to head home. Turning into the circuit at Elsham, all I am only thinking about are my bacon and eggs breakfast; it has been another quite trip. It can be trips like this that can lull a crew, into a feeling of complacency that could be their undoing. Though to be honest, mining trips like this are usually four and a half hours of flying to and from the target, with ten minutes of excitement over the drop zone. These are totally different from the constant battle flying the breadth of Germany before dropping the bomb load, then fighting your way home again.

Its Sunday, we are not listed for flying so we spend it in the mess having a quiet pint. The mess had a dartboard; there were dominoes or cards, not sure if there was a chess board. Some Sundays a dance would be organised with Waffs or crews girlfriends from the local villages invited. The Dining room would be cleared of tables to create an area to dance. Music would come from a Record player or from an impromptu group around the piano, Accordion or any instrument someone could play. The bar itself was a hatch in the wall through which drinks could be ordered and served up. I have talked about fear among aircrew. But there was one time all male station personnel feared, it was when the C.O. called a general muster. Male personnel would be assembled for an identification parade. This was the normal procedure, when a female civilian found she was in the family way and was looking for the father. The appearance of some airmen underwent rapid alteration, hairstyles were changed, moustaches disappeared, false teeth were removed. Though on most occasions, this subterfuge failed with the offending airman was bought to book to face up, to his responsibilities.

Kiel Bay 15th May Monday flying with Strangers

Tonight, Fred Brownings crew are not on the board for ops, they are sitting in the mess. We were waiting to head into town, as there are five crews already listed for a gardening trip. Without warning the door of the mess opens, an officer call's to Jack, "We have a wireless op down sick, get your kit, you are replacing him". It's not a happy situation, but he resigns himself to the fact, there is nothing he can do but follow orders.

In the Op's room he gathers the gen about the raid, a mining trip to Kiel Bay. Later that evening, after a half hour air test in the afternoon, he boards the Lancaster with six strangers. Over the North Sea he is disturbed by the amount of chatter over the intercom, I can only hope it will stop once the Danish coast is reached. This is completely at odds with the way our crew operates under Fred Brownings. But if this is the way this crew copes with the situation so be it.

Crossing Denmark Jack leaves his wireless station to stand in the astrodome, to be an extra set of eyes watching for Jerry night fighters. I can see we are now well out into the Baltic, so Jack returns to his station leaving the gunners to their chatter, as we fly on to Kiel Bay. Approaching the target, the HS2 which we will use to place the mines fails. This means we cannot drop the mines with any accuracy, so the Skipper decides to abort the mission, we will return to base. Turning back into the Baltic we head north away from Kiel, before finally turning west for home. Crossing Denmark again, I stand in the astrodome to watch for fighters in the distance are aircraft exchanging tracer to the north over the Danish islands. But when I mention it, the gunners comment is "it's a long way away", but it still shows there are fighters about. At this moment Jack has in his mind Bert Burrill's experience with the crew he had left, to join Fred Brownings. This crew aged me by ten years during that raid, recalls Jack and I never forgot them, I often wondered if they survived their tour. Arriving back at Elsham we find there are two aircraft missing from the raid, one from our squadron the other from 576 Squadron.

103 Squadron
The Crew of Lancaster ILL963   PM-D

P/O	K.W. Mitchell	RAF		Kia
Sgt	D. Howells	RAF		Kia
F/S	W. Kelly	RAF		Kia
F/S	R.A. Tapp	RAF		Kia
F/S	C.F. Bish	RAF		Kia
Sgt	D.F. Pegrum	RAF		Kia
F/O	T.K. Wright	RAF		Kia

576 Squadron
The Crew of Lancaster IME576 UL-X2

F/O	E.J. Presland DFC	RAF		Kia
P/O	A.E. Slade	RAF		Kia
Sgt	A.W. Knapp	RAF		Kia
F/O	M.L. Abramson	RCAF	Kia	
F/O	C. Ashcroft	RAF		Kia
Sgt	B.J.J. Hudson	RAF		Kia

Sgt	R.E. Leatham	RAF	Kia
Sgt	A.G. Wright DFM	RAF	Kia

The weather has turned really nasty, but we are not complaining we are off to Sunny Scunthorpe for a night off. As it happens, we get three nights off as the poor weather continues to disrupt operations.

Orleans 19th May Friday U Uncle

Since the mining Op on the 15th the weather has been awful. On the morning of the 19th the cloud lifts slightly, though there is a constant drizzle which wets everyone and everything. Out on the dispersals, the ground crews are scurrying about, so it looks like an Op is on the cards for tonight. Sure enough we are called to the ops room; here we find the target is the railway marshalling yards, at Orleans in France. Our contribution will be eleven Lancaster's out of a total of 118 aircraft taking part in the raid. We take off at 22:00Hr into the overcast which quickly enveloped our Lancaster, Ron calls out a heading, Fred sets off for Reading. Here there is a course change to Brighton on the south coast. Out into the channel we cross the French coast near Rouen before heading South East for Orleans. Because of the cloud there is little flak with no fighters to be seen, but as we pass to the south of Chartres the sky brightens and starts to clear. By the time we reach the target the Pathfinders flares can clearly be seen ahead so we quickly drop our bombs on the markers. We now continue on the same heading towards Tours before a sharp turn to the North toward Le Harve where the cloud returns to envelop us. Fortunately, when we arrive over Elsham Wolds the sky has started to clear making our landing much easier. In the debriefing we find all our squadrons aircraft have returned safely, it has been another good night for the squadron. Last night there have been a series of raids across France with 900 Bomber Command aircraft taking part. The Command losses are 7 aircraft, with fifty one airmen losing their lives, the rest are either taken P.O.W. or evading.

If we take the time to stop and look at the numbers involved last night, there were over seven thousand young airmen in the sky over France. There have been occasions when this number was as high as 8000 though the norm would be more like 5000. In the morning we are told Fred is leaving us, but only a far as the Officers billets, he has been promoted to Pilot Officer. As a crew we are delighted for him but very sad he will not be there in the sergeant's mess to talk to.

Duisburg 21st May Sunday U Uncle

It's Sunday morning but there are no hangovers from the Saturday night out, last night was spent quietly in the mess. We have been busy these last few weeks, as unknown to us we are on the run up to D Day so there will be no let up. We gather together for breakfast to notice the dispersals are bussing with activity for an Op. In the afternoon we congregate in the Ops room to find the target is Duisburg the industrial heart of the Ruhr. We are to provide eighteen Lancaster to the total of 510 aircraft taking part in the raid. The C.O. talks about the importance of the raid, then the Intelligence Officer gives the latest on the defences we will find on our route to and from the target. When the Met Officer steps up, he is full of bad news there will be heavy cloud, all the way to the target, with some improvement on the way home. The meal before takeoff is eaten in silence, as a crew we are aware how tough this raid is going to be. Take off is 22:00Hrs, we climb through cloud toward Mablethorpe before setting out across the North Sea for Duisburg. We cross the coast to the north of Amsterdam then, follow a series of course changes that curve to the South terminating at Duisburg.

The cloud over Germany makes it difficult for the defences, the searchlights cannot penetrate it and the fighters will have trouble finding us. Though the flak is different, its radar controlled so can be fired blind at us, as we approach. When we reach the target, the pathfinders are having trouble illuminating the aiming point, they have to resort to sky markers. Fred makes an approach running up to these; Norman drops our bombs as accurately as he can. Then it's the wait for the photo flash to fire, though I doubt if there will be anything on the film but cloud. As we leave Duisburg Fred reports breaks in the clouds, the searchlights are starting to penetrate, then as we fly on the flak starts again. We begin to lose height when our Lancaster rocks under the impact of flack, there have been at least two hits somewhere on the aircraft. Everyone reports in as ok, as Arthur our flight engineer scans the fuel gauges for any losses. Once we are away from the Ruhr, Fred climbs back to the safely of the cloud as we head back to Elsham, Arthur reports no fuel loss thank goodness. We must follow a new curved route to the West of Dusseldorf then Eindhoven to cross the coast north of Rotterdam. The rest of our journey is uneventful; we are relieved when the wheels finally touch the runway, then taxi back to our dispersal. Fred is quickly out of the aircraft, onto the tarmac looking at our damage; there is a hole in the underside of the starboard wing. Its 03:30Hrs in the morning, but the ground crew appear from the darkness to welcome us back, Fred shows them the damage. Our ground crew chief say it can be fixed, but they will have to check for any internal damage. We leave them to get on with it, we report for debriefing and a mug of hot tea with a Tot of something in it.

After our breakfast, we hear there are two aircraft missing from the base, one from 103 the other from 576 Squadron. Overall, there are twenty nine aircraft missing from the force involved in this raid on Duisburg, that's over 5% of the total taking part.

103 Squadron
The Crew of Lancaster IME722 PM-E

P/O	T.I. Jones	RAF		Kia
Sgt	D. Sharpe	RAF		Evd
WO2	E.S. Moran	RCAF	POW	
WO	B.A. Davis	RAAF		Evd
Sgt	C.R. Francis	RAF		Evd
Sgt	M. Pickles	RAF		Kia
Sgt	W.E. Jones	RAF		Kia

576 Squadron
The Crew of Lancaster IDV365   UL-Z2

F/O	E.H. Stansel	RCAF	POW
Sgt	R.W. Ball	RAF	Kia
F/S	A.W. Cooper	RAF	Kia
F/S	H.L. Arrowsmith	RAF	POW
Sgt	G. Webster	RAF	POW
Sgt	C. Lister	RAF	Kia
Sgt	L. Green	RAF	Kia

Flying at night on ops, day after day, fatigue drains aircrew to the point that they can fall asleep on a raid, despite the intense cold (-40C). Sitting in the turret the gunners stare out into the dark sky, searching for the slightest sign that will reveal the incoming night fighter. Because the eyes have no point to focus on, they become disorientated their vision suffers. To break this lock up the gunners have to refocus on the tail plane or wingtips. To alleviate this tiredness problem the medics can prescribe wakey, wakey pills to be taken when needed. Aircrew quickly realise these pills will keep you awake, but need to be taken with caution. Sitting at a dispersal waiting for the off is not the best time to take one. If there is a mission scrub then you spend the rest of the night with your eyes wide open like a child's wax doll, sleep becomes impossible. So, if you need a pill, you wait until you are approaching the enemy coast before taking it. Even then there is a cost, taken too often aircrew can find they return to the billet, then fall asleep for fifteen or twenty hours before they awake. I know these pills were available but I can't remember many aircrews taking them often, if at all. Some of the best air gunners in the air force were ex farm workers; they have lots of experience shooting Pheasant's, Grouse or Rabbits. Their natural eye for shooting at moving targets makes them ideal gunners. To keep their eye in practice, when there was no operations on that night the will disappear into the darkness of the local country side with a shot gun. A few hours later they will reappear with a bag full of food for the cooks to prepare. Often the camp would be visited by a gamekeeper from the local estate, who would complain that the Lord of the Manor was losing game birds to poachers. Our camp Commander would assure him it was nobody from the Base but, if they could catch an airman poaching, he would be dealt with.

Dortmund 22nd May Monday U Uncle

A new day arrives; we troop into the ablutions block, to restore us to functioning human beings. These places were not somewhere you spent a lot of time in. They were cold, the water was not very hot, it was often wet underfoot. There never seems enough hours of sleep in a day, but a good swill quickly gets the blood circulating round the system again. From that moment on, we are only thinking of food; we arrive in the mess like a swarm of locust eating anything and everything placed before us. Then when we have drunk our fill of hot tea, we are ready to face the day. Out on the dispersal the ground crew have been working miracles, U Uncle is repaired, as confirmed by the smell of fresh paint. They also report that the armourers are preparing the bomb trolleys, for an Op tonight, but they don't know where yet.

Leaving them to it we going back to our billets, here some of the boys write letters home or try to read the papers. Mainly it's to relax, recharge our batteries in readiness for the nights Op. Before we know it, it's time for the trip to the Ops room; we file in to find out our fate. Dortmund is the name on the board; we are briefed on the route for the raid, before the met Officer gives us the weather report. It's predicted to be clear, all the way to the target. Fred has been informed his crew are listed to be in the first wave over the target, we are to ensure it's well alight for the following waves. Darkness has fallen, we are out on the dispersal waiting for the off. Standing looking up into the open bomb bay of the Lancaster, I am always amazed by the size of the bomb load this aeroplane can carry. A four thousand pound Cookie hangs there with very little visible means of support, around it are the boxes of incendiaries. These are 108 of the 30 Lbs plus 1170 of the 4Lbs in the bomb bay. The theory behind the bomb load is that the Cookie lands first blowing off the roofs, the windows or doors of buildings. Then the incendiaries fall into the buildings setting them alight, this renders large areas of industry unusable for the German war effort. Fred's voice breaks into my thoughts as he calls us to board our Lancaster the Op is on.

Around me the ground crew are taking up their positions to start the engines. Take off time was 22:01Hrs, as we leave the Lincolnshire coast, our gunners are commenting on the number of aircraft they can see in the sky around us. Dortmund our target is 30 miles west of Duisburg still in the Ruhr valley where we bombed last night, so they are going to be ready for us. Crossing into Holland from the North Sea our route is complex we zig, zag, toward Osnabruck. Then we run west toward Hannover before a turn south west direct to Dortmund. We are half an hour from the target and the searchlights are coming up ahead of us. Approaching the target both gunners are reporting fighters in our vicinity, but they have not picked us out yet. We have started the bomb run when Ken Smart reports a fighter attacking a bomber to starboard. The other aircraft is also on the bomb run but it is putting up a fierce defence against the fighter. That wonderful uplift as the bombs are released, followed by the aircraft banking away from the target comes as a relief. We are on our way home but we are not out of the woods yet.

Around us the flack is coming up with the searchlights still hunting for us. Fred is weaving about trying to anticipate where they will be when we get to them. Our return route is back to Hannover, then West toward Amsterdam. A sharp turn to the North West takes us clear of the City out into the North Sea. Then once again we are in darkness, with the Dutch coast behind us. As we cross the North Sea again there is cloud gathering, which by the time we reach Elsham Wolds the ceiling is down to 500ft. This is just another unwanted ordeal, for tired aircrew to endure at the end of a long trip. In the debriefing supping our hot tea, we are shocked to hear the other crew's talk of pitched battles with night fighters plus the heavy flack. We look at each other in wonder, have we been to a different target from the rest of the Squadron.

Tonight, the Squadron provided fourteen aircraft, to the total of 360 taking part in the raid. Out of this total we lose two Lancaster's from 103 Squadron and one from 576 Squadron.

103 Squadron
The Crew of Lancaster ILL946   PM-Z

F/L	G.A. Morrison DSO	RAF	Kia
Sgt	H. K. Grant	RAF (USA)	Kia
F/S	C. Jackson	RAF	Kia
F/S	F. J. Goodale	RAF	Kia
Sgt	K.D. Crothers	RAF	Kia
Sgt	J.N. McKenna	RAF (I.R.)	Kia
Sgt	A. Tuffs	RAF	Kia

103 Squadron
The Crew of Lancaster III   ND629   PM-G

P/O	W.J.D. Charles RCAF		Kia	
Sgt	A.E. Lee	RAF		Kia
F/O	O. Wright	RCAF		Kia
F/O	L.S. Kennedy	RCAF		Kia
P/O	D.F.A. Wiener	RAF		Kia

Sgt	V. Davies	RAF	Kia
Sgt	H.A. Shephard	RAF	Kia

576 Squadron
The Crew of Lancaster IME687 UL-S2

P/O	R.R. Reed DSO RAF		Kia	
Sgt	A. Taylor DFM RAF		Kia	
F/O	G. Hallows DFC	RAF		Kia
F/S	M.A. Saruk DFM	RCAF		Kia
F/O	W. Murphy DFC	RAF		Kia
Sgt	S.S. Greenwood	RAF		Kia
F/L	F. Hill OBE DFC	RAF		Kia

Coming back from a raid crew's would return to their billet, climb into bed then fall asleep without any problem. As a group, aircrew were no different from any other gathering of young men, with all their habits, flatulence, belching, sweaty feet and snoring. Among our crew we were lucky in not having anyone who snored. However, there were occasions when one of the other crews did have someone who could rattle the windows. One occurrence of this was where the individual concerned was loud, very loud. We tried all the usual tricks, stuffing our ears with cotton wool, even wearing a flying helmet to deaden the sound with little effect. Then one night, I fell into a deep sleep for a couple of hours, only to wake to the sound of this airman's snoring. I reached under my bed to find a shoe, to throw in his direction, when I saw four of his crew mates gathered round his bed. They carefully lifted the bed with their friend in it, slowly carrying him down the billet then outside into the open air. There they left him to snore, to his heart's content, though I can't remember what the weather was like at the time.

Aachen 24th May Wednesday U Uncle

The calendar says it's Wednesday our target is Aachen and I have no recall of this raid so it must have been a fairly uneventful one. I recall from my log book we did two raids on this target and that on the second one we were attacked by a night fighter. Again, I have to consult the Squadron ORB for information. The target was Marshalling Yards so we would have used a 1000lb mix with 500lb MC bombs. According to the ORB our route to the target was Elsham to Orfordness, then to Dunquerque. From here the route was South East toward Luxembourg before heading due North to Aachen.

Checking with Chorley I find there were three aircraft missing from the base, one from 103 two from 576 Squadron. Out of the total force of over four hundred aircraft that attacked Aachen that night, there were twenty five aircraft lost to flack or fighters.

103 Squadron

The Crew of Lancaster III		ND624	PM-F
F/S	D.E. Tate	RCAF	Kia
Sgt	W. McCulloch	RAF	Kia
F/S	J. Williams	RAF	Kia
F/S	E.H. Calvert	RAF	Kia
Sgt	D.J. Jones	RAF	Kia
Sgt	R. Holmes	RAF	Kia
Sgt	W.D. Kirton	RAF	Kia

576 Squadron

The Crew of Lancaster ILM120 UL-T2			
P/O	G.A. Langford	RAF	Kia
Sgt	G. Shutt	RAF	Kia
WO2	E.A Mason	RAF	Kia
Sgt	R.S. Dickinson RAF		Kia
Sgt	K.H. Hodgkinson	RAF	Kia
Sgt	A.E. Bachelor	RAF	Kia
Sgt	G.J. Cooper	RAF	Kia

The Crew of Lancaster III		NE171	UL-Y2
F/S	D.G.C. Thorpe	RAF	Kia
Sgt	D. White	RAF	Kia
WO2	A.A.J. Tremblay	RCAF	Kia
Sgt	H. MacD Mundy	RAF	Kia
Sgt	R.E. Smith	RAF	Kia
Sgt	J.W.C. Labelle RCAF	Kia	
Sgt	N.W. Green	RAF	Kia

Commission Board

Now well into his tour at Elsham, Jack has been put forward for a commission so he appears before a board headed by a Wing Commander. On the 25th May the board subjects Jack to a serious, question and answer session, then just as he thinks things are going well, comes the body blow. The Wing Commander spots my appearance before the Bridgnorth Magistrates, "Not the sort of behaviour we expect from an officer" is his comment. My promotion was deferred. As he receives commiserations from his crewmates, they find that Ops are not on tonight. So Jack is off to drown his sorrows with a night out in Sunny Scunny. Scunthorpe the nearest large town, was your typical Northern Steelmaking town, with its ample supply of pubs. On its high street stands,

'Oswald's' the RAF's pub; aircrews from the many stations in the area, were drawn there to meet with their fellow airmen. It was also a magnet in the area, for all the single young ladies and a lot of the temporary single ones, to mix with these young flyers.

Getting to Scunthorpe could either be, the bus from the airfield main gate, or by train from Barnetby-le-Wold. Aircrew arriving at Barnetby railway station would stow their bikes in the hedge back, opposite where the train will stop on its return. Having had a good night out at the 'Oswald' pub, Jack makes his unsteady way back to Scunthorpe Station, to catch the train to Barnetby. At the station he meets his old pal the Squire who is also three sheets to the wind; they attempt to board the last carriage of the train. Inside are gathered other airmen from Elsham who blockade the doors, they refuse to let the pair in.

Hanging out of the windows they shout good humoured abuse at them. Finally, Jack and the Squire give up, they walk to the next carriage, but as the Squire climbs aboard, he is muttering retribution. Jack follows him into the carriage, slamming the door behind him. When he turns, he sees the Squire opening the door on the opposite side of the train. He checks all is clear, then climbs down onto the track. Following him Jack tries to get him to return to the train, "Not until I have had my revenge" he ducks under the buffers. As he struggles to unhook the coupling he shouts to Jack, "Don't just stand there, give me a hand or we will be here all night". Jack slips under the buffer to join the 'Squire' they quickly uncouple the last carriage, from the train. Now the deed is done he helps Jack up into the carriage before climbing back aboard himself. The smile on Jack and the Squires face says it all. Hanging out of the train window, as it leaves the station, the pair wave back to the airmen, who suddenly realise they are being left behind. Sadly, their glory is short lived, the train is halted at the next signal box. It then reverses back to Scunthorpe, to pick up the last coach and guards van. Having recovered the lost carriage, the train sets out again for Barnetby. Sitting in their compartment, the pair realise that when they arrive at their destination the mob in the last carriage will come looking for them. As the train stops at the station, Jack and the Squire climb down from the train on the opposite side to the platform. They quickly run to the rear of the train then dodge behind the hedge. As they watch, the airmen from the last carriage begin searching the train looking for them. Unobserved the pair quietly grab two bicycles from the hedge to set off for the airfield knowing the hounds will be close behind.

Aachen 27th May Saturday U Uncle

After Thursday's trip into Scunny, it's a quite night in the mess for our crew; we will have to wait for a pay parade, before our next outing.

146

Saturday morning finds an Op on the board; it's a return trip to Aachen to finish the job we started on Wednesday. Late in the morning, we have to take part in a fighter affiliation exercise. The Lancaster we are to use is T Tommy belonging to Gerry Chase's crew. As we arrive at the dispersal Gerry's crew are waiting; "If you break anything you will be in deep trouble" they tell us. "It will be nice for you to fly a fast Lancaster instead of that lame duck you use" they called. I just gave them my usual Churchill two fingered salute. We took off then flew out to sea to rendezvous with the fighter, after about thirty minutes the fighter had not appeared. I signalled the airfield to be informed the exercise has been cancelled we are to return to base. On our return to the dispersal, we were the ones to hand out the banter, "That aircraft was so slow I nearly fell asleep at the controls" joke's Fred. "I was worried my maps would go out of date before we got back" said Ron our Navigator. Then as we walked back to the mess the armourers drive past with the bomb trolleys. They were loaded with 1000 lb and 500 lb M.C. bombs again but this time only twelve aircraft would take part. Takeoff was 23:45hr; we head for the target, ours is one of six raids taking place simultaneous tonight. The total number of aircraft involved will exceed eleven hundred. We cross the North Sea with a force of over 450 aircraft, 300 of these will break away to attack a target in Belgium.

Our group of 160 aircraft mainly Lancaster's will continue to Aachen's railway yards. As we cross the enemy coast at Rotterdam our gunners are scanning the sky for fighters. I join them for as long as I can. Then in what seems like a very short time we are approaching the target, apart from seeing the searchlights and the flack we have arrived without incident. Norman's voice on the intercom giving Fred course corrections shows we are on the bomb run. Then the welcome upward surge as the Lancaster rids itself of its burden. Fred turns away from the target as soon as the target photo is taken, it's just in time. Bert Burrill's warning call, "Corkscrew starboard" heralds the end of our run of good fortune. Tracer from the incoming fighter; is answered by both gunners giving him a hot reception. This time it's not a short combat, he must be turning with us as the shooting seems to go on for a long time; then he is gone. Our Lancaster returns to level flight; I move back into the astrodome to provide another pair of eyes, as we continue to fly south toward France.

Ken Smart our mid upper reports aircraft exchanging fire to starboard, as I look there are faint flashes in the distance below us. Ron our Navigator breaks into the silence, to give Fred a course change east to Lille then Calais. As we cross the coast, I give an audible sigh of relief. We arrive back at Elsham Wolds without further trouble to join the circuit and land, it's then I suddenly realise we have just completed our twenty first trip. After de-briefing then breakfast we return to our billets for a good sleep.

The morning brings us news, there are two crews missing from our Squadron, but the word is we have wrecked the rail yards.

103 Squadron

The Crew of Lancaster III		ND362		PM-Q
S/L	L. Ollier DFC AFM	RAF		Kia
Sgt	J. Ray	RAF		Kia
F/O	G.P.J. Kimmins RCAF		Kia	
Sgt	F. C. Mustoe	RAF		Kia
F/S	W.A. Clevey	RAF		Kia
Sgt	M.J.H. Vedavato	RAF		Kia
Sgt	N.P. Warlow	RAF		Kia

The Crew of Lancaster III		ND925	PM-C
F/L	T.G. Leggett	RAF	Kia
Sgt	W.A. Edwards	RAF	Kia
F/O	R.H. Beer	RAF	Kia
F/O	A.A. Wilks	RAF	Kia
F/S	L Ireland	RAAF	Kia
P/O	P.C. Gore	RAF	POW
F/O	A.V.M. Jones	RAF	Kia

Family Disaster

The date is the 5th June 1944, Jack and his crew are waiting, for their next operational trip, from Elsham Wolds. The morning post arrives; with a Telegram from home. My initial excitement is dashed when my father's words tell me of the death of my brother in an operation in North Africa.

Flight Sergeant Thomas William Spark (RAFVR) was serving with 216 Squadron; they had been tasked to deliver aircraft to North Africa. They flew from England out into the Atlantic then across the Bay of Biscay, this would reduce the chance of any contact with enemy fighters, then to Gibraltar. From there it was a short run to Algeria their destination. Here in North Africa, he would join his Squadron in flying supplies to all areas of the front line. After his allotted tour of duty, he waited for a term of leave back to blighty.

Sitting at the desert airstrip his thoughts would be of he his wife Doris, their two year old daughter Corel and the imminent arrival of their second child (a son, Colin). The following day a Dakota III, of 216 Squadron, arrives to ferry him home. Boarding the aircraft, there were already people there having been picked up at other airfields along the way. As the Dakota takes off, everyone settles down for the long flight, which sadly would not be completed. The wreckage of the aircraft was found later, in the Atlas Mountains, twelve airmen, an Army Lieutenant Colonel and a Captain, were lost.

Fred my skipper noticed my shocked expression, by the fact that the colour has drained from my face. He immediately takes me to see my signals leader Flight Lieutenant Ron Stewart DFC. Ron is a New Zealander with 50 operations to his credit despite his 23 Years. After reading my Telegram he promptly tells me to wait in his office, while he goes to see the C.O. When he returns, he is holding a 5 day pass, "Get yourself home Jack, don't worry about your crew I will fly in your place".

Back in Carlisle, Jack and his parents are coming to terms with their grief, at the loss of Thomas, but joy at the birth of his son, their new grandson Colin. Jacks mum Ellen is devastated; she confides in Jack that she was always fearful for both of her son's lives, but at least she thought that Thomas was out of danger in his role in transport command. This brings back to Jacks mind the last time he and his brother met; it was when both their leave passes coincided.

It was at that meeting, his brother implored him to join 216 Squadron, to become a transport wireless operator. "It's much safer than the flak and fighters you will face every night in bomber command". I was at an O.T.U. at the time; how green the other man's grass can appear. Our family life has been turned upside down by my brother's death, but as we grieve the war goes on. Relatives and friends call with their condolences, but also tell us of the news of the D Day landings. Having a death in the family is never easy but there is always a funeral to bring a sort of closure to the loss. During the war you do not even have that comfort; Thomas will be buried in the Military Cemetery in Oran. Our family will just have to come to terms with the emptiness.

Then days later, as always happens in war, Jack is back on his way to Elsham Wolds. As I stood on the doorstep mum was in tears, she gave me one of those hugs only a mother can give. Dad was more stiff upper lip, his only comment was "Watch out for yourself Lad", then he shook my hand, but his face could not hide what he was thinking. Back on the squadron we are preparing for a raid on the French port of Le Havre. In his absence the crew had completed two additional Ops. One to Flers on 9th June, the other was to Gelsenkirchen on 12th June with Fl/Lt Ron Stewart taking my place. Though his extra trip to Kiel Bay, with another crew meant he was only one Op behind his own crew. Sadly, I did not get chance to thank my Signals Leader, he had been posted to 617 Dambuster's Squadron. It was also Fl/Lt Ron Stewart who originally recommended me for my DFM, including my ultimate successful commission.

Later long after the war, I uncover in the Australian National Records, a copy of the report into Jack's brothers accident

The Board of Enquiry reveals the following conclusions.
(a) Dakota F.D. 886 was flying on a routine transport flight from Biskra to Oujda on the morning of 3rd June 1944. It left Biskra at 0634Z hours and crashed into the side of a mountain at 0855Z (see para 5 for exact location). The mountain top was covered in drifting cloud at the time of the   crash.
The aircraft was climbing steeply when it crashed. There were sixteen persons killed including the crew of four, one passenger survived. The aircraft was totally destroyed in the crash and subsequent fire.
(b) Five minutes before his own signalled E.T.A., the pilot took advantage of a hole in the clouds over which he had been flying for some considerable time - to get below them. He must have thought he was very near his destination because at this time the signal "Landing" was received at Oujda. Upon breaking cloud the aircraft was seen to circle in a wide valley apparently lost and with the pilot undecided. It then followed a road in a North-Easterly direction for five or six miles. Oujda from this valley bears Westerly. The outlet of this valley and the hills to the East were clear of cloud. Finally, and unaccountably the aircraft was seen to turn to Port and climb into cloud away from the road and the valley which was clear and where the visibility was 4 to 5 miles below the cloud. Almost immediately afterwards the crash occurred. The pilot did not request further briefing at Baskar for Oujda although his log book he had only once previously flown this leg and that was three months before. The aircraft has crashed south of the Officially briefed route at a point on the direct track from Biskra to Oujda. The court feels that pilots should give more attention to briefing when they are comparatively new to a route. The Pilots Flying Log Book reveals that he had flown an average of 108 hrs per month for the last six months which included 13 hours night flying each month and a total of 172 operational hours in India in a period of six weeks. He returned from India on 27th May having completed 128 hours in that month. He started this his last flight at approximately 0100Z hours on 2nd June. The court considered his flying excessive and a contributory factor.
It must be assumed that the navigator's dead reckoning was been relied upon too much for the purpose of navigation as it is known that the radio was operating satisfactorily and that no wireless aids were even requested by the aircraft. It is felt that more use should have been made by crews of these navigational facilities (which are always available) especially in conditions of cloud covering mountainous country as were obtained at the period under review.

(c)   Although no recomendations are called for, the court is to allocate under its terms of reference responsibility if any. The court is of the opinion that.

i   The pilot is responsible for the accident in that he committed a gross error of judgement, possibly occassioned by fatigue, by flying blind unnecessarily when uncertain of his position.

ii.   The navigator was to blame for poor navigation in that he did not use all the means at his disposal and allowed the aircraft to be 40 miles from destination on his own E.T.A. there.

iii.   The officer commanding, 216 Squadron, should have ensured that instructions contained in 216G/1433/1/Med dated 20th April 1944 had been carried out. Copies of signals (attached at appendix 'G') show that no such medical examination the case of Flying Officer Thompson took place. The relevant clause of the 216 Group instruction referred to above is contained in Appendix "g" "b".

Reference has already been made to the Court's view on the excessive amount of flying as Captain of Aircraft which this pilot concentrated into a short period immediately proceeding the accident. The court has examined two wristlet watches which were found at the scene of the crash. Both were dented and both have stopped at 1055hrs (local time i.e. 0855Z).

The Court is of the opinion that Regional Control (Oran and Algiers) showed little if any initiative in knowing the whereabouts of Dakota F.D.866 during the flight or in helping to locate it after the Official "Request News" had been originated by R.A.F. Station Oujda. The court has covered its Terms of Reference as issued from H.Q.284 Wing for Summary therefore see appendix "H".

The above report is repeated as typed, with errors and misspelling exactly as found in the records.

A remarkable fact from this tragic accident is that one man, a Sgt D Wilcock RAF 1213938 survived with only a broken ankle.

Le Havre Raid 14th June (day) Wednesday U Uncle

We are at breakfast when we are told that we are to do our first daylight raid; the target is the harbour of Le Havre on the French coast. As we leave the briefing the station commander grabs Gerry Chase, "Where the Hell is your navigator he was not at the briefing". Gerry made an excuse; he promised his navigator would be there for the take off. He promptly heads back to the billets with the rest of his crew; here Ginger their navigator was still half cut from the previous night. With the help of the crew they dressed their giggling crewmate, before carefully transporting him to the dispersal. I remember watching them lift him into the Lancaster as Gerry came over to talk to our crew. Gerry said as it was a daylight raid, could they formate on our Lancaster after takeoff then follow us to the target. Fred readily agreed as he had flown with Gerry since pilot training and wanted to help him out of this fix. Fred hangs back in our dispersal waiting for Gerry's aircraft to appear on the Peri track. When it does, we slip out in front of him and head for the runway. Take off was 20:00hrs and as we climb away from Elsham, we start to notice the other aircraft around us. Some are only a few hundred feet away, but the overriding image is of the sheer number of them. We suddenly realised, this is how it has been on our night time raids, but the darkness had concealed the danger from our eyes. Bert Burrill now reports T Tommy flying behind and to port of us, he comments, "I only hope they don't have to put Ginger over the side in a chute today".

The German navy are operating motor torpedo boats from Le Harve, attacking our shipping supplying the Normandy landing forces. Our bomb load is all H.E., to do as much damage as possible to the docks and the E boat pens. As we reach the south coast ready to cross the channel our gunners report fighters approaching. Thankfully it's our Spitfire and Mosquito escort, but we realise they will not be able to stop the flack coming up. Sure, enough as we run up to the target, the flack starts to appear in front of us, great big black puffs of smoke which thankfully is scattered. Norman has taken his place down in the nose of the Lancaster lining up on the flares. I don't think we took an aiming point photo, as Fred turned away from the target immediately the bombs were released.

In seconds we are heading away from the target back over the channel. At the time, we were not aware that 617 Squadron aircraft had dropped a large number of 22,000Lb Tallboy Bombs. These were to break the reinforced concrete roofs over the E boat pens; I would have like to have seen that, they must have made a hell of a bang. Back at Elsham Wolds, we are debriefed and relieved to find all twenty, of the Squadrons aircraft have made it back safely. Ginger never knew a thing about the raid, he slept on the rest bed all the way there and back, unaware he had completed another Op

Sterkrade 16th June Friday U Uncle

Standing in the Ops room our target is Sterkrae/Holten; people looks at one another completely puzzled, "Where is it" comes the question. We have never heard of anyone talking about this place. The signals officer starts to explain; tonight we are to attack a German synthetic oil plant, the enemy is running short of refined fuel and oil. This facility is producing alternatives from coal; our job is to stop them. As we lift off Elsham's runway at 23:00Hrs, the low cloud swallows our Lancaster and the ground disappears from view. We climb blind to over ten thousand feet before it starts to break up; then we turn to cross the North Sea. Approaching the Dutch coast the cloud is gathering again, but the searchlights are appearing as is the flack. The route over Holland is close to Arnhem, our gunners report fighters in the vicinity attacking bombers. Fred is steadily weaving our Lancaster, watching the searchlights ahead trying to judge where they will be when we reach them. Ron the navigator warns Fred we are approaching our last turning point, as both of our gunners are reporting lots of fighters in the area. They are also reporting a number of aircraft going down in flames, but are unable to identify then as friend or foe. Fortunately, the fighters have not latched onto us yet, then the cloud thankfully closes in on us again as Ron gives Fred a course change. Running up to the target, the flack is very heavy and accurate, our Lancaster is rocked by close bursts that are invisible in the cloud. Norman's voice on the intercom announces that the pathfinder's flares are only a faint glow through the cloud. "Put our load as accurate as you can", instructs Fred. There is a pause then the Lancaster lifts as our bombs drop clear, though we continue to fly on waiting for the photo flash to go off. "Another wasted piece of film" comments Fred as he banks away from the target to head for home. The flight home is done in thick cloud; Fred is weaving our Lancaster to make it difficult for a ground controller to home a fighter onto us. Once over the North Sea we feel the pressure is off, but the cloud is going to make landing at Elsham difficult, a diversion may be on the cards. Twenty one aircraft from our Squadron had set out with a similar number from 576 Squadron. All of these aircraft will be now returning to the airfield in cloud hoping to get down quickly; we are all an invisible danger to each other. As we begin to circle the field, Jack listens to other aircraft getting permission to land, then it's our turn, Fred wastes no time in lining up on the runway. We get a double bounce touchdown before U Uncle rolls to the end of the runway, then we taxi to our dispersal. On the ground our gunners are talking about the number of aircraft they had seen being attacked by fighters, they think it has been a bad night for bomber command. In the debriefing, other crews are reporting being attacked by fighters, with sightings of a number of aircraft being shot down.

By the morning we find there are three aircraft missing from Elsham Wolds, one from 103 Squadron with two from 576 Squadron. Out of the three hundred and twenty aircraft taking part in the raid thirty three are missing. History reveals, 77 Squadron at Long Sutton are missing 7 Halifax's from their total of 23 aircraft, a devastating loss for them.

103 Squadron

The Crew of Lancaster ILM173 PM-M

P/O	M. Lambert	RNZAF	Kia
Sgt	D.L. Whamond RAF		Kia

Sgt	D.J. Lawler	RAF	Kia
Sgt	G.J. Ware	RAF	Kia
Sgt	J. McMinn	RAF	Kia
Sgt	F.R. Hardy	RAF	Kia
Sgt	R. Fitchett	RAF	Kia

576 Squadron
The Crew of Lancaster III   PA997   UL-D2

P/O	A.L. Puttock	RAF	Kia
F/S	L.R.S. Templeton	RAF	POW
F/S	T. Jefferson	RAF	Kia
F/S	J. Brown	RAF	Kia
F/S	D.W.G. Warr	RAF	POW
F/S	H.E. Lillicrap	RAF	Kia
F/S	C. Philp	RAF	Kia

576 Squadron
The Crew of Lancaster IME810 UL-K2

F/Lt	G.E. Stockdale	RCAF	Kia
Sgt	D.E. Fabb	RAF	Kia
F/O	D.E. Fuller	RCAF	Kia
F/O	D.W. Stewart	RAF	Kia
Sgt	J.K. Gray	RAF	Kia
F/S	R.A. Jack	RCAF	Kia
Sgt	E.H.J. Morgan	RAF	Kia

The loss of the 576 Squadron Lancaster of F/Lt George Edward Stockdale is particularly relevant. George was the cousin of my biographer David Crawford. During the research into his cousin our mutual friend Adrian van Zantvoort finds a German combat report relating to the loss of the crew. This report is typical of the new Luftwaffe night fighter weapon 'Schrader Music'. These aircraft were fitted with twin upward firing 20mm canon. This allowed them to attack from the blind spot below the Bombers with devastating results. The combat report is as follows.

Luftwaffe Combat Report for 17th June 1944
Date   17th June 1944
Time   01-34
Oblt, Johannes Hagar was patrolling in a Heinkel He219 night fighter North West of Deelan airfield at an altitude of 4000m (13000ft).
        I was instructed by ground controllers to fly on a course of 360 deg to intercept a bomber stream returning to England, which I did. My radar operator Fw von Bergen reported picking up an aircraft on our Lichtenstein airborne radar. The target was approx 2.5 kilometres distance

at 4100m (13500ft) flying a course of 300deg. Following my radar operators instruction, we approached the target, a British four engine bomber. Our He219 was fitted with two twenty mm cannon in the rear fuselage, mounted behind the Crews Canopy, pointing upwards and forward at an angle of 60 - 75deg. My approach from directly below the bomber made me invisible to their rear gunner. Matching my speed to the bomber I slowly climb till I was about 100m below it. Leaning back in my seat I looked upward and use the cross hair markings in the roof panel of the canopy to line up on the bomber. The first burst of canon fire saw strike's along the fuselage, starboard inner engine which caught fire, the bomber banked to port and I followed maintaining my position below it. My second attack saw further hits along the fuselage and wings resulting in a fierce fuel fire causing the aircraft to dive vertically with its port wing down. As it passed in front of my aircraft, I started my third attack from 100m using my forward firing machine guns and canon. The bomber then entered cloud and I broke off my attack, shortly after a large glow was seen below the cloud as the aircraft struck the ground. No-one was seen to leave the aircraft during or after the attacks.

The attack must have been a devastating one as all of the crew were found with the Lancaster. Such is the fortunes of War that only five days later Fw von Bergen was killed in an air combat in another He 219. Johannes Hager however survived the war dying in Germany in 1993 aged 73.

Originally the Lancaster was fitted with a dorsal turret armed with twin 303 machine guns. The gunner sat on and above the guns he was expected to search for enemy aircraft by looking into a periscope. This ran down between the gunners legs with the viewing lens sat between the guns on the outside of the fuselage. It was a disaster from the start, the ability to see anything at night was abysmal. At this time Lancaster's were being fitted with the new HS2 scanners. As the only place these would fit was where the turrets were, the turrets were abandoned. From this moment on the Lancaster was vulnerable to attack from beneath and the Luftwaffe took full advantage of this.

Married Lady and my best Cap.

When Op's were scrubbed, crews would head for Scunthorpe with its pubs, here they could forget the war's horrors, if only for a few hours. There was also the hope of meeting a local girl then go on to a dance. Aircrew could be noisy and drink a lot too much, but complaints were few, locals realising these lads may not be back tomorrow. One evening in the Oswald, Jack meets an attractive young lady; they spend the evening chatting and downing a few drinks. Having noticed there is no wedding ring on her finger, he asks if he can walk her home, she agrees.

Stepping outside the pub they walk arm in arm down the main street, suddenly she yells "Oh no, it's my husband". Coming toward them is a burly steelworker with trouble written all over his face. Not wanting to get into a barny with a local civilian, Jack turns on his heels to leg's it. In the rush to outrun this irate husband, his cap fly's from his head but with his pursuer close behind, there is no chance to retrieve it. "I only remember It was my best cap which I had to be replaced, at my own expense".

Pas de Calais Recall Monday 19th June U Uncle

It's a miserable day the weather has been awful, but there is a raid on the board for our Base. The target is a flying bomb launch site in the Pas de Calais area, one again we are to have a fighter escort so there will be only the flak to worry about. Take off is early afternoon, we climb away from the airfield to head south in cloud toward the target. We have been airborne for forty five minutes when I receive a Recall signal; Fred brings our Lancaster round to return to Elsham. It looks like a night in the pub for our crew; no one is going to complain about that though.

Six Girls in Harmony

When we were a bit short of spending money which was quite often, then staying on camp was our only choice. Here we would enjoy a sing song with a crowd gathered around the piano with someone of variable ability pounding out a tune. How the piano continued to play is a puzzle, aircrew would bring a pint of beer for the pianist plus a half for the piano, poured into the works. The alternative was a game of darts in the mess or into the Cinema, to watch the latest RAF's moral boosting epic. As a piece de resistance, there could be the presentation, of an ENSA show. Many servicemen unkindly attributed these initials, to mean 'Every Night Something Awful'. Over a period of a week or so, posters proclaimed the arrival of the next ENSA show, 'Six Girls in Harmony'. The accompanying photos show a group of very attractive young ladies, so the venue is well attended by airmen including Jack, all waiting in anticipation. But as the lights dim, the curtains part to reveal six ladies of mature years, with violins and a cello's dashes their dreams. Jack starts to leave his seat with other airmen, but are confronted by the C.O. "Sit down, I have no intention of enduring this on my own", so back they had to go.

Pas de Calais Mimayocques Thursday 22nd June U Uncle

Three days of poor weather ends with an Op on the board, we are going to the Pas de Calais to complete the raid that was cancelled on Monday. The target is a daylight raid on Mimoyecques a V1 launch site with it's stores depot fifteen miles to the south of Calais. Our aircraft U

156

uncle is loaded with eighteen 500lb Medium Casing bombs to destroy the concrete and steel launch ramps of these flying bombs. Take off was at 13:41 hrs, with Sq/Ld Van Rolleghan leading twenty one Elsham Wolds Lancaster's from 103 Squadron. We head south then as we cross into Kent our fighter escort arrive on cue; they will keep any German fighters away from our group. We have started to realise fighter command has taken total control of the airspace over Normandy, but the flack is a different matter. Running up to the target Norman comments at how light the flack is, considering the Pathfinder flares are going down ahead of us. He loses no time in putting our H.E. into the centre of the flares before Fred turns back to the channel for home. There were over Two Hundred and Thirty aircraft taking part in the raid, thankfully all aircrew have returned unharmed. My logbook shows this was our twenty fourth operational trip, I start to think we will reach the end of our tour.

Saintes Friday 23rd June U Uncle

It's Friday morning, we are to do another op today, I am hoping it's another daylight raid to France, as the armourers are loading H.E. bomb's again. In the operations room any thoughts of a milk run disappear, the target is France, but it's a night raid on Saintes railway yards. Saintes is on the Bay of Biscay, we will be in the air for seven and a half hours. We take off at 22:15hrs into a clear sky to head south into the dark.

Our route is to Upper Heyford then down to the south coast. We cross the coast at Bournemouth then down the channel, passing to the west of Guernsey. There are six hundred aircraft in the air tonight. Four hundred of them will separate from us over the channel, to attack flying bomb sites along the French coast. The other two hundred will continue into the Bay of Biscay, there they will split up to attack Saintes and Limoges. Standing in the astrodome, I watch our gunner's turrets slowly turning searching for incoming fighters. Around us in the clear sky, I can see a handful of the bomber force flying around our Lancaster but I am wondering; where are the other one hundred and ninety five. Below us I can see the sea with the French coast in the distance on our port side; it is a deceptively peaceful scene. The French coast at Lannion passes below us, now it's out into the Bay of Biscay near Quimper.

It's a short run along the coast to pass to the North of La Rochelle, before the final turn South to Saintes. The run onto the target came as a surprise as there was no flack to greet us. Ahead the pathfinder's flares were clearly visible so Ron quickly lines our Lancaster up on them. Ron's call 'Bombs gone' is followed by the wait for the target photo, then U uncle banks steeply away from Saintes, back towards the Bay of Biscay. Out over the sea our crew are puzzled but relieved at the same time, it has been an anticlimax where were the fighters, it has been too easy. But we have to avoid complacency, there is a four hour flight ahead of us, anything can happen before we are home. Onwards we fly as the Bay of Biscay slips behind us. We retrace our route to Quimper then, the short run over France to Lannion, the English Channel now stretches out ahead. Then we are back over the south coast at Bouremouth and on to Upper Heyford, as sky starts to brighten behind us. Approaching the Lincolnshire Wolds, I contact the airfield for permission to land; Fred gives us a smooth touchdown for a change. At the debriefing some crews are saying what an easy trip they have had, while others talk of night fighters patrolling the sea off La Rochelle. Of the twenty aircraft we contributed to the raid tonight, all have returned safely, thought the force as a whole have lost two aircraft.

The Oster Milk Tin.

Once aboard a Lancaster on the way to a target, the only toilet facility is an Elsan behind the main spar and you had to be very desperate to use it. At Twenty five thousand feet it was so cold that if you touched anything metallic with the bare skin you will stick to it, so crews had to be resourceful. As Jack sits adjacent to the Navigator, they find their own solution to this age old problem. They find that an empty Oster (powdered) Milk tin, with a lid, it will fit neatly under the steps in front of the main spar, where the spare aerial reel is stored. When required this tin could be accessed without moving very far, just the job they think, until one night. The Op is a long one; we are about an hour from the target, when Ron the Navigators hand appears from under his curtain. Rapping twice on Jacks table is the signal for the tin; removing the lid he passes it under the curtain to the Nav. A short pause then the curtain is drawn back, the tin placed on the floor for Jack to replace the lid. "Fighter corkscrew port", calls the mid upper gunner the Lancaster stands on a wingtip then plunges, Jack and Ron sit transfixed. Now obeying Newton's laws of motion, the tin first rises to the astrodome, then as Fred our pilot brings the Lancaster back on an even keel. The tin turns over in midair cascading it contents over Jack and Ron, this last movement is the tin obeying, 'Murphy's law'. "I can't remember if the fighter opened fire or not", recounts Jack. "We were too busy watching that dammed tin".

Fred Brownings has called a crew meeting; here he announces we are losing Bert Burrill. Because of his operations with his previous crew he has completed his tour so he is being screened. Bert has already asked to continue to start another operational tour, but it will not happen immediately. His request will still have to go through the system.

Flers Sunday 25th June

Sunday morning, after a leisurely breakfast we make our way out to the dispersal. We arrive as the armourers are positioning the trolleys under our Lancaster; they are loading 500lb medium casing bombs. Norman baker our bomb aimer wanders over to talk to them, as we walk round our Lancaster to talk with the ground crew. We are hoping to get an idea as to where tonight's raid may be. The only clue is that the fuel load is small, so we are not going far, another flying bomb launch site, in daylight we hope. Fred and I sit talking about the way the war is going; we are both of the opinion that at last, we have the Jerries on the run.

Later back in our billets some of the crew are writing letters home, others are rereading letters from loved ones. Things have really swung in our favour, in the short time since we arrived on the squadron back in February. By lunch time we realise that a daylight raid is off, we would have had a briefing by now. Fred has been informed he has a stand in rear gunner for tonight's raid it's a J. Woolard. In the late afternoon we walk over to the Ops room, here we find the Op is a flying bomb site, at Flers in France. Take off time is to be 01:45hrs, so we have a few hours to kick our heels. It's well after midnight when we arrive at the dispersal, the wind is freshening but the sky is cloudless. Standing waiting for the all clear, the cold is starting to sink in, we move to the side of the ground crews hut for shelter. Fred is with the ground Chief signing the Form 700 accepting the aircraft as fit for duty. We get an OK, the raid is on so we board U Uncle, once inside we are out of the wind, but it is not warm by any stretch of the imagination.

A Lancaster is all metal so it quickly becomes cold after the sun sets, only when the engines are started will warm air blow into the fuselage. But up in the air at altitude, the engine heaters will fail to warm anyone but me. Once more we set off south, I think our Lancaster does not need navigating, Reading, Selsey Bill out into the channel, she can almost find her own way. The weather is good with scattered cloud, but the wind is shifting about, Ron is busy with course recalculations. From the coast we head into the channel toward Bayeux, at the last minute we turn to Fler. Approaching the target there is a lot of searchlight activity though the flack is very light. Both gunners are reporting fighters in the area, as tracer is being exchanged in the dark sky. Fred's tactics of keeping our Lancaster jinking about stops, as we commence our bomb run. Flares from the pathfinder's aircraft marking the aiming point are falling up ahead, as Norman in his bomb aimer's position takes over control for the final run in. The pause before the release seems an interminably long time, before we feel the bombs drop, then another wait for the target photo to be taken. Fred brings our Lancaster round to head back to the coast at Cherbourg and the relative safety of the channel. Our return run back to

Elsham Wolds is uneventful, so as we arrive at debriefing there is the feeling we have had another easy trip. All of our Squadron aircraft have returned safely, but 576 Squadron have lost one of their Lancaster's.

576 Squadron

The Crew of Lancaster III		JB460	UL-V2
F/O	J.W. Alcorn	RAAF	Kia
Sgt	J. Mannion	RAF	Kia
Sgt	T.E. Hayes	RAF	Kia
F/S	R. K.Begg	RAAF	Kia
Sgt	T.R. Roby	RAF	Kia
Sgt	J.B. Cowie	RAF	Kia
Sgt	A.T.T. Morrell	RAF	Kia

We have a few days break, so a trip into Scunthorpe is the order of the day. As a crew we have become aware that new crews are pointing us out in the pub. The fact that we are approaching the end of our tour is probably something of a comfort to them. If we can do it then they can, may God help them. Arriving back at the Drome there is a bit of a flap at the main gate, someone has stolen the fire bell from the guard room wall. Next day the MP's find it in a dustbin, outside one of 103 Squadrons huts. Whoever removed it or put it there, is never identified but the word goes out about the consequences of a reoccurrence of this sort of behaviour. On an airfield, aircrew would spend their sleeping hours in a billet, which they have to share with other crews. There could be up to thirty men in a hut.

Some of these crew members we got to know, others would arrive on the base, settle in then fail to come back from the next raid. At this point the committee of readjustment would come into the hut to remove all the possessions of the lost airmen. Before returning personal effects to an airman's family they would have to closely scrutinise the contents. It was not unknown for airmen to have a girlfriend as well as a wife. So any incriminating evidence would be removed before it was returned.

Chateau Benapres Wednesday 28th June

We have had two days of rest, but are now on the board again for a night raid. The stand in rear gunner has been changed our new man is Sgt Jock Murray. In years to come, Jock would become President of the Elsham Worlds Association, but that is in everyone's future. Our target tonight is another flying bomb launch site in the Pas de Calais area. Walking away from the briefing the crews are talking about the raid, how many more of these sites are there. It's been three weeks since the D Day landings; we thought they would have all been overrun by ground troops.

160

The weather is grim, it's been raining on and off all day then, as we ride out to our dispersal, it starts chucking it down. We climb into our Lancaster immediately to get out of the downpour, once inside the aircraft we are dry. I sit at my radio station listening to the drumming of the rain on the thin shell of the fuselage, it's very noisy. Through my small window, I can see the ground crew sheltering under the wing preparing to start our engines. Water is running in streams from the trailing edge of the wing. These lads really are the unsung heroes of a bomber station, working in all weathers to keep us in the air. One of our ground crew spots me looking down from my window. He promptly gives me the thumbs up, then a very rude V sign, which I return. Fred climbs aboard with Arthur our flight engineer; they move into the cockpit, we are ready to go. Ron has been sitting on the rest bed, waiting for the skipper and Arthur to board. His Navigators position in the aircraft blocks the access to the cockpit completely. So he has to wait for them both to pass before he comes forward to take up his position. The bark of the first engine starting brings U Uncle to life, the power turrets are turning, I know the heater will soon be working. Take off was 01.30hrs, we climb into cloud before heading South to Gravesend here the cloud is breaking up as we head towards Eastbourne. It's a short run across the Channel, then a course change to the target. Ahead there are a few searchlights waving about, but again the flack is nonexistent. Then we see the pathfinder's marker flares raining down. We lose no time in dropping our bombs into these flares, before getting out of the area heading south toward Rouen. Another course change sees us heading back out into the Channel. Again we have to negotiate the searchlight belt, but the lack of anti aircraft fire can only mean one thing, fighters are roaming about us. Crossing the channel we fly North East to Brighton, then it's onward to Reading, before heading to Elsham. As we land I look at my watch, we have been airborne for three hours forty minutes.

In the debriefing room everyone for a change is in agreement, it had been an easy run. The talk among the crews is that we must really have the Jerries on the run, that's why there is so little opposition. Twenty one aircraft took part in the raid and all twenty one have returned. My log book shows I have completed twenty seven trips, dare I start to hope we will complete our tour.

Neuville au Bois Friday 30th June
We rise very early, shave, wash, then head off for our breakfast, I comment to Ken Smart on the amount of activity out on the dispersals. The armourers are bombing up the aircraft, for another daylight raid on a V1 flying bomb launch site. Before we head for our briefing, Fred informs us we again have J. Woolard as our stand in rear gunner. Our briefing is a

161

short one, the target is Neuville au Bois to the south of Abbeville in France. We will have a fighter escort from the south coast to the target then back again, the weather is expected to deteriorate but should be clear over the target. Take off is 05:30 hrs, we head south with the cloud increasing, by the time we reach the south coast we can see nothing below us. If we had a fighter escort we never saw it. Ron gives Fred a final course change with 10/10 cloud all around us, then on the run up to the target I receive a message from the master bomber. We are to bomb on HS2, the marker flares are totally invisible in the cloud, I passed the message to Ron our navigator and the skipper. Norman Barker our bomb aimer takes up his position in the nose, here he waits for Ron's signal to drop our bombs. When they go Fred immediately turns away to head south to Rouen then out into the channel, the photo flash is ignored as it will show nothing of interest.

Our return flight to Elsham was done in 10/10 cloud, which fortunately was not low enough to cause a problem when we had to land. All of our Squadrons aircraft have returned to base, we have had another uneventful trip. This trip was my twenty eighth raid, but the rest of my crew have now completed twenty nine. Our next trip will be the crews last, but I will have to do one more with a different crew to complete my tour. Unanimously the crew decide to do an extra trip, to make up my total to thirty, I feel very humbled by their decision.

Fortunately, the powers that be, take the matter into consideration, they announce that our next trip will be the last for all of Fred's Crew. We went into Scunny that night to royally toast the stations C.O. (JR St John DFC) "God bless him".

Orleans-les-Aubrais Tuesday 4th July 44 'The Wager'

One crew among the number at Elsham Wolds was Gerald Chase's lads; they were particular friends of Fred Brownings crew. Fred and Gerry were Pilots who had come through training together as were the other trades; Jack and the Squire were the Wireless operators in the crews. The crews had both arrived at the station at the same time they flew the same number of Ops. One unusual feature of Gerry Chase's crew is that they completed all thirty trips of their tour in the same aircraft, ME674 T for Tommy a Lancaster B1. On nights out both crews exchanged the usual banter that friends enjoy; each trying to outperform the other. This is what led to the 'WAGER'.

In the pub one night just before their final trip, both crews were arguing over which Lancaster was the fastest, when the bet was made. The first crew back from this last trip would collect 7/6p (37.5P) from each of the losing crew. It was the 4th July 44, but the American Independence Day was not on anyone's mind, Orleans was to be the final sortie but more importantly there was money at stake. Out from their dispersal Fred's Lancaster works its way around the perimeter track, they arrive at the threshold just as Gerry Chase's Lancaster, thunders down the runway. Fred promptly swings our Lancaster onto the holding point then waits for the green light from the control van. When it comes, he opens the throttles to powers down the runway, with the flight engineer holding the throttles wide open while we climb away from the base. Gerry's aircraft has disappeared into the darkness, with the other eighteen aircraft from the base. We head down the country to Upper Heyford, Lyme Regis, then over the Channel. Arriving at the French coast we fly toward Rennes, then the final turn to Orleans. Fred asks for a precision run-up to the target, let's do it right first time, in and out in one go. Timing it just right the navigator gets them to the target just as the markers are going down, though the flak is very heavy with fighters about. Dropping our bomb load into the centre of the target Fred waits for the photo, then he banks the Lancaster into a tight diving turn, the race is on. Our return route is a long one Angers, Rennes, Lyme Regis then Upper Heyford to Elsham. "I never, saw Fred thrash the engines, during our time at Elsham", says Jack, but tonight it will be different. The Flight Engineer Arthur is taking them, right to the limit; we have plenty of fuel so he is pushing the Merlin's hard. Fred is watching the altimeter, keeping the nose down, losing height gradually, to increase the airspeed. Reaching the last turning point, the navigator gives Fred a new heading for Elsham we are on the home straight. Crossing Northampton onto Grantham, we are back into Lincolnshire. ETA fifteen minutes announces the navigator as Jack tunes into the Elsham Control tower. The Wolds shouts Fred our spirits are high, then over the ground set, Jack hears those ominous words "T Tommy pancake" Gerry's crew are home. As Fred's crew arrive at the debriefing room, Gerry's boys are standing waiting with extended hands for their seven and a tanner's. The question remained, how did they make it back so quick, they must have really flogged the engines on the way home, is Arthur our Flight Engineer's opinion. Days later it slips out; on the return journey Gerry Chase flew a straight line course from the channel to Upper Heyford missing out Lyme Regis. They totally ignoring the return route laid down at the briefing, we did not get our money back either. All of our Squadron aircraft have returned safely, but 576 Squadron have lost one of their Lancaster's.

576 Squadron

The Crew of Lancaster III		LM532 UL-A2	
P/O	D.F.J Baxter	RCAF USA	Kia
Sg/t	J. Pender	RAF	Kia
Sg/t	E.J. McCloskey RCAF		Kia

Sg/t	D, Shoobridge	RCAF	Kia
Sg/t	A.H. Treadwell RAF		Kia
Sg/t	R.F. Hillman	RCAF	Kia
Sg/t	E.W. Bookhout RCAF		Kia

Fate can be a cruel lady; having served Gerry Chase's crew for the whole of their thirty op's tour, Lancaster ME674, PM-T Tommy was handed over to another crew. With 258 flying hours to her credit, she is lost just nine days later in a mid-air collision with a 550 Squadron Lancaster over Revigny. Sometimes the crew not the aircraft are lucky, after all Jack recounts our M Mother of 'Mother always brings you home' renown. This aircraft served us well, but M is the thirteenth letter of the alphabet, I didn't tell my crew that at the time though. With the end of our tour the O.C. of 'B flight' signs off my log book I have 161 Hrs daylight flying and 231 Hrs of night flying. Having finished our tour the crew will disband, to be assigned to separate training units. But for the present we will celebrate our survival in style tonight.

The hardworking ground crew was rounded up and are taken to 'Oswalds' in Scunthorpe to get plastered and "Man oh man could they supp ale". Next morning with sore heads we were given travel warrants; we go home on leave to spend time with our family and friends. There are times in our lives we do things in all innocence and today I am about to make a big mistake. One of the crew is going into the village to send a telegram home to his folks so I go with him to let my family know I have finished my tour.

As we arrive back on the camp I have misgivings about my action, but the deed is done. When I arrive home it's to a great welcome, but Aunt Lillian takes me to one side. She was visiting my mum when the telegram boy stopped outside the front window, fearing the worst she dashed to the front door before he knocked. The relief when she opened the telegram was incredible; she rushed into the kitchen to tell my folks I was coming home. I could not thank her enough, as I remembered how badly my Mum and Dad had taken the telegram, with news of the death of my brother only a month before. Settling in at home, Mum is over the moon at my transfer to a training unit. With the war looking like its coming to an end, my six months off an Operational squadron is very good news. Though I don't tell her of the dangers of training new pilots, who are preparing to go on to an operational squadron. I must admit that I am more relaxed at the thoughts of moving to Sandtoft without the stress of going on bombing raids.

1667 O.T.U. Instructors Course Sandtoft.

After a few days leave Jack returns to active service and his posting to the Operational Training Unit at Sandtoft in North Lincolnshire. As the train pulls into the station at Sandtoft, Jack hauls his kitbag down from the luggage rack, then steps down onto the platform. As the train disappears down the track, a lone RAF airman stands on the opposite platform. "The airfield, are sending transport for us, but it may be a while, they are busy", he shouts. Crossing the tracks he introduces himself, "Sid Gunn, Flight Engineer", let's find a drink. Stopping at the station entrance, they prop their kit bags like corn stook's in a field then set off for a nearby pub. "The driver will see our bags there and know where we have gone" remarks Sid. An hour or so later, the slightly tipsy pair return to the station; outside a WAAF driver is spitting feathers. "Where, have you two been, the C.O. was waiting to see you an hour ago, your both in deep trouble". Back at the Drome in the C.O.'s office they both attempt to appear sober, but the smell and the vertical instability give's it all away. They are both given a severe dressing down, words like a disappointment, a disgrace plus a few we can't print here were used. But from that moment on Sid is Jack's new best friend.

After completing a tour of Thirty Op's, crews were screened to be sent to Operational Training Units (O.T.U.) to teach new crews. Here they will pass on their experiences of flying on Op's to sprog crews, hopefully to help them survive their tour. Unfortunately, it was found that being experienced and being able to put that knowledge across to new crews, was a different thing. So it was decided to take tour expired pilots then, teach them how to instruct new pilots. This was to be tried at Sandtoft, at what was to become a, 'Flying Instructors School' (F.I.S.) in 'D' Flight, the 'A', 'B' and 'C' flight are conventional O.T.U's.

Our Instructors are W/Cdr Barker, Sqd/Ldr John Marshall, Plt/Off Joe Munsch, Flt/Lt Carey and Plt/Of Clark. Then at the end of the course, it would be Sqd/Ldr Marshall, who would do the final checks on trainees. When we were introduced, I remembered P/Of Clark from my operational training days at Lindholme. Sadly however memorable he was to us, we were just faces in a steady stream of trainees' there. Settling in to the new routine on the O.T.U, Jack finds his skills are not in great demand, his sole purpose in the aircraft, is to make contact with the ground when required. My first flight is with F/Lt Edwards, then two with Jack Currie, doing Instructional Flying Exercises. Jack Currie is a pilot who Jack holds in the highest regard, he has a lot of hours in his log book, with a proven war record behind him. I remember sitting with Jack Currie one evening in the pub, we are swopping tales of Operational flying training. He recounts a tale of his training days and a flight sergeant called "Bill the Bast**d"; I immediately ask what he looked like. Sadly it's a different Bill and Jack Currie comments "There must be lots of training flight sergeants called Bill who were all Bast**ds". Most of my time in the air was spent just sitting listening to the BBC home service, as we are flown round the countryside, by Pilots teaching other Pilots. We turn up at the Ops room each day to find out who we are listed to fly with, this week I do five exercises with F/Lt Carey a New Zealand Pilot. There are five different Instructional exercises that have to be practiced, followed by a final check from Sq/Ldr Marshall.

A new day dawns, it's Thursday the 10th August 1944 with another training flight to do: it's Jack Currie in the driving seat. Jack Spark settles himself down at his radio station below the pilot. The Merlin engines are started, pre-flight checks carried out, then Jack Currie taxies the Halifax round the Peri track to the main runway. A short stop, then with a roar, the engines power them down the runway; without a bomb load the Halifax lifts readily into the air, the training exercise begins. Jack Spark relaxing at his station checks the radio, while up in the cockpit.

Jack Currie now takes the Halifax through a series of circuits and bumps with the pupil pilot. Then he turns the aircraft away from the Circuit, to instruct him in teaching complexities, of flying on three engines.

Jack Curries voice on the intercom, announcing the end of the day's instruction, brings Jack Spark back from his BBC Home Service listening. He sees from his position in the aircraft nose that they are now near, Doncaster flying over the River Don. This is no accident, Jack Currie is seeing a young lady from this area, he is about to pay her a visit. Dropping down to low level, they streak down the Don towards their target, Jack Spark glances out of his window and is surprised to see a local bus. Although a distance away, he can still see clearly, the faces of the passengers, staring back from above, on a hillside road. The Halifax banks to starboard toward a field, in which stands a farmhouse; the roof flashing beneath the aircraft. A tight turn then they beat up the house for a second time.

Making a more leisurely circuit this time, a woman appears outside the farm, waiving a white cloth over her head. Jack Currie waves back as they pass overhead; having achieved the object of the exercise we head back home. Still flying low, Jack Currie spots a field ahead, with what looks like POW.'s building a hay stack. Down goes the Halibag diving toward the farm workers, we are almost on top of them before they hear our approaching aircraft. Like sailors deserting a sinking ship, they leap from the haystack, onto hay wagons or the ground. The crew are all peering back as far as the limited rear vision the Halifax will allow. Everyone on board is laughing fit to burst, when a cry goes out, 'HILL', they turn to be confronted by rising ground with trees directly ahead. Jack

Currie hauls the column back; he banks to port to avoid the trees when a violent shudder runs through the airframe. From his seat, on the port side of the fuselage, Jack Spark has a front row view of the incident. He watches in disbelief as the port outer engine scythes through the top of the field hedge as everything appears to go into slow motion. There is debris flying in all directions, the Halifax seems to come to a complete stop, then slowly it picks up speed again. At first, I thought we were about to pile into the field, but somehow we are still flying. The aircraft starts to vibrate badly, as the pilot heads back to Sandtoft with the crew very quiet and subdued.

Entering the circuit, Jack Currie puts the Halifax down smoothly then he stops at the end of the runway, the vibration seems worse on the ground. Climbing down from the aircraft, Johnny Walker the flight engineer walks round the port outer engine, he then returns to the cockpit to report. "The radiator has foliage sticking out it, plus all the prop blades are missing about six inches from their tips, it's not good", but Currie is not convinced. He taxies round the perimeter track to line up on the main runway, opening the throttles the aircraft takes off again. As they become airborne, he applies the brakes, to stop the main wheels rotating, before retracting them, but the vibration continues, that's not the cause.

He returns to the airfield to land taxiing back to a remote dispersal, the ground crew are quickly on the scene inspecting the damage. Jack Currie tells them of a bird strike and possibly of clipping the top of a tree; he then walks back to the billets. Later in the mess, the Flight Commander is talking to Jack Currie about a bird strike he once suffered, and the shock at the damage it caused. However, in the afternoon, he is visited by the Chief Technical Officer, with a large box, full of hedge debris taken from the Merlin's radiator. His comment to the Commander is, "If Flight Lieutenant Currie has had a bird strike, they were nesting when it happened". This results in Jack Currie being hauled over the coals by the C.O. before being transferred immediately to 'B' flight, here he will be someone else's problem. After the excitement of that day, we soon settled back into the routine of Instruction, an air of normality returned.

Today I received a letter with an invitation from my old pal Dennis Langhorne. He and his fiancée Cecilia Jardine are getting married; they both want me there for the ceremony in Carlisle. They believe the War is coming to an end, so have decided to look to the future together. Before I can reply to confirm my attendance, I will have to wangle a three day pass.

SID and the LEED Visits

Weekend leave is normally too short for Jack to travel home, so he is left to amuse himself locally, this is where his new pal Sid Gunn comes to the rescue. His home in Armley Leeds is close enough to be reached on a Friday, then back again on the Sunday before night fall, so Jack is invited to meet the family. What Jack does not know is, Sid's father is a Cemetery superintendant, living in a large old house at the entrance to the graveyard. Standing at the bottom of Green Hill Rd it is one of the 'Three Rests'. At the top of the hill is the 'Travellers Rest Pub', below it the 'Old Workhouse' known as the middle rest.

Then there is the "Cemetery" which is called the final rest. Despite the spooky surroundings, Jack finds a friendly family who welcome him as one of their own. Nights out in Leeds are a revelation, I had never seen so many pubs and wearing an RAF uniform gets you into places without question. One dance hall I remember was "Armley Baths" a local swimming pool by day then a dance hall at night, when the cover over the pool was rolled out. It was an enormous place with people dancing on that floor over the pool; it had to be seen to be believed. Sid's dad is a man with an easy going manner, but a wicked sense of humour. His mother is your typical quite spoken Yorkshire mum, a good cook and housewife, who in reality rules the roost. Arriving one weekend Jack retires early, leaving Sid chatting with his parents, later that night he wakes in a cold sweat. Someone is moving around outside the house, looking across the room, he see's Sid fast asleep in the bed opposite. The sounds of footsteps on the stone path below the bedroom grow louder, then the creaking of the gate hinge, there is no way Jack is getting up to look. The startling sound of the back door rattling in its frame is followed by the footsteps going away, a relieved Jack finally slips back into sleep. Next morning at the breakfast table everything appears normal, so he brings up the noises that woke him from his dreams. Sid father immediately allays Jacks fears, oh! dont worry about him, he never gets in I always keep the door bolted. It's only after there is a repeat of the events the following night, that Mrs Gunn lets the cat out of the bag. "It's the local Bobby, who checks the doors on his rounds" nothing spiritual, just another of Mr Gunn's wicked little tricks.

Back on the Base its Tuesday the 26th September 1944 and as I walk into the Ops Room, the sound of a familiar voice brings me wide awake. My old Skipper Fred Brownings is standing talking to F/Of Clark, the instructor greets me with "Morning Mr Spark". Fred turns; his face is a picture of surprise, "Jack Spark so this is where you ended up". F/Of Clarke is puzzled so we spent the next few minutes explaining to him how we know each other. That evening we sat in the Pub lifting an elbow to old friends; he tells me that our rear gunner Bert Burrill, refused to be screened at the end of our tour. He immediately volunteered for another tour and was still flying on ops with another crew; his dislike of the Germans was so strong. We spent the next three days on flying exercises together; then Fred was tasked to fly with another crew.

17th October 1944 Jacks Medal

It's the 15th October, I have a six day leave pass to travel home to Carlisle, after an overnight stay I continue on to Barrow in Furness. I had been promising to visit my mother's sister, aunt Lilly for months so now I was not on operational flying, it's a good time. Tuesday morning at aunt Lilly's, a telegram arrived from my parents. Dreading the contents I opened it, what a surprise to read "Congratulations on your award of a Distinguished Flying Medal" Signed Mum and Dad. To say what I was shocked was an understatement I thought there must be some mistake, so I set off to buy a copy of The Times. Walking into town I called at every Newsagents asking for this national paper, mostly my answer was "The Times, in Barrow in Furness". "You have more chance of finding a Conservative Club in Moscow". But eventually I did find a copy, sure enough there it was in the announcements. I was very pleased, more so for my parents sake plus the fact that the rest of the crew, had also been given gong's. We had a good celebration that night in one of the local pubs. After a few days I returned to Carlisle, to spend time with my parents, before returning to Sandtoft. They were over the moon at my award, but I was thinking about being able to take them to Buckingham Palace, where I would be presented with my DFM by the King. It was while I was on leave, I met up with an old school friend Jean Campbell, her Dad's a post man and they have just moved into Herbert Street. We start walking out together, trips to the pictures or into town for a drink, she helps me catch up on news of old school pals. But all too soon I am on the train headed back to Sandtoft.

It's the end of October 1944, Sq/Ldr Marshall has just signed off my logbook for the Month. I have 139Hrs day flying plus 32Hrs night flying with 'D' Flight, he now informs me they are moving personnel about. There is another Instructors Flight 'E', on the base flying Lancaster's so some of the Officers and NCO's of 'D' flight are moving to it, I am one of them. The C/O is to be Fl/Lt Clark with F/O Munsch, Rudge and Fl/Lt Hing a Malasian Pilot making up the team.

Hold very tight please Ding Ding.

During one of his many trips to Leeds with Sid Gunn, Jack goes shopping in town one morning, with his pal. The town is busy, the local indoor market is crowded with people buying food. Then people start to mutter about getting home. It transpires the local corporation buses have been abandoned by their crews who have gone home over a dispute with management. As both these pals start walking back to Sid's home they are stopped by a local police officer who informs them they are being recruited to help. The managers of the bus company are to drive the buses we servicemen are to become temporary conductors, to get people to and from work including getting the shoppers home. I was given a conductors bag but no tickets, "Just ask them what their fare is, then put the money in the bag" is the instruction. At the end of the afternoon, they end up at the bus depot, here he meets up again with Sid, "What do we do with the money" is the pair's question. "Keep it as compensation for your help" came the Managers reply, the pair go home a lot happier and richer than they set out that morning.

On Monday 11th December 1944 Jack attends his second Interview for a Commission this time at Sandtoft. His interrogators are the Unit Commander of 1667 O.T.U., Wing Commander R. Attwater plus the station Commanding Officer, Group Captain J. Nelson. Sitting in front of these officers, Jack is totally non-plussed by the whole thing, expecting to be deferred once again. The questions start coming which Jack replies as honestly as he can, then as he fears the W/Cdr hands the C.O. a copy of form F121. This gives details of his offence in Bridgnorth Magistrates court, Jacks heart sinks then he is surprised by the C.O.s laughter. "Well Mr Spark, if every officer, in this air force, who took a leak behind a hedge, was deferred, we would be very short of leaders". He promptly signed and approved, my commission, which will still have to go to, Air Officer Commanding No.71 Base for final approval. On the 13th December 1944 Jacks appointment, as a Pilot Officer was gazetted on the 31st January 1945. My first job on being commissioned was to travel to London to be fitted out with my Officers uniform. Sitting on the train from London to Newcastle, Jack contemplates his commission to 'Pilot Officer' as he travels home on leave.

Walking across Newcastle Station, to the Carlisle train, Jack spots the familiar outline of his father leaning against the cab of his train. Puffing on his pipe he is surprised by his son's voice asking, "I hope you are going to give me a smooth ride home tonight". As they exchange news of family and things back home, his dad takes in his son's new officers uniform. "So you won't be joining me on the footplate then", "Not likely Dad I have my First Class ticket so I am going to get my head down, don't forget to give me a shout at Carlisle". My mum's face when I arrived home was a picture, the last time I saw that look on her face, was my first day going to work, before the war. She could not wait to go into town next day, but only if I was wearing my uniform. It was just the same with my girlfriend Jean, she would not be seen out with me without my Officers uniform, whereas I just wanted to wear something relaxing. Jean and I are becoming close but I have told her, I will not make any commitment to her until the war is over. My decision was brought about, by what happened to my brother, seeing the heart ache his loss caused. At the end of my leave, I set of for Sandtoft but totally forgot I had a first class ticket.

I had entered a second class compartment when another airman, a flight sergeant commented on my not being in first class. Thanking him I made my exit to the first class carriage.

A night out in the Plough pub at Sandtoft airfield, Jack meet's with a fellow Cumbrian, this airman stationed near York, owns a motor cycle. The coincidental meeting allows Jack the occasional trip home on the pillion of this Royal Enfield Bullet. This bike he remembers left him with a numb posterior after the long ride back to Carlisle, made longer by the wartime lack of lights. Sometime later this airman is posted abroad, so Jack is offered the opportunity to buy the Enfield which he jumps at. Now with his own transport, trips to Leeds with Sid no longer rely on hitching a lift. Arriving early at Sid's home one Friday night on the new bike, they both tuck into one of his mums wonderful home cooked meals.

While they sit drinking tea afterwards, the talk somehow turns to Ouija boards, but Jack Immediately urges caution. "I tried it once with school mates, it frightened the living daylight out of us, it's not something I would try again". Pushing him for more details, the family ask how the board is laid out; he reluctantly describes the letter and number position plus the yes and no. As he climbs the stairs to get ready for a trip into Leeds, paper and scissors are produced and a replica board is fashioned. Standing shaving in the bathroom, the laughter from downstairs is audible; however after a few minutes, there is silence from downstairs.

Standing at the bottom of the stairs, Jack looks across the room, Mrs Gunn is sitting by the fire, the rest of the family are clearing the board remnants away. Sid hurries upstairs to change as Jack slips into a chair, to read the evening paper awaiting his pals return. Later in the pub Sid reveals all, it started out light heartedly, but when the glass spells out answers to questions then actually names people, it all changed. My Mum recognised a name, the details revealed frightened her, she immediately broke away from the group, refusing to continue. This event was never mentioned again, but Jack is sorry he allowed himself, to be talked into showing the family the board layout.

Operation Eggs for Breakfast

Whilst at Sandtoft the War draws to an ends, the station becomes a ghost town on weekend when aircrew get leave then disappear into town to visit friends or travel home to see families. One particular weekend sees Jack as duty Wireless Officer on Saturday the duty Flying Officer is Flight Lieutenant Hing a Malaysian. Sunday morning the 8th April 45 sees them both at breakfast in the Officers Mess, the menu includes powdered eggs due to the shortages. This almost inedible substance is not well received, F/Lt Hing is not a happy man, "Jack after breakfast we will go to collect some fresh eggs". Right Sir, "I will organise some bikes, we can go round

171

the farms", "Bikes" replies Hing "I'm not riding a bike". "There's an aircraft outside wanting to be air tested". "Do you think you could get us, to the Isle of Man", "Yes Sir I believe so". Then with a Flight engineer rounded up, the three of them, set off in a Lancaster, for the Isle of Man. The weather is fine, Jack gets them there without incident; he even manages a view of his old stomping ground, the Lake District on the way. Approaching Jurby airfield, Flt/Lt Hing shuts down the Port outer engine, he instructs Jack to contact the control tower, inform them of our three engine landing. Down on the ground, a fire tender turns out along with the blood wagon, taking up station beside the runway approach watching for the aircraft. The Lancaster executes a perfect touchdown then taxies to the dispersal nearest the control tower. As Flt/Lt Hing climbs down from the Lancaster, a party of officer's welcome him like the prodigal son returning home. It now transpires; he had served at Jurby eighteen months before and is held in high regard by everyone still serving there. An RAF car is produced to allow the three visitors, to be chauffeured around the local farms collecting eggs, which are carefully placed in containers packed with straw.

Returning to the airfield, the trio are treated to lunch in the mess, before climbing back aboard the Lancaster we set off for Sandtoft on all four engines. For the next few weeks, Jack appears in the mess every morning, with two fresh eggs for breakfast, to the curious stares of other airmen.

The Long Walk

There are no fresh eggs for George Silva as he sits in barrack 31a at Stalag 17B in April 45. The winter has been hard very hard; the barracks have had any wood that was not supporting anything vital, stripped to provide fuel for the stove. Even so there are cases of frostbite among the prisoners. Our food is nothing more than a rehydrated cabbage soup, which has been watered down to make it go further. The only protein is provided by the presence of grubs or worms which we avoid looking at. Our secret radios are reporting allied advances, in Camp the Germans are getting very jumpy.

As the war against Germany progressed, the Russians were working their way up the valley to the eastern part of Austria. They were close enough to our camp for us to sometimes see the flashes of their big guns. When the night was clear we could also hear them. Our German guards were becoming quite apprehensive; we had heard from a few of them that they were afraid for their lives, for the Russians were getting very close. The German officers of our camp think that if we move to the West, we would be moving towards Gen. Patton's troops, who were coming from the western part of Austria.

We were then told through our camp leaders, that we would be leaving camp probably in the next two or three days. Since we would be walking we should consider what and how we were going to carry any possessions we need. For those people that had been here for a long time, who had also been receiving packages from home, there was a lot to decide on. I had been here in camp a bit over a year now, so I only had one package from home, so my choice was food, blankets, my logbook plus a few incidentals. As soon as the rumour had started about our move, I began to save my daily ration of bread, so that I had six slices of bread plus some canned food from the last food parcel we had received. How to carry that, all I have would be my pockets.

My friend that I had met on the night I got to the camp over a year ago, came over he asked how I was going to carry anything on the walk, I admitted that I didn't know. He said that he had an extra shirt that I could use to make a sort of backpack. He brought the shirt along with a needle and some thread, first I had to sew the cuffs together. Then with the shirt buttoned up, I stitch the bottom of the shirt together front to back. Now I can put the shirt arms over my head across my chest to carry it. What a great friend he was, in the backpack I had space for my logbook including what food I had saved. There was plenty of space for his things so we decided that we would share carrying it. Now we were ready to vacate quickly, all we had to do was roll up our blankets. Everyone in camp wanted to say goodbye to the friends they had made while here, so the curfew was lifted which caused a lot of activity up and down the street.

Everyone was going to say take care, see you soon. Fred my bunk mate decided that we would stay close together on the march and not get separated because there were so many of us. It turned out to be one of the best decisions that we made, as later on I had a great need of his assistance.

Preparing to leave camp

The camp held about 4500 prisoners which would be too large a group to control, so we were divided up into groups of about 500 which set off an hour or so apart. In getting ready to leave the camp there was a lot of confusion, everyone wanted to be with their friends. My crewmate Dick Thayer is somewhere in our group as I have seen him moving about with one of his hut mates. So when the guards had us in a position ready to walk out, there was a lot of movement in the ranks, as people moved to where they wanted to be. As we prepared to move out, there was a rumour that the Russians were only about 20 miles from our camp as there was so little resistance in front of them. Of course what made our guards worry more was, they had heard that the Russians were breaking through the small town of St-Polle. The plan was that we were going to march for 50 min. and rest 10 min, we were to walk for 4 miles then stop for lunch.

173

Before we started to walk after lunch our guards decided to have a roll call, but when there were hoots of discontent they decided that perhaps they would wait until the next morning. After a little confusion the march eventually started, on we went marching then resting alternatively, the lunch stop when it came was only long enough for those of us that had food to eat it.

That first night we spent in a farmyard so we were able to bed down in a barn. During the day though, the farmer was careful to move all his cows away from our area, so no milk for us tonight! Next morning the lucky ones of us, who had been able to think ahead and store a little food, had an advantage over those who did not. Our guard decided that this was a good time to have a roll call, but they were dismayed because they found of the 500 in our group, there were 29 missing. Of course it made everybody roll with laughter, though I don't remember ever finding out what happened to those fellows that went missing. During one of our stops, we heard that the Russians had bombed the Krems railroad yards. We were now walking along the Eins River getting close to Linz; this was supposed to be Hitler's hometown. But as we were across the river from it, we did not walk through the city. The march continued through farm country where again we stayed on a farm overnight, although the farmer would not allow us to sleep in his barn. The weather was little balmy that night so I strolled across a field, to my surprise I stumbled on what looked like a sugar beet about the size of a large apple. I quickly ran back to where my bunk mate was to show him my treasure. That night we cooked it and thought it tasted very good, next morning everyone was out walking in the field looking for beet.

The morning after our big feast we started to march about 9:30am, It wasn't long after that I began to feel not so good, as the day progressed I got to feeling worse, It was not long before I had to stop walking to seek a spot where I could eliminate my breakfast. The guards would not tolerate stopping along the route unless it was a scheduled rest stop. My bunk mate had eaten the other half of the vegetable that I found, but it didn't seem to bother him at all. I struggled along until our scheduled rest stop; there I managed to relieve myself as best I could. My problem continued most of the day, but by the time we stopped for the night I desperately needed a bath but of course there was no water. We did manage to find a very small stream and although it was cold I was able to clean myself up a bit. By morning I felt better, at least I was a lot cleaner thanks to the help of my friends. At our lunch break we were told that we did not have very far to go to where we will be staying. Little did we know that our so-called home was in a small forest? We were to cut down limbs from trees in order to make a shelter of sorts to live in. My friend borrowed an axe; with it we cut enough branches from trees to make us an adequate shelter.

They guards did not make any attempt to feed us, so we had to have whatever we had put aside in our backpacks. I had saved four slices of our bread ration, some crackers or K rations from our last food parcel as well as one square each of a chocolate bar, which was our dinner.

Next morning breakfast consisted of a slice of bread with a mug of soup, followed by a mug of coffee; then we are back on the road, marching west. During the day we have to be constantly vigilant for approaching traffic, from either direction. There are trucks or cars moving toward the advancing Russians, there are also trucks bringing injured soldiers back from the battle. The drivers of these vehicles have little regard for our band of POW's, if we do not get out of the way they would run us down without a second thought. Onward we march, only when the sun is getting low in the sky can we see an end to our day, as the Germans shepherd us into another field for the night. After a long delay we are served more soup with a slice of bread followed by a mug of coffee, not much after covering almost 25 kilometres. Huddled together in groups for warmth we spend another bitterly cold night in the open air. When the morning comes, we have to spend time massaging our legs, to ease the stiffness in our joints. Breakfast is two slices of black bread then, as we line up for coffee, the German guards start shouting to get us moving. They seem to be determined that we cover 25 to 30 kilometres a day; they try to urge us along by shouting "Rous, Rous Ruski kommen".

We have been marching for about an hour when it starts to rain; it rains all day and I am thinking about the miserable night we are going to have. Then someone up above smiles on us, the Germans are herding us toward a large barn out of the wet. I found a nice corner with a pile of straw in it, then slump to the floor exhausted, though I must not fall asleep. If I don't stay awake when the food is distributed, they will pass me by so I won't get anything at all. When it arrives, its Barley soup again, with one thin slice of bread then more coffee, the only good thing about it is, it's hot so it brings warmth to my cold body. Now I gather as much straw as I can around me, then cover it and myself with my two blankets, I fall fast asleep. After the open fields of the days before this is luxury; I sleep like a baby in a feather bed. Next morning I wake refreshed but hungry; some of my fellow POW's are suffering with colds or flu they are not fit to march. After a breakfast of more soup and bread, with a mug of coffee, the guards tell us we are to rest here for today then restart tomorrow. I take the opportunity to find some water to wash myself, my feet are sore after the marching, but they are holding up well. The rest of our day is spent getting as much rest as possible; we are going to need it tomorrow.

Morning comes but after breakfast some of our guys are still not fit to travel, they will have to remain in the barn until they recover. The rest of us are rounded up, we are on the march again. By the afternoon, we have crossed the river Danube as it starts to rain. In a short time we are all soaking wet, the cold is starting to seep into my bones. The rain is still beating down on us, as later in the day the Germans lead us to a cluster of farm buildings, we are to bed down here for the night. We have covered another thirty kilometres today, but our supper is a meagre slice of bread with a mug of soup with what looks like carrots in it. On one of the days we marched, I remember it was about mid day the Germans called a rest stop. There was a group of Jews being marched along the road in the opposite direction; they have also stopped to rest. They just sank to the ground in the field then, some of them started to eat the grass like cattle. At the end of the rest period they were ordered to continue their march; slowly they formed up and started to move off again. Left behind were nine stragglers too weak to continue, despite the urging from the soldiers. To our horror the German guards shot them all dead, as they lay on the ground; the depravity of that callous act has stayed with me ever since. There was almost a riot as our guy's rose as one to protest. Only the fact, that the German guards had rifles they were only too willing to use them stopped it becoming an all out battle. Further along the road, we were passed by horse drawn carts, following behind the Jewish prisoners, it was loaded with bodies. The Germans were gathering up the executed Jews as they went along. We all despised them for their brutality and inhumanity. It also brought a feeling of dread, for the safety of the guys we had left behind in the barn.

A few more days of marching followed, then to our surprise the Red Cross people arrived with food parcels for us. What they saw of our conditions made them very angry, they remonstrated loudly with the German Officers. They informed the Germans they would be reported, for the way we were being looked after, they would have to answer for our treatment. Though for us it did not matter, we were too busy watching the food being unloaded, from the trucks they brought with them. There was the luxury of the additional blanket's they distributed, to keep us warm at night. We break open the food parcels, to carry the contents as best we can, as the Germans want us on the march again.

That night after being fed we prepare to bed down in the open air again, fortunately it's not raining. I am woken by the sound of an air raid to watch the searchlights with the sounds of the guns in the distance, the guards just mutter "Ruski's". Day after day we continued to march, sometimes it rained other times it was sunny, but it was always cold. One morning we are halted by a convoy of trucks heading to Krem's. Suddenly there is a lot of shouting, one of our guards has been run down by a truck and killed. The Germans are saying he was pushed by one of our group of POW's which was denied by us. We are quickly marched on by the remaining guards, as any trouble from the troops on the trucks, will reflect badly on them with the Red Cross people. The only highlights to our days were the nights we got to sleep in a barn, or any similar building.

Thankfully the Red Cross having found us, did not forget our hardships, they regularly searched us out to bring more food parcels, "God bless them". One food drop saw us with a mixture of U.S. and French packages. We could not read the French labels on the cans, but there were pictures on them, which took the guesswork out of the contents. Though at that point we would have just eaten anything that was in the tins we were so hungry. Its Thursday 27th April, we have been marching all day through towns and villages. The local inhabitants gazed at our rag bag column with varied reactions. Those in the small villages just looked on wondering who we were. But those who had been on the receiving end of our bombs called out 'Terrorflugen' (Terror Flyers) as they shook their fists at us. By mid afternoon we arrive at Branau; our guards lead us to a wood where to our amazement we are told that this is our destination. Our supper sadly is only bread and coffee with what we have left from our parcels, we can only hope it improves tomorrow.

Over the next few days we just made the best of the situation, thought the arrival of some French food parcels helped improve things. On Wednesday 2nd May we meet with some British POW's who tell us the allies are close by our location, this news really cheers everyone up. Today is Thursday 3rd May 1945 we have had a miserable breakfast of bread and coffee, before spending the rest of the day watching for our liberators. We spent a lot of time standing on the bank watching the military activity of Patton's third armoured division in the distance across the river. We yelled and waved our arms hoping that we would be noticed. We found that they knew that we were there, because one day someone had said to us that he'd heard a Jeep horn. We laughed, we thought that he was hallucinating but later that day a jeep drove up with an officer driven by a corporal. They tell us that the war was just about over, that we were once again in the US military; also in the next couple of days a Red Cross truck would be here to administer medical help to anyone that needed it. Next day G.I.'s arrive in our camp to disarm the Germans then take them prisoner. We all stand cheering, as some of them are given a good beating by our G.I's, who relieve them of their rifles. They had the deluded idea, that the allied armies would join with them, to fight the Russians. What a celebration there was that night in that patch of trees that had been our home for a few days. Then the army arrive in force with field rations to hand out, to tide us over while things get organised. Sunday morning, we are on the move to a warehouse on the edge of the town, here more field rations are handed out. Amazingly during the whole of this march, Ben Phelper had continued to take photographs of our makeshift camp sites and other points of interest along the way. This would be used to create a truly historic document of the Second World War. Our change of accommodation also allows us the chance to wash and shave, to suddenly start to feel human again, after the degradations of the last few weeks. Suddenly the realisation of what we have been through, over the last twenty six days hits home. Our group of four thousand five hundred prisoners have marched over two hundred and eighty miles since we left Krems. When a register of the survivors is taken we are five hundred men short of the original figure, we can only hope the rest have escaped. But for those that were taken ill at the start of our journey, we can only hope they were taken good care off by the Germans. Down the road a bit were a couple of small villages, some of the boys felt they would walk down to visit with the people that live there. Most of them were delighted to see the Americans and hear that all was going well with the military. I did not participate in going to town because, although I felt much better than I had for a while, I thought It would be better to stay quiet because no one knew where were going from here. True to their words, the medical people did show up to administer help to anyone that needed it. I was given Sulfa drugs, which made me feel much better than I had for quite some time.

When my buddy came back from his second trip to the village, he brought back some fruit. He had an apple, a few grapes with some cherry plums. They were not quite ripe, but I dared to eat some of them, but only because we had the medical people nearby.

Next we were told that we are to be flown to a first aid station in France; here we would be given healthy foods in order to get us healthy enough to withstand a trip across the ocean. We were told not to become impatient because we had to regain our health in order to make the long trip across the Atlantic to home.

Robert M Cook

In Stalag Luft 1 the German Commanders, were also starting to worry that the Russians were getting very close. In response they start to organise our evacuation from the camp back into Germany. What they had not considered, was the reaction of the barrack leaders. They totally refused to vacate the camp, we will remain and wait for the Russians was their reply, in a way I think the Germans were pleased.

It meant they could pack up and leave immediately. When they had gone, we set about making white arm bands with the words POW's written on them in Russian, to avoid any confusion when they did arrive. In an attempt to avoid conflict the POW'S Commander Colonel Zemke sent a scouting party to seek out the advancing Russians. On the 1st May 45 the Russians arrived to much celebration. But there were doubts over the Russian intentions, so the allies immediately organised a rescue mission. On the 12th May the first party of American military arrived in a B17 to set up the evacuation of the prisoners. Over the next few days B17's ran a shuttle service to remove all the POW's. The Americans were flown to camp Lucky Strike in France, with the allied POW's being flown straight to Britain. The first prisoners to be flown out of Barth were the sick and injured, this included Robert Cook whose weight had fallen to 100 lbs. He was so weak he had to be carried on a stretcher to the aircraft. These aircraft would land and keep their engines running as there was no restart facilities for them, prisoners would have to be quickly loaded before the B17's would make a rapid takeoff.

VE Night End of WAR in Europe

Back in England the 8th May 1945 was V.E. night, Jack having heard the news on the morning radio; he later joined the crowds up at the "Travellers Rest" pub for a night to remember. We really celebrated the end of a nightmare that evening, the drink flowed until all hours, I can't remember the landlord ever calling time. Then in the early hours, Sid's family and I trooped in total disarray down the hill to Cemetery House. Mrs Gunn unlocked the front door, everyone but me entered the house. a remember trying to negotiate the path to the front door when either Leeds suffered its first Earth Quake or my legs lost contact with my body. But I found myself looking up at the stars on my back in the bushes, laughing like an idiot. My brain must have still retained some coordination as I sat up thinking, "Where is my dental bridge, it's not in my mouth". Fumbling about in my pockets, I fished out a box of matches to start a search among the shrubbery for the missing denture. When the Gunn family finally realised I was missing, they found me still crawling about in their flower beds rapidly running out of matches. A torch was produced then with the missing item recovered from the bushes, we all went inside. Later that night laid in bed, I can still hear Mr and Mrs Gunn laughing loudly, in their bedroom down the hall.

The War in Europe may be over, but at Sandtoft the flying training continues, the word on the station is we could be going to the Far East. It's the end of May 1945, I am bringing my log book up to date, there are 22.5 Hrs daylight and 5 Hrs night flying this month. As I look at the bottom line, the totals so far are, 355 Hrs daylight plus 278 Hrs night flying. My instruction time at Sandtoft is lifting my daylight hours back above the level of my night flying hours. June is approaching, I remember that in a few days time it will be the first anniversary of my brother's death, it has passed so quickly. But I try to remember the good times we shared before this war started. We are into the 1st June; training continues with a three hour night flying exercise, F/Officer Cartwright is the instructor. Night flying is not as relaxed as the daytime, I can't sit listening to the BBC, darkness is every flyers enemy. After that night exercise, we will not fly again until the end of June then, it will be a Cooks Tour for the ground crews. Monday 25th June we are off to the Ruhr but there will be no shooting today, our crew consists of a pilot, navigator, flight engineer plus me the wireless operator. The bomb aimer's position and the gun turrets are manned by ground crew plus three others sitting on the day bed. After takeoff we head across the North Sea, the weather is clear, in no time at all we cross the Dutch coast at Rotterdam. Now it's on to Arnhem still inside Holland before we head for Germany, this is what the ground crew have come to see. Actually it's what I have come to see as. Although I have completed a tour of ops against Germany, the raids were in the dark at twenty thousand feet.

This is my first opportunity to see the damage that has been done. Essen is the first German city to come into view, but it's Cologne that I am interested to see. When it does the damage is dramatic, especially at the two thousand feet we are now flying. The city is a sea of rubble with what is left of the buildings standing among it all. Then Cologne Cathedral comes into view, amazingly it appears undamaged among all the devastation around it. But onward we fly; Aachen is next on our tour, by comparison with Cologne it's a much smaller place but I recall we bombed it twice. The ground crew are asking questions they are pointing out damage on the ground. Though at the speed and height we are flying, things are flashing by to quickly to give an answer in time. Our Lancaster is now turning west again, the next place on our tour is Antwerp, we are back over Belgium.

All too soon we are over the North Sea on our way home, but the ground crew are still talking about what they have seen. Once we arrive back at Sandtoft they disappear to tell other erk's about the trip they have just flown. I can't remember how many aircraft were involved on this Ruhr Tour, as it is not noted in my log book, but there were quite a few. There is no flying for the next ten days, then on Friday the 6th July we do the Ruhr Tour once again, for the ground crews who missed out on the first trip.

Today is 15th August 1945 we have not flown for over a month; we are about to find out why. That evening the end of the war with Japan is announces in America, VJ day has arrived but it leaves me wondering where I go from here. I would only fly twice more from Sandtoft with the last but one exercise was with F/Off Charles Wearmouth on the 29th September. Charles had like myself flown a tour of operation from Elsham Wolds, so we had many a chat about our time there.

Jean Cambell Jacks first wife   Jack Spark at work

Jack's Shop Fire

Jack & Dorothy's Wedding
Dorothy's two brothers are far right Darly, Muriel, Norma & Billy Young

Jack & Dorothy   Jack Feeding young Colin van Zantvoort

Gloria Silva Mack   George Silva   Fletcher Rohden

Adrian and Ingrid van Zantvoort with Dorothy and Jack Spark

Jack's Office

George's Office

Mailly le Camp 2006 Jack is the tall man in the front row, Jimmy Graham is to the left both representing Elsham Wolds. French Veterans behind them.

Marjorie Hiller, Jack Spark, Dr John Washbourne & Gp Cpt Don Hiller

Jack Spark at Reg Tailby's headstone

George Edward Stockdale 576 Squadron

George and Betty Silva

Dr Bill Hossack and Margaret Crawford with Jack Spark

Gloria & George Silva at Mill Ave Art Festival 2013

George aged 93 & two of his Brothers 2013

David & Elaine Frampton

Regular gatherings of Jacks friends in Grantham

Left to Right Julie Blichmann & her husband Ted Fore, Terri & Rick Moore
Cousin of Fremont Granade, Jim Thomas Stephanie Lopez, Robbie Thomas
daughter of Gerald Poplett & Finally Pascal Bulois.

The 452nd Bomb Group Memorial with its Honour Guard.

RAF Elsham Wold's Veterans Reunion 2006

Although during the war he was on 576 Squadron, where as I was with 103 Squadron.

Camp Lucky Strike

In France George Silva and his fellow POW's are being tended to in preparation for repatriation to the States. We were flown to camp Lucky Strike near Le-Harve in France, here we would be able to have as much good food at any time of the day or night. Of course, most of us ate too much, so suffered stomach cramps plus all the other things that overeating causes. Along with the good food, we were given all the eggnog's we could handle. Slowly, we began to forget about the food problem of the past, to once again enjoyed waking up in the morning knowing that we were free. When we were not eating I walked around the camp looking for someone I recognized from the 452nd or the 728th Squadron.

I thought that our pilot Lieut. Cook could be here, but I wasn't successful in finding him. I did find out later that indeed he was there, but there were just so many of us. However pleasant the conditions were in the rehab camp we are all itching to get home. We're told that when there were enough people fit enough to travel they would be put aboard one of the Liberty ships at the wharf to sail home. Because of my problem on the walk with dysentery I was detained almost 3 weeks longer than some of the others. When Robert Cook was brought into camp Lucky Strike he was immediately hospitalized. Here the medics stabilized his condition and put him on the road to recovery. He would need to be put onto a nutritious diet to cure his scurvy and help rebuild his emaciated body. Like George this would not be a quick process and his treatment would have to be continued when he returned to the States.

Crossing the Atlantic

Our health has improved over the last three weeks, since the first three ships left for home. The Camps Health Council decided that those of us that had to stay for more treatment are now well, so as soon as the ships return we could get on board to sail for home. We waited impatiently for two days until a liberty ship tied up to the dock, but the captain told us that he was preparing to leave on the morning tide.

There had been very little reason to get excited until now, but the news that we would be getting on board the ship to sail in the morning raised our spirits. Since there were only about 30 of us that were left behind, because of our bouts of dysentery, we were going to have plenty of space to move about on the ship. About 7:30am the next morning, the ships engines were already running as we boarded, then went to our allocated cabins, when we arrived back on deck we had already pulled away from the dock to start on our way home. About the second day out we noticed the ship was not moving so I asked the sailors why this was.

We were told that they had just blown a boiler which would take most of the day including part of the coming night to repair. So there we are sitting in the middle of the ocean, 30 plus ex-prisoners anxious to get home with nothing to do, but wait until the defective boiler was repaired.

It took the greater part of the day and night to be fixed. Then in the early hours of the morning of this second day we are moving again, but because the repair is a temporary fix we can only maintain half speed, but at least we are heading homeward. We also receive word from the captain that we would not be stopping at New York Harbour, but we were going to sail on to report in at Newport Virginia, a matter of one or more additional days sailing. A special meal was prepared by the crew of the ship for us, which we all enjoyed very much although we were disappointed that it would be another day before we landed. Then we were told that we would be loaded onto a military train to head for California. That news received three hip, hip, hurrahs as most of us who came from California. The feeling on the ship was much lighter from then on, songs broke out we were even dancing with each other. We spent a lot of the time finding out which city each of us came from, there were 22 that came from the Oakland area the same as myself, so we all promised to keep in touch. Later I found out from a sailor that some of us would not be going straight home, but stopping at Long Beach for rehabilitation.

Therapy

Therapy at Long Beach was about eating the proper, or the best foods for those of us that had suffered from a bout of dysentery while on the long walk from Stalag 17b. We were advised that we would be detained there for only a short time until they were sure that those of us that were stricken more severely than others had completely recovered. After 10 days or so of treatment we were released. I was given 28 days of furlough before having to report to Hamilton Field Air Force Base in California for my next assignment.

I boarded a bus to Ukiah where I was met by my brother who drives me home to Mendocino, here my mother, father, brothers and sisters were awaiting my return. As one can imagine there was a tearful but happy reunion then, everyone had questions. I told them that I would try to answer them all but not tonight. Tonight I was just going to savour the feeling of being home.

Hamilton Field Airbase

My leave was about over, my next assignment is to Hamilton Air Force Base in Sonoma, California on September 12, 1945. When I reported in to the base I was given a choice of living on the base or living at home in Oakland and commuting. I chose the home option; my stay on the base would be for about three weeks, while I was awaiting my discharge. On October 19th I was taken to McClellan field in Roseville, near Sacramento. There I received my discharge from the United States Air Force, though they did provide me with a ride into San Francisco. From here it was a short bus ride to Oakland, arriving in the bus station, I called my home to ask for someone to come down to the station and pick me up. While I was waiting I walked out of the station looking up and down the street where I'd started my journey four years earlier. I took a deep breath, I WAS HOME!!!

After the war George was informed about the U.S. Air Forces rehabilitation services, giving him alternative employment options. At first he was set on becoming a Barber and the military would fund his equipment costs to start his business. However back home he met up with the owner of a local chain of butchers shops. He was looking to train people; he was willing to teach George to become a qualified meat cutter. I agreed to take up his offer, a decision I would not regret. Without hesitation I contacted the Air Force, the Barbers tools were replaced with the tools of a meat cutter.

George Silva Peace Time

When George retired in 1982 he had spent the last 37 years of his working life in this trade with the last 23 years at Safeway Stores. During that time he had also met and married Betty Silva who already had a four year old daughter, as a family we settled down to my new life as a civilian. Over the years they would raise daughters Lisa and Gloria, watch them both marry and bring grandchildren into the world. In 1999 Betty drew my attention to a clipping in the paper that local airfield was hosting a visit by restored WW2 aircraft, one of these was a B17. So that weekend we both visited the field and although all of the planes were good to see the B17 was the one I was here for. A sum of $6 allows both of us to look round the inside, Betty was shocked at how little room there was inside, I also found it was smaller than I remembered. But to be honest that could be down to my being a little larger than I was in 1944.

Robert M Cook Peace time.

Robert M Cook was repatriated from camp Lucky Strike in June 1945 and would return to his home in Los Angeles, California. Robert would remain if the US air force. Over the coming years he and his family would move around many air force bases in the US. There were also secondments to US bases in Europe and North Africa. This last one was to Marrakesh, Morocco where they spent over four years. He would finally retire from the air force as a Squadron Commander of a tanker unit in 1965. Then in 1998 Robert attended the 452nd BG Reunion, here he would meet up with George Silva for the first time since 1944. They spent the few days catching up on what had happened to them both since 1944. Sadly just four years later in 2002 Robert M Cook would succumb to a brain tumour. This was such a cruel, cruel end for a man who had devoted so much of his life to his country, his family and friends.

Richard Thayer Peace Time.

Richard L Thayer would return to the family farm in Hope Indiana. Here he would see for the first time the Purple Heart, Silver Star and Bronze Star he had been awarded, he had also been nominated for the Medal of Honor. In 1947 Richard Thayer stood for the post of Sheriff of Bartholomew County, he was successful in being elected to the post. As Sheriff he lived in a house with the Jail attached, part of his responsibilities there was to see any prisoners he had in custody were fed. This duty fell to his wife Evelyn who was expected to cook the food for the inmates. Their first child Gordon would be taught his basic alphabet by one of these prisoners in the cells in those early years. Richard was held in high regard by the community he served, as did the prisoners in his charge.

One of these would comment that the only person in Bartholomew County capable of beating Dick for the Sheriff's job would be his wife Evelyn. Dick Thayer would continue to hold the position of County Sheriff until 1950. Then not content with serving as Sheriff, Dick would stand for the position of Mayor of Columbus Indiana, he was again successful, he would hold this position from 1952 through to 1956. During his time as Mayor his family would grow to include a daughter Margie and the twins Tim and Kim. Later he would serve as a Bartholomew County Councilman for many years, truly a lifetime of service to his Country and his community. Dick's niece, Susan Thayer Fye currently serves on the Bartholomew County Sheriff's Merit Board following in her Uncles footsteps.

Winding down.

At the start of October 45 Jack Spark is called into the C.O's office to be told of his movement to 17 O.T.U. as an equipment officer. But with the end of conflict in the world, things are winding down quickly, my stay at 17 O.T.U. last only a few weeks. Then it's off again to Blyton, here I am officially re-allocated to ground duties as an equipment officer. I have just started to settle in when I am off again, this time it's to Bicester as an equipment officer. Unbelievably after only a week I am moved to Headquarters 56 Wing, thankfully this time it lasts until the spring of 1946.

On the 10th April Jack is called before the C.O. who informs him of his new relocation, "I see you have previous experience in a stores

196

depot Spark". Well they are in need of officers to help run No.14 Maintenance Unit up in Carlisle, It's a bit out of the way but someone has to do it sadly you have drawn the short straw. I could not believe my good fortune, but quickly told the C.O. we all have to do our bit, however tough it was. I could not pack my kit bag quick enough, in readiness for my move back home.

Arriving at 14 M.U. on the morning, of 14th April 46 the WAAF officer was welcoming, but informed me, it would be difficult to find somewhere to billet me. My comment that, I would find somewhere, in town myself was met with laughter, but she wished me luck. Standing at the front door of 24 Herbert Street, my mother was surprised to see me, but glad of the extra money, the RAF paid for putting her son up at home. This new posting also meant I could continue seeing Jean every day. My duties at 14 M.U. were the running of No.2 Site under the command of Group Captain Boldero though my first encounter with this officer was not an auspicious one. There was a Commanding Officers parade every Friday; I was listed to officiate in the weeks following my arrival. That morning saw the C.O. standing on his podium in front of the flagpole, I was stood facing the squad of airmen marching toward me, when they reached the C.O. I ordered "Squad Halt" which they did.

It was at this point that things started to go wrong, as I needed to turn left to face the Flagpole I ordered "Squad left turn" which they did. As I gave the order I knew I had made a mistake, the Squad were now standing, with their backs to the flagpole and the C.O. The look on the C.O.'s face confirmed my worst fears; my Command "Squad about turn" rectified the situation but the damage was done. Later in the mess he commented "Bloody good start Mr Spark", my apology was accepted, but I knew I could not make a second mistake. One week later the C.O. informed me that the RAF need to close a surplus Maintenance Unit at Lissett on the Yorkshire coast, then transfer the stores back to Carlisle. I was appointed to oversee the operation travelling to Bridlington to manage the closure. It was a something and nothing job in reality; the local stores people handled everything with ease, after all this is what they did every day. In a short time, I was back at 14 M.U. where there had been a few changes.

One of these included my transfer, to No.5 site where I had started, as a stores clerk back in 1940. My first instinct after settling in, was to seek out my old pal, Charlie and Mr Sorrel; unfortunately Sorrel had moved on so was not to be found. But as for Charlie, I was walking through the main store, towards his office, when he surprised me by appearing, from a side aisle, right in front of me. At first he apologised, for nearly colliding with me, then as he looked me in the face, a slight sign of recognition came over him. But only when I spoke to him, did he realise who it was, "Jack Spark, as I live and breathe so the Jerries didn't get you then". We spent the next two hours, in his office, supping tea and catching up on old times, while dipping into his ample supply of biscuits. The amount of spares we were handling at 14 MU was diminishing as the war effort wound down. Then one day a telephone call from the main gate, informing me I had a visitor, could I collect him. A bit puzzled I arrived to find my old pal Dennis Langhorne in uniform waiting at the gatehouse to see me, he had heard that I was here and he was on leave. I spent the rest of the day, showing him round the depot, before having Lunch in the officer's mess to catch up on his war. He had just completed a duty tour in Libya, so I told him about my brother's accident in the Atlas Mountains. At the end of his visit, I took the trouble to rustle up some transport, to take him home with the promise of a night out in Carlisle to celebrate. He also informs me he is being demobbed so intends to go back to College to become a pharmacist. His wife Cecilia is working at Holloways chemists in the town and they would like to run their own shop in the future.

May 1946, things are really becoming quiet at 14 MU and Jack is looking to liven his life up. He rejoins the Cumberland County Motor Club where he competes in the "Velocette Cup" a motor cycle reliability trial. Here he gives a good account of himself, riding his 500cc Royal Enfield Bullet. However his enthusiasm for the sport wanes, as his back injury starts to cause him problems again. The RAF site medical officer gave me the once over, but said "We need an expert opinion on this back of yours Mr Spark". Later, in July while at home Jack receives a travel warrant and a letter from the air ministry, instructing him to report to Harley Street, for a medical examination. In the accident, with the B17 Fortress at Dunsfold, returning from Berlin, Jack injured his back. At first he ignored it, but as he continues with his tour, it is not improving. Doc Henderson notes the condition he suggested that it needs attending to as soon as possible. It is on his recommendation that Jack now travels by train on the overnight sleeper, to London and Harley Street.

Walking into the waiting room with the aid of a walking stick he is greeted by the Surgeon Mr Young. "Now Mr Spark, let's have a good look at you"; a thorough examination was followed by a trip to the X-ray department. After viewing my X-rays with a further bit of prodding and checking on the range of my movement, he said I could get dressed. Then into the consulting room, "Ah well, Mr Spark you're not too bad", "How old are you" came the question, "Twenty four Sir". "Well you look near forty four, but by the time I have finished, you will be twenty four again plus you won't need that stick". "I want you to report to St Peters Hospital Chertsey in Surrey, where you will find, you are not alone in having this condition". "I will be along next week to operate on that dodgy back of yours". "Don't worry I have done this operation before on hundreds of patients and I have never lost a one".

On arrival at St Peters, I booked in at reception to be escorted to the ward by two porters, one carrying my case, the other pushing my wheelchair. This miserable pair, were known by the airmen on the ward as, "Mutt and Geoff" (deaf) because whenever you called them, they never seemed to hear you. The other lads, on the ward were full of tales, about the Doctors, the nursing staff and the operation, I was about to undergo.

On the evening before my operation, the talk on the ward changed, the question, "Has the angel visited you yet", which left me puzzled. Then about nine o'clock, this nursing nun arrived at my bed, just as I was about to try to get some sleep. After spending some time talking to me, reassuring me about my operation, she knelt at my bedside to pray for my soul, should I not come through it. When she finally left, the rest of the boys on the ward were convulsed with laughter, by my facial expressions while she was at my bedside. Apparently, they had all gone through this ritual, with this well meaning religious lady. Two days later, Jack is in the recuperation ward with his back problem resolved; attending to his needs, are a team of St Thomas's nurses. Later he is moved to a small ward in which two other servicemen are also recovering from surgery; they will remain here for a number of weeks. One day during this period the ward sister came into our room, she informed us she was bringing a Group Captain into our room. He had been operated on and was in recovery, our unanimous reply was she needn't bother we don't want him in here giving us orders. To calm us down she agreed to put him in a private room on his own. But a few days later she announced the Groupie was feeling low he needed company, so we would just have to like it or lump it. I remember his family lived locally so his wife visited regularly with their small boy. The Groupie's son was a great fan of the Lancaster so he promptly told him to talk to me as I flew in one. From that moment on, the young lad spent every visit to the hospital, asking me questions about my bomber raids to Germany. He was a canny kid and I looked forward to his visits, as my own family were too far away to come and visit me.

Having reached the stage, when they can now partially sit up in bed, the four invalids are keen to know, about an upcoming party, in the hospital. The ward sister dismisses all hopes, of them attending the venue, but promises to see their needs will be catered for, but will say no more. Sure enough the evening of the party arrives, the ward becomes quite, apart from the squeak of a trolley, coming along the corridor. Then like an angle of mercy, the Sister appears in her finest ball gown, pushing a trolley, on which sits a barrel of Best Bitter with four glasses. By repositioning our beds, one patient can hold a glass, while the one on the other side of the barrel, turns the tap, then it's a simple task to pass the full glasses to each other. Medicine never tasted better, or was more eagerly imbibed in.

During his time in hospital the Distinguished Flying Medal which has been awarded in October 45 was brought to the Hospital. To applause from the nurses and patients the Sister pins the Medal to Jack's pyjamas, though it is a moment of great sadness. Having lost his brother, he was hoping that he would be able to give his parents a treat, by taking them to the Palace, to watch him receive the DFM from the King. But as we all know in war; 'time and tide waits for no man' plus the visible pleasure, written all over the Sisters face, was some compensation. The time for Jack's release was clearly approaching, when the sister finds him playing cricket in the ward using, a rolled up newspaper as a bat and bread rolls for a ball. "Clear this mess up at once she orders" everyone jumps to obey. "You Mr Spark are going home" she informs me as I whisk her off her feet, giving her a big kiss at the same time.

A few weeks leave, being pampered by mum, enjoying her home cooking and going for a pint, with my dad. Life is becoming a lot better for Jack, he is starting to walk much easier plus outings with Jean have raised his spirits. My time at 14 M.U. fly's by, then in late 1946, people are being demobbed in large numbers, though Jack is hoping to stay in the RAF. However, due to his back injury, plus the large pool of people the RAF have to pick from, he finds he is being released back into Civvy Street. He applies for and gets a job as an assistant manager at Jackson's the Tailors in Carlisle in 1947. His courtship of Jean Campbell continues, they become engaged. In the summer of 1948 they are married in Carlisle; his best man is an old school friend Jack Caruthers. After a short Honeymoon they move in with Jacks parents, while they search for a home of their own. Houses are in very short supply after the war so they start saving to buy a house if one becomes available.

Sitting at home one night, Jack is visited by his friend Jack Caruthers an Engineer who has been called out to fix some faulty pumping machinery. The pumping station is out in the country so he asks Jack to come with him for company. They drive out into the wilds where his pal looks at the equipment and soon fixes the problem. Setting out for home they stop off for at a country pub for a swift pint. Leaving the Pub later, a man and woman are standing outside, they ask for a lift back into Carlisle having missed the last Bus. As they set off for home Jack is chatting to his pal who is driving them back to Carlisle. Into the dark night they go, then as they round a sharp bend the car runs into the back of an unlit, broken down truck. Another motorist comes across the accident; he summons an ambulance and the three men are transported to hospital.

The woman just disappears into the night leaving behind one shoe like a modern day Cinderella. She was sat behind me in the car and of course seatbelts had not been invented yet. So in the crash she was thrown forward into me, I went through the windscreen. Jack suffers lacerations to his head needing over thirty stitches to the scalp, fortunately in the hair line which will not show when they have healed. (Though now in his eighties with receding hair it is becoming visible once again). I remember coming round in the hospital as a nurse was finishing the stitching she had a badge on her uniform. "Doncaster Royal Infirmary", I said out loud. "What am I doing in Doncaster", "Your not, came the reply I have just moved to Carlisle so I am waiting for a new uniform. At least you're not suffering from concussion". All three of them are now admitted to the hospital, they have been allocated beds in the same ward. Then at visiting time the man they had given a lift to is visited by his wife and mother in-law. The wife is not the woman from the Pub, so the Mother in-law spends visiting hour quizzing Jack about the night of the accident. Not wanting to get involved Jack diplomatically claims he can remember nothing of the incident. When he is finally released from Hospital, Jack goes back to work throwing himself into his life back in Civvy Street.

It was about this time I received a letter from my old skipper Fred Browning he has set up his electrical business in Worthing again, he has also married his girlfriend Florence Parrott. They have set up home in Worthing, they are expecting their first child, he extends an open invitation for both of us to visit whenever we can. I write, congratulating them both on their marriage and the good news about their baby, but I am afraid a visit will have to wait awhile.

Then one day, Jack hears of a house about to come on to the market, with his wife rushes to view it before someone else can snap it up. The property is a double fronted cottage on the Kingstown Rd for the princely sum of £300 ($1200), It has stone floors with only one bedroom. By today's first time buyer's standards, it was not much to look at, but after the war, we were thankful to find anything. With the help of a schoolmate who is now a brick layer, Jack spends his spare time labouring for his friend to extend the cottage. It quickly grows as an extra bedroom along with a bigger kitchen; I have never worked so hard in all my life. Every muscle in my body ached at the end of each day, but the sight of our efforts growing in front of my eyes was wonderful. Settling in with his wife in their first home, he feels he is finally getting back into civilian life. In the 1950's Jack buys his first car a used Ford 8, this car is already fifteen years old.

New cars are still very expensive and in short supply, as everything that is being made in the country is for export, not for home consumption. Then out of the blue in 1958 Jack is appointed Manager of his own shop in South Shields on the opposite side of the country. In this old car Jack travels the 90 miles each way to Tyneside every week to run his new shop. It was a long journey in those days there were no motorways, the only road is the A69 Military Road which was just a single track. I remember that I always carried a 5 gallon tin of oil in the boot, my old car was reliable but it burnt oil at quite a rate. Once on the road I could buzz along at a fair old speed with no one able to overtake me mainly due to the cloud of smoke coming from the exhaust. When he arrives at South Shields there is an air of tension, as the resident assistant manager is resentful, at not being appointed manager. Sometime later however, he confides in Jack that he was not really ready for the responsibility, he quickly becomes my right hand man. Having settled in Jack spends some time in South Shields, looking for a permanent place to live. He brings his wife Jean with him, together they choose a house in Newlands Road, Cleadon Village on the outskirts of South Shields.

Their old house is put on the market; it sells quickly so the contents are promptly loaded into a removal van to be transported to our new house. Here they set about building a new life in the North East of England. Together they start laying out the garden of this new home, to create a haven of peace they can both enjoy after a long days work. Jean is also busy organising the décor for their new home, after the privation of the post war period. It's nice to have a choice when buying things in the department stores. Jacks new shop is also growing, there is plenty of work in the area, he is steadily building a list of regular clients, life is starting to look good in South Shields.

Then in September 1959 Jack is telephoned at work by his family from Carlisle, there has been an accident involving his parents. They are both in hospital seriously ill, Jack and Jean rush back to Harraby. When they arrive the full horror of what has happened is plain to see, both parents have be run down by a motor car.

My 74 year old mother Ellen has massive head injuries; she had taken the brunt of the impact with the car. My father 77 year old Matthew was also hit by the car, although his injuries are less, they are still life threatening. Jack and Jean spend days moving between his parent's bedsides, but on the 30th September Ellen Spark loses her fight for life. Jack and Jean are devastated but have to continue to hope for Mathew who is still unconscious. For another 6 weeks they sit by his bedside to pray, but sadly he succumbs to pneumonia and passes away on the 10th November 1959. We all realise we will have to face the death of our parents, but to lose both of them so brutally, is just unbearable. Our family and friends gather round to support both of us; relatives take over the organisation of the funerals. Over the next few weeks, there is a multitude of thing to organise. Then when it is all over, we return home to South Shields, still in a state of shock at what had happened.

Trying to come to terms with his loss Jack throws himself into his work, to repay the company for their understanding at this time. Jacksons my employers gave me as much time off as I needed; there was never any pressure on me, to return to work. Slowly we begin to rebuild our lives as Jean continues to turn our house into a home. Around us the world is changing, the era of the swinging sixties is here. The young people of Britain have a new found wealth with a zest for living, the clothing industry is booming. On a Saturday I am measuring over a hundred suits, with the new Italian styles doing very well. Things are improving at work, so I decide it's time for a few changes we buy our first new car, a Ford Prefect. We use it for outings and holidays in this country, life is becoming good again. Trips across to Carlisle though, to see Jeans parents in Harraby are a difficult time for me, I lived across the road with my parents. But there are new people in our old house, it's not the same anymore, life is moving on.

Some of our trips to Carlisle we use to visit Alston we meet up with my old pal Dennis Langhorne and his wife Cecilia. After the war Dennis went back to College to train as a Pharmacist. He finally qualified at Heriot-Watt College Edinburgh, as had his wife during the war. They had both originally moved to Gainsborough in Lincolnshire where they worked together. Then in 1949 they moved back to Carlisle running their own Pharmacy in Harraby. Finally they moved to Jack's family home town of Alston where they still own the Local Chemists. Jack and Dennis have continued to keep in touch over the years often meeting in Hexham with their wives for lunch. Things are so good in South Shields, our shop is doing a roaring trade, but I still take time to enjoy, what we have worked for. Thursday is my day off so with Jean I start to explore the Northumbrian country side. As we tour round the area, I begin to notice the wonderful rivers and lakes, this is good fishing country.

One of my regular customers is Bill Wilkinson, a local police man who is also a keen angler; he introduces me to one of the local lakes where he is a member. There is nothing to compare with fishing for unwinding the stresses of the working day, Bill is also good company. He introduces me to the joys of golf, at first it's just the odd round with business friends. To my great surprise, I find I have an aptitude for the game, so I join the South Shields Golf Club. Here I meet up with other local business men to get involved with the charitable organisations, in the area. One of these is Probus, a group dedicated to raising money for local or national charities. Jean is also getting involved, helping me with the charity work; we are quite busy, becoming part of the community.

Cleadon village where we live is a very picturesque little place, there are a number of nice pubs with plenty of restaurants to enjoy a meal. We are also not far from the coast, with its good stretches of sandy beaches where we can walk, to blow away the cobwebs. It was in 1961, that I noticed Jean was becoming tired very quickly, after a few weeks the condition is getting worse. A trip to the doctors, revealed a problem with her kidneys for which she was prescribed medication. But as the months went by the condition worsened then in 1963 Jean was rushed into Newcastle Royal Victoria Infirmary. Here she sadly passed away aged only 41 years, Jack was devastated, in the last four years he had lost both his parents, now his wife. My wife's parents and her sister came over from Carlisle to give me support, but I began to feel there was a curse on me. They stayed for a while to help me, but in the end I realised there was no easy answer, I have to start getting on with my life.

Work again provides a distraction for me, somehow I found myself involved with the Cleadon Village players. At this local but well established theatrical group, I began helping out back stage, painting scenery or moving props between acts. There was even one or two appearances on stage as a butler or the like, handing out drinks but little in the way of dialogue.

Golf became another outlet to throw myself into, I played as often as I could then when I wasn't, I had a fishing rod in my hand. Slowly I am coming to terms with living on my own. With the shop running like a well oiled machine, trade continues to pick up nicely; I found life was at least settling back into a routine. During the week the assistant manager and the other assistants are left to measure customers to gain experience. In the background Jack is keeping a watching eye on his staff offering advice or guidance when required. Then on a Friday and Saturday Jack comes into his own, nobody can match him at measuring people for suits. He also built up a customer base of regulars; South Shields was a busy port in those days. The ships Captain's or Officers would call in for suits, with money no object for these discerning customers. We would keep a special book for these regulars, with all their measurements recorded for later use. There would often be letters in the post from a foreign port from an Officer asking for a suit to be made up for them. They would specify a date when the ship would be docking in South Shields so they would call in for the suit.

One local businessman was a good customer, he would order a couple of suits a year, arriving on his own for measuring. Then one day he arrived with his new wife, this lady was from Germany, and she would moan about everything. Her husband would look at me then, just beam that smile of resignation, all we married men know. On one occasion they arrived, I started to go through his cloth option for his new suit. He had selected a cloth but his wife did not like it or much of the others he chose, she commented, "We have a much better choice in Stuttgart". It was at this point I queried "Ah! You are from Stuttgart", "Yes" she replied "You have been to Stuttgart". I replied "I have been there on three occasions, but found the local people, not very friendly". "Probably because we were dropping bombs on them, so they would not be"; she sat down to not speak another word. After that her husband came for his suits on his own, I think he was as relieved as I was.

The new year of 1965, was a turning point for me in many ways some good, some not so good. Because of my Probus charity work I would be often spend time talking to the manager of 'Boots the Chemists' organising events. One day I was looking for the manager but ended up talking to one of his female buyers, from the cosmetics section of the shop. Over the next few weeks, we passed the time of day, on a number of occasions, but it was her manager that mentioned one day that she was single. Dorothy was tall dark haired and very good looking; eventually I plucked up courage to asked if she would like to go out for a drink. To my surprise she accepted, over time we became regular visitors to local restaurants or theatres. As we became close, I found she had two brothers, Billy who was a policeman and Darly who worked for the Inland Revenue (IRS). But this did not deter me, as on Saturday 10th July 1965 Jack married Dorothy (Jack was 42 Dorothy was 37).

It will come as a shock to people in today's enlightened times, but Dorothy as a married woman could no longer work at Boots the Chemist. Company policy dictated that they only employed single ladies; though the men could be married. How the world has changed. This new start for both of us included a move to a new bungalow in Mill Grove South Shields, which was built on the side of the Cleadon Hills. I could always find my way back to our new home, as behind it on the hill top stood, 'Cleadon Tower'. This Victorian Chimney is over one hundred feet tall (30m) it was part of a water pumping station. It could be seen from anywhere within a five mile radius. Our new home had one other advantage; we were only five minutes from South Shields Golf Club. I was never a gardener but Dorothy loved it, I helped or should say I did the heavy lifting or digging if pushed. Over time the garden became a riot of colour which was a credit to Dorothy's efforts.

The 9th August 1965 is burned into my memory forever, the morning started out as usual with the arrival of the Assistant Manager at 08:45am. Wilf Alderson opened up the shop for the staff and put the kettle on for a brew of tea; at 09:00am I arrived to the greeted by the assistants. I walked across to my office to sort through the morning mail, then to organise the day ahead. At 10:00am I left the shop to talk to the Manager of 'Boots the Chemists' next door. I had been gone about fifteen minutes, when our shop junior came rushing up to me "Mr Spark the shops on fire". Calming him down I said "All right young man, I am coming now", thinking it was just a fire in a waste bin. I followed him back to the shop to find it full of smoke with a lot of flames from the store room at the back. I ushering the staff outside, before rushing into my office, to grab the accounts books and measurements records. As we stood on the pavement, the fire brigade arrived to start tackling the growing blaze. I then found one of my assistants, had received burns to his hands and face.

When the ambulance people arrived, they attended to his injuries outside the shop, before transporting him to hospital for treatment. Despite the best efforts of the fire brigade, the shop was completely gutted so I report the situation back to head office. They authorised me to find temporary premises, as quickly as possible. After a thorough examination of the scene, the fire brigade attributed the fire to a faulty heater in the store room. Our local press had a field day at my expense; I remember the Shields Gazette had a headline which read. "The day Mr Spark wished he was called Smith or Jones or anything, other than Spark". I did not let this phase me though; I had to concentrate on finding alternative premises to trade from. Fortunately there was an empty shop in Fredrick Street, a little further out from the existing shop, in what is known locally as the Arab quarter.

These temporary premises will suffice until the old shop is rebuilt. South Shields has been a busy Sea Port, with a diverse spread of people from many parts of the world since the 1880's. This area for the shop has become well known, for its Middle East and Asian restaurants, with their wonderful array of foods on offer. The temporary shop has become established doing well in fact, but Jack was watching the new shop rise from the ashes of the old one. As he prepared to reopen this new shop, tragedy was to rear its head once again. Jacks assistant manager, Wilf Alderson was working at the Fredrick Street shop; he was a keen follower of horse racing. This particular day, he hit a winning streak winning a large amount of money. After work he went to collect his winning, then out on the town to celebrate. In the morning, his lifeless body was found behind the Black Prince Pub in the town, his substantial winnings were missing. Sometime later, a local man was arrested to be charged with his murder. After a long trial, he was found guilty then sent to prison. At times like this I wonder what is wrong with our community, here was a hard working young man just trying to make his way in the world. Then without warning he is gone, this is not what we fought the war for, it is such a waste of a life.

Sunday morning and I am up early, Dorothy is going to her green bowling club with friends. So, Bill Wilkinson is picking me up in half an hour to go fishing at Hallington Reservoir. It is only an hour's drive to the lake; we are both looking forward to a good days sport. The sun is up by the time we arrive as there are only a few cars in the parking area, we will have the pick of the best pitches. Standing on the bank, there is not a sound, other than the birds singing, or the occasional moan of cows in the fields. At first I am content to just get my casting arm warmed up, but an unexpected strike brings that feeling of success. I quickly net the trout then continue to cast keeping an eye open for movement of the fish coming to the surface. Bill is standing a little way to my left; he gives me the thumbs up at my early success. Sadly there follows two hours of famine, but the fish are still feeding, as Bill has pulled in what looks like a big one. We continue until lunch time when we both stop, to eat our sandwiches and take a drink of tea, from the thermos flasks. The early sun has given way to light cloud so I slip my sunglasses into my pocket. A breeze is also getting up, as the afternoon progresses, with no further sign of catching another fish. Hoping to change my luck I move my position on the bank to try casting into a different area. As I bring my rod back over my shoulder the line flicks back and forth across the water as I look for a likely spot to hit.

Suddenly a gust of wind catches me in mid cast, I feel my line snake across my face, instinctively I close my eyes. Then a stinging pain in my left eye makes me shout out with the shock. It takes all my concentration not to touch the eye as I know that can only make things worse. As I slump to the ground on the bank my pal Bill arrives, he takes a look at the damage. The hook has gone through the lower eyelid, but does not appear to have touched the eye, but I can now feel the feathers of the tied fly irritating my eyelid. Other anglers have gathered round, as Bill quickly snips the line attached to the hook. Then we slowly walk back to the car, our fishing gear will be packed up by the other members of the angling club. When we arrive at the Hospital A and E a doctor takes a close look at the injury, before I know what is happening the hook is snipped in two and removed. Thankfully the eye is only bruised so should recover in a day or two, but the doctor asks why I was not wearing glasses. He then proceeds to gives me a well deserved lecture, on the number of people he has treated, for this type of injury. My air force training has taught me to sit, listen and say nothing, until he has finished, I then thanked him profusely before heading back to the lake. As we drive home Bill says he thought the doctor was a bit harsh, but I am thinking, it's nothing to what Dorothy will say, when she sees me. From that day on I always wore some type of eye protection when I went fly fishing, as did Bill.

Year 1979

The world of tailoring is changing rapidly, suits sales are shrinking rapidly, people are adopting a more casual dress. In response Burtons have adapted to meet this demand as the shop in South Shields stocks up with a range of Jeans and casual shirts. Although the mass market side of the business is changing the company realise there will always be a demand for suits. In response to this Jack is asked to take over a bespoke shop in Shields to satisfy this demand. In his new position Jack feels the stress of running the high street shop diminish, He has a steady supply of regulars to keep the business profitable, life is becoming more relaxed. Unbeknown to Jack at this time, miles away from Tyneside the RAF Elsham Wolds association was being formed.

The Shields shop is doing well I am still enjoying my work; the bespoke side of the business is very fulfilling. The interaction with the customers is so good compared with off the peg sales. Here the customers just call in pick up a pair of jeans, pay then leave with very little communication. But I suppose this is how the world wants to shop and it pays the bills for the company so we have to accept the way it is. There are again changes in Jacks world when in 1982 he is asked to take over the running of the Sunderland Burtons Shop. This again is the bespoke side of the business which is in need of his magic touch to boost flagging sales. Throwing his full efforts into this new challenge he quickly achieves an improvement much to his relief he has not lost his touch.

During 1983 the War Years resurface as Jack is contacted by Alan Cooper who is in the process of writing a book about the Berlin raids. The book is to tell the full story of the assault on the German capital and is to be called "Bombers over Berlin". A lengthy interview follows in which Jack relives the night of the 24th March 1944. This story is included in the final edition of the book published in the January 1985.

Life is good, but Jack is aware of his advancing years. Then in 1986 his is offered the chance of early retirement. His long service with the company is much appreciated so his final settlement is a generous package. Retirement is a strange thing; it is always approached with some trepidation, as any major event in life is. But eventually the reality of relaxing with Dorothy to enjoy life without having to march to someone else's beat sounds great. In April 1986 Jack aged 63 retires. We have been happy in our home in Cleadon Village but Dorothy has spotted a new house which is closer to her family. This new place in Wardley Gateshead is smaller than our present bungalow but is quite big enough for our needs. So in 1989 we up sticks to move, hopefully this will be for the last time, meanwhile we have the new garden to reorganise.

For a number of years now Jack had been a member of the Air Crew Association. From his friends there he hears of the existence of the

Elsham Wolds Association. He quickly makes contact with Shirley Westrupp, to become a member. In letters to his Canadian Crew mates he passes on the news, with both Norman and Ron follow him in joining. My first visit to the Elsham Wolds Reunion in 1991 was a revelation; I had of course received the weekend itinerary. The Saturday morning was just listed as tea with cakes at Shirley's house. I remember following the road to the house that morning, then being surprised to see a large field allocated for parking. In this field there were already thirty or so cars. Her garden was filled with lots of old people like myself; some of whom I recognised others only when they introduced themselves. Shirley herself was the Secretary of the Association, who had been a WAAF driver at Elsham Wolds. That day was the start of one of the best weekends I have had for a long, long time. For the Saturdays evening's Reunion Dinner more Veterans had arrived during the day. The meal was excellent then, we had the opportunity to sit, exchange stories swop photos with people I had not seen for nearly fifty years. There was also a few glasses of beer involved.

Returning home from the Elsham Wolds Reunion in 1993 Jack stopped to refuel his car then grab a bite to eat. As he stood on the forecourt of the filling station, he was surprised to hear the sound of a four engine aircraft approaching. To his astonishment, a B17 Flying Fortress flew over at no more than five hundred feet. His mind immediately went back to the Dunsfold crash with the 'Passionate Witch', one question came to him. I wonder if any of its crew survived the war. On his return home he perused the entry in his flying log book of the Dunsfold accident. The thoughts of the American crew would not go away, so he contacted the U.S. Embassy in London. There a very polite young man listened, as Jack recounted his tale of the B17 crash in WW2, which he promised to investigate. Three weeks later, Jack had started to think they would not be able to find the information; after all it was almost fifty years ago. But to his amazement one evening the telephone rang, the same man apologised for the delay.

He then informed Jack about the sheer number of aircraft called the 'Passionate Witch'. The best solution he suggested was to write to the 8th Air force records office in Iowa for which he provided an address and phone number. Then he joked, "Mr Spark we have been looking for you since 1944, we have a bill for the B17 you wrecked". To my utter amazement, the cost he quoted was almost $240,000, but they did not expect payment. At first this seemed an inordinate amount of money for a Flying Fortress. Later I realised that back in 1944 a Pound was worth about four Dollars, so in real terms a B17 cost £60,000, not much more than a Lancaster. As I did not want to wait I promptly phoned the number he provided and spoke to one of their personnel who took details of my query. A few weeks went by without any news, then another call brought forth the news Jack had been waiting for, the B17 was part of the 452nd Bombardment group.

There were three survivors from the crew of ten, the Pilot, one of the gunners then low behold the Radio operator. Unfortunately they had no forwarding address for any of them, Jacks heart sank, It's another dead end. However, the voice continued, this group has an Association based in Richmond Virginia for which he had an address he suggests I write to a Mr Whitte there. Over the next few days I penned a letter to the American Association with a brief account of the Dunsfold Crash and my search for the crew of the B17. It was a cold March day in 1994; as I arrived home from work, Dorothy greeted me with, "Who do you know in California". A large envelope, with a U.S. post mark plus a 452nd Bomb Group sticker on it, set my pulse racing. Inside was the latest newsletter from the U.S. association. Part of it was given over to my story about the "Passionate Witch" crash and my search for the crew; it sadly brought forth no replies. The summer of 1994 saw the first visit by one of my Canadian crew members Norman Barker; he was here for the Reunion in August. Dorothy and I showed him the sights of the North East of England which he really enjoyed seeing. Then at the August bank holiday Norman gets his first taste of an Elsham Reunion.

He was totally overjoyed, meeting with people he remembered on the station during 1944. Chatting with ground crew including the Motor Transport WAAF's, he was rejuvenated. Later in September all three of us travelled to London for a short holiday, which included a trip to the RAF Hendon Museum. The sight of the Lancaster standing proudly on display was just what these two Vets needed to complete a memorable visit. He promised to return another year with Ron Walker and all their wives. As I stood looking into one of the display cases, I became aware of two people standing by my side. The young man asked about my connection with the RAF, he seemed delighted to hear I was a Bomber Command Vet. He introduced himself as Adrian he was visiting England with his wife Ingrid from the Netherlands. Adrian van Zantvoort to give him his full title was a member of the Air War Study group in Holland, he had a million questions to ask. He left a deep impression on Jack so before the end of the day they exchanged addresses promising to keep in touch. True to his word, Adrian wrote back when he returned home with numerous letters being exchanged about Jack's time in Bomber Command.

In the February of 1995 Jack attended his annual medical check up with old friend Dr Brumby. Here he is informed that he has become Diabetic so he will have to be careful with his diet to control it. This has one benefit in that Jack's weight falls by 10 Kilo's to 81 Kilo's which improves his mobility. The 7th May see's the 50th Anniversary of V.E. Day. In memory of the day, Jack joins a large contingent of Veterans from all branches of the armed services at Newcastle Cathedral. Here they hold a Service of Remembrance followed by a Parade through the Streets of the City.

On the 22nd June Jack revisits the Diabetic clinic where he is warned not to overdo it on his forthcoming holiday to Torremolinos on the 29th. The end of June arrives with Dorothy and Jack heading for Newcastle Airport to fly out to Spain for a two week break. At the Hotel the facilities were tremendous, a sumptuous room, an open air pool with a bar plus the restaurant has a great menu. Our days are spent sitting by the pool soaking up the sun, though Dorothy makes sure I watch my intake of the food and drink. Every day we spend time wandering around the local sights to provide me with exercise as a means of burning off the excess calories. The break is very welcome, the predictable weather a bonus, then just as we are getting used to it all, it's time to return home, Hey Ho. Arriving back from Spain Jack finds a letter from the local hospital. For eight months he had been waiting for an operation on his right hand to cure a contracting tendon. This has caused two fingers to curl toward the palm making the holding of a golf club almost impossible. He is booked in for the 25th July but should be discharged the following day. In meanwhile I have been invited to give a talk to the Newcastle Aero Club on Bomber Commands air war.

The talk was well received; it even results in a flight in one of the clubs light aircraft. Dorothy decided not to join me, "If it does not have a drinks trolley you can count me out" she comments.

The 20th August 1995 saw Adrian and Ingrid visit Britain, in particular the Yorkshire Dales, before eventually travelling to Edinburgh. On route they called in to visit Jack and Dorothy. Jack proudly shows Adrian the local Sunderland Air Museum even managing to arrange a visit to the Air Sea Rescue station at Boulmer on the Northumbrian coast.

Saturday of the August Bank holiday weekend, Dorothy and Jack travel to the Elsham Reunion. The guest speaker this year is to be Don Charlwood from Australia. Don was a Navigator with 103 Squadron during the war, who wrote two classic books about his time at RAF Elsham Wolds. His first "No Moon Tonight" has become the must read work on Bomber Command. He later follows it up with "Journey's into Night". As a writer Don has managed to capture the very essence of a Bomber Station and the people who served there. His talk on the Saturday night after Dinner was both informative but reflective. Australia has now become a multicultural country. But the new arrivals; do not have that same affinity with the old commonwealth, that Don's fellow servicemen had during the war. As he travelled to schools to give talks to the young people there, he finds he is in for a shock. They question why we were involved in a foreign conflict; sadly I don't think they would have understood my answers. Sunday morning we were up on the old airfield, for a service of remembrance finishing off with the finale, a flypast by the Lancaster. She came sweeping up the valley, making the sound that only four Rolls Royce Merlin engines can make, truly awe inspiring the crew gave us three low passes before leaving to visit another venue.

It's now the 5th September the operation I had on my hand is improving. Hopefully I will be able to play golf soon, but fishing this year finishes on the 31st October so I may miss that target. In the meantime I have content myself with watching Dorothy play indoor green bowls with her ladies club. Over the last few months I have been busy communicating with my friend Adrian in Holland. He is searching for families of aircrew, from Bomber crash sites discovered in the Netherlands. These volunteers are building a memorial to the memory of these aircrews who died helping to liberate their country. I find the work of these fine young people very uplifting, they represent everything we fought for.

Sunday the 30th October, tomorrow is the last day of the fishing season. So with my pal Bill Wilkinson I set off to the lake one last time, I'm glad I did. Just as the day is drawing to a close I get a bite to land as 5 Lb 4 Oz Rainbow Trout, my best catch of the season. Bill will be the one who will get the pleasure of eating it that night. Now with the onset of winter, I will have to rely on Golf for my recreation, weather permitting. Early in December I received a letter from Adrian inviting Dorothy and I to visit Holland next year and stay with them. In my reply I accept, but have to say we are both going to Canada in June for four weeks. We have been promising for a long time to visit my crew mates to see some of their country. The year comes to an end with our usual Xmas and New Year celebrations with Dorothy's extended family. I love these family gatherings, they remind me of the Christmas's I had as a kid back in Harraby.

It's the first week in March 1996, our Aircrew Association in Shields has organised a five day trip to Scotland. There are twenty five of our members plus their wives on the coach. We are going across to the west coast to Oban, Fort William, Isle of Mull then finally to Inverness. Oban brings back memories of my childhood when as a family I travelled this area with my parents. The towns have changed a lot since those days but the scenery has not, it's spectacular.

Saturday 16th March and Jack is visiting Elvington air museum near York. Today there will be a talk by General Leutnant Gunther Rall of the German Air Force. This German Ace flew in the Battle of Britain then later on the Russian front. His final posting was to defend Germany in the closing months of the war against the incoming bombers both day

212

and night. He has 275 kills to his name mostly on the Eastern front; he himself was shot down on eight occasions. This last of these was by an American fighter which resulted in him being taken prisoner, by the advancing Americans. It was a very interesting talk from a remarkable man who was very lucky to survive. Later in the evening I found myself in his company so I asked where he was on the night of 24th March 1944. "Why" he asked, "Where were you, Over Berlin in a Lancaster" I replied, "Getting seven bells knocked out of us by a night fighter". We both laughed "Fortunately he said it was not me, thank goodness I was fighting in France in 44". It was good I thought, to be here forty years later with no trace of animosity toward a fellow flyer, who was doing his job at the time.

Its Saturday the 30th March 1996, I am travelling with four other members of the Northumbrian branch of the Air Crew Association to Elvington again. Today they are unveiling a reconstructed Halifax bomber appropriately called Friday the 13th. This Halifax flew a hundred and twenty eight raids with 158 Squadron from Lisset during the war. She was displayed for a short time at Oxford Street, London in 1945 then cruelly sent to a scrap yard. The fuselage was found in the Outer Hebrides (Scotland), the wings were salvaged from a Hasting passenger aircraft. The engines were donated by the French Air force with the tail wheel assembly being found in a field near Paris. Quite a jigsaw of bits but the finished job was spectacular. There were three thousand present with a number of veterans from Canada who flew with 158 Squadron. They even had the Canadian High Commissioner to do the honours, a memorable day for everyone.

In late April we receive a letter from Adrian with the news that Ingrid has given birth to a boy who they have named Colin. I immediately phone them at home in Holland, we both congratulate them it's great news. He also asks if Dorothy and I would come to visit them in Holland. In response Jack and Dorothy travel to Holland in June they are delighted to see the new baby Colin. Dorothy has brought a few presents for the new baby one of which is a Peter Rabbit door plaque. One surprise for Jack is Adrian's Research room. Here there are scores of letters asking for help about relatives lost over Holland during the war. This dedicated young man is carefully researching the details provided to find the complete details of the circumstances of their family loss. Now it's Adrian's chance to show them the places of interest. There were visits to safe houses with the opportunity to meet families, who had hidden RAF air crew shot down during the war. They visited Rotterdam, Amsterdam, Maastricht then Bruges in Belgium, the shock for Jack was the reaction of people in Holland. As a Veteran of Bomber Command they held him in the highest regard, they talk to him about stories of "Operation Manna". This was the period toward the end of April 1945. The Germans were retreating, taking with them all of the food in Holland. As a consequence the Dutch people were slowly starving; they had resorted to eating the flower bulbs to survive. When Britain realised what was happening, they organised food drops, using Lancaster's and Halifax bombers. These flew at low level with the bomb bays full of loosely bagged bread, flour, all the staple foods that would sustain the people.

Germany was warned that these food drops would take place. They were also told that any attempt to stop them by firing on these aircraft would result in war crime charges on those responsible. Crowds of people stood in the fields of Holland to pick up the food being dropped by the RAF and the USAAF aircraft. Returning crews talked with immense pride plus a few tears at seeing the roofs of houses on which locals had painted two words in English "Thank You". The Dutch have never forgotten this act of kindness; they teach it to the children in school, who help to look after the graves of those flyers who never left Holland.

In few weeks it will be Adrian's birthday, Jack has a surprise for him. He hands over his WW2 Irvin flying jacket that he wore on operations; the smile on Adrian's face says everything. During this visit Adrian learned of Jacks attempt to find the crew of the "Passionate Witch" so he decides to help with his own search. Through his contacts in Holland, England and America he set about finding the crew for Jack. To his great surprise he managed to find the Skipper of the B17, Robert Cook. He was interested in Adrian's quest though he had not seen the other two surviving crew members since the war, but promised to help find them.

On returning home Jack has to see a consultant about a recurring problem with his right hand. His grip with the index finger is failing which makes playing golf difficult. The specialist thinks he can loosen the knuckle joint without having to operate again. He also informs me that my age (74 now) has a lot to do with it. "My hearing is not getting any better either, apparently listening to four Merlin engines, hours on end has taken its toll. I wonder when that happened, Ha Ha."

My membership of the Northumbrian Branch of the Aircrew association results this year in my being seconded onto the Committee. My new title is the Publicity and Welfare Officer, wow I have to keep in touch with members who are in poor health. Though to be honest with my Diabetes, associated eye problems and deafness, maybe I should be one of those to be receiving help. Well winter is coming so Dorothy and I have booked a few days holiday in Wales. Our trip is based at a hotel in Chester then we will have days out visiting places of interest around Wales. The weather is kind; we see Llandudno and Llangollen at their best. We have never been to North Wales before, unless you consider my getting lost over the mountains in 1944 at twenty five thousand feet as visiting. In places it's a bit like the Lake District only more spectacular. It's been a great trip which has refreshed us both. October is coming to an end; I have been searching for information on a flight engineer friend of mine with no luck.

In an attempt to resolve it I ring me old pal Jack Currie. To my surprise his wife Kate answers the phone then, she stuns me with the news that Jack had passed away on the 19th, my birthday. This news completely takes my breath away. I have to sit down to continue the conversation. Kate tells me he suffered a massive heart attack; we talk for a long time, I can only offer my condolences which seems so inadequate. When I eventually come off the phone Dorothy is concerned at my appearance, I tell her about my sad news. He was a great man, who wrote a number of excellent books about bomber command, one of which he signed for me included an apology for the incident over the hedge, he will be greatly missed.

George and Betty on Holiday

It was at this time that George and Betty have decided to take a Holiday to Europe; they book a cruise around the Mediterranean. They flew from California to New York then on to Heathrow in London. "What a pity we had not come into contact with Jack at this time, we could have made a visit to him and Dorothy, but as they say C'est La Guerre". From London we flew to Athens to pick up our ship. We had a great time touring the Greek Islands and the rest of the Mediterranean; It was something special for the both of us. Then as a finale we sail through the straits of Gibraltar out into the Atlantic to end our trip in Lisbon, Portugal. It was a poignant moment for me, to visit the country where my father had been born.

Back home in Wardley Jack continues his association with the local snooker club on Thursday evenings. In the winter of 1996 he has a good run in the annual competition as he succeeds in winning the Club Members Trophy. He also continues his love of fishing spending many weekends with his pal Bill Wilkinson. Winter 1996 comes; it's a cold one that seems to go on for a long time. Eventually spring arrives; Dorothy and I are off to the South coast for a few days break in Folkestone at the end of April. We have outings to Canterbury to see the Cathedral; there were plenty of shops to keep Dorothy happy. On one of the trips out I spot a road signpost which reads Maidstone. I remembered that's where our rear Gunner Bert Berrill came from before the war. That evening in the Hotel I found a Maidstone Telephone book, low and behold there was a B Berrill listed. I took the chance to ring the number, a woman answered. I said I was looking for a Bert Berrill who was a gunner in a Lancaster bomber during the war. "My Bert was a gunner in the RAF would you like to speak to him" she replied. "Yes I said would you ask him if he knows a Jack Spark". A very excited man came on the phone "Is that you Jack". We spent the next hour talking about what had happened since the end of the war. I also promised that we should get together some time in the future.

Back home in Wardley I was reading a book about 617 Squadron (Dambusters) which set me thinking about my Signals chief Ron Stewart a New Zealander. At the next Aircrew Association meeting I talk to other members to find one of them is in touch with one of his crew in New Zealand. Letters are exchanged with an appeal being placed in the Ex Service magazine for Ron Stewart. A number of weeks pass; I start to think we are getting nowhere. Then to my surprise one morning a letter drops on the door mat, it's from Ron Stewart. He tells me all about his time after the war, now 76 years old he owns an ocean going yacht called 'Three Sisters'. In it he sails around New Zealand and the islands in the Southern Pacific. Sounds like he has it all organised for his retirement. We continued to correspond for a number of years with the occasional post card from some obscure island or other. There was an open offer to visit him in New Zealand to go sailing but my back and legs could not have stood the 23 hour flight. Actually Ron was the one who recommended me for my DFM and for a commission. Both of which came through after I left the Squadron. Well I had another surprise this week with a letter from Ken Smart our mid upper gunner. He had been in touch with Bert Berrill who gave him my address; he is keen to arrange a meeting of the three of us. I write back agreeing to work out a meeting date as soon as we get back from Canada.

It's now August 97; Adrian has arrived with his family by ferry from Holland. The next few days are spent travelling around the North of England. We visit the Lake District which must come as a change from the flat land of Holland. Then while Dorothy takes Ingrid and Colin shopping in Newcastle I take Adrian to RAF Boulmer an old WW2 airfield. It is now home to 202 Squadron a Helicopter search and rescue unit; we are shown round by F/Lt Sue Ashton the Liaison Officer. I also have a surprise for Adrian; a few years ago I gave him my Irvin flying jacket. From an aircrew friend I have been given the matching trousers to make up the complete suit, Adrian is delighted. Then after a few days Adrian, Ingrid and Colin have to continue on their trip south to Lincolnshire then onto Norfolk. He is looking to add to his knowledge of lost aircrew he is researching, a very dedicated young man.

Now we spend a few days relaxing before we have to start packing for our visit to Canada to visit my crew mates. Having flow on holiday before I have taken the trouble to book Club Class this time, it is so worth it. Plush seats with plenty of leg room plus tea and biscuits at 35 thousand feet; it was never like this in a Lancaster. Canada what a country, we are staying with Ron Walker who is now 81; Dorothy and I are made to feel like one of the family.

After a day of rest we meet up with Norman and Margaret Barker he is 82 then it's off to see Niagara Falls. Wow, is too small a word to describe the falls, the noise it makes is something else. It's incredible to think that the water has been flowing over the edge like it does for hundreds of years. I start to realise how small our own life span is in comparison with what I am looking at. Later we all went for a bit of retail therapy for our wives; Dorothy was like a kid in a candy store. They really know how to make shopping a memorable experience in Canada. Then in the evening we all went out to dinner, another treat for us. Dress was more casual than we would do in the UK with the choice of dishes mind boggling, as were the prices. The next two weeks were a blur of large city vistas then spectacular views of wild forests or huge lakes. All I could think of was the fish there must be in the rivers and lakes all free for the taking. Sadly the trip is coming to an end, I start to realise this may be the last time I will see my old crew mates.

At the airport on our day of departure there are a few tears, but a firm commitment to keep writing. On the flight home Dorothy and I talk about this visit, what a memorable time it has been for us both. Over the years I have been corresponding with both of the air gunners from the crew. We have always promised to meet up, but it has never happened. Then in January 1998 Ken Smart and Bert Berrill contacted me to arrange a meeting in the Railway Tavern outside Kings Cross Station in London. Early on Saturday morning I catch the train from Newcastle and arrived in London just before lunch. There waiting for me on the platform are two men from my youth, Fifty three years had changed them. But the young men I knew from the war were still there inside. The pub served up a wonderful lunch which was followed by a few glasses of something with alcohol in it.

We spent the rest of the day exchanging photographs and stories about what had happened to each of us since the war. I relate my letter from Fred Browning a few years ago to them but sadly in the move to South Shields his address has been lost, so we have had no further contact. The only one of our crew I have not seen or heard from is Arthur Richardson our Flight engineer, he just seems to have disappeared. I inform them about the formation of the Elsham Wolds Association and how successful it had become. I promised to send them details so they could join. Then sadly it was time for me to catch the train home. Thank goodness I had a three hour train ride to sleep of my alcohol intake before I arrived home.

Received a letter from Adrian in Holland today he has details of our old Lancaster M Mother ND572. Apparently she was repaired to fly

217

for another year with 57 Squadron as DX-F. Then on 1st February she collided with a 207 Squadron Lancaster EM-N over Ruskington Lincolnshire. Both aircraft were on a training exercise. Just one of the hazards of war time flying, the sky is full of aircraft that can appear at the drop of a hat. There is never a time to totally relax your concentration.

It's now June 1998, Dorothy and Jack are off for another holiday, this time its Lake Garda then Verona in Italy. The Hotel is on the edge of the lake with a great view of the mountain in the distance. Just to be able to sit then chill out as they say, without having to think about preparing lunch or any other meals. Each morning after breakfast, we spent drinking coffee while soaking up the sun. Then we are off on one of the guided tours of our list. Verona was the most memorable with its Plaza's and Castles.

The Lamberti Tower was tremendous; the view from the top was described by the guides as spectacular. However the 300 plus steps did not appeal to Dorothy or me to be honest. So we contented ourselves to a slow casual walk around the Plaza's looking in the shops. We also took the opportunity to sample the excellent Italian Ice Cream on sale. Looking round at the architecture I could see there had been some rebuilding since the war. At times though it was difficult, to notice it immediately. I know Bomber Command did bomb Italy on many occasions but our crew was never asked to do it. In fact I can't honestly remember any Italian raids while I was at Elsham.

452nd Reunion

In the summer of 1998 Robert Cook the pilot of the Passionate Witch attended the 452nd Bomb Group annual reunion. Here to his great joy and surprise he finds his radio operator George Silva, they spent the evening recounting what had happened since Chateaudun. Fortunately Robert Cook had not forgotten his promise to Adrian van Zantvoort and that weekend he showed George Silva the letter about Jack Spark. George had joined the 452nd Bomb Group Association in 1985 but he had not seen Jacks letter printed in the 1994 newsletter. He was intrigued by Jacks story enough to make contact with him in October 1998. Jack was delighted to receive a letter especially as it came out of the blue so to speak. The icing on the cake for Jack was that George was the Radio Operator of the "Passionate Witch"

Air mail letters are exchanged between George and Jack over the next few years including photographs of our families and both their crews. Christmas and birthdays we allowed ourselves the luxury of a Trans Atlantic phone call. At the moment one of our grandchildren is staying with us, he works for Apple Computers and is working for a while at an office nearby. He was always encouraging me to get a computer, but when

218

he talks about the benefits I have very little understanding, his words are a foreign language to me. One thing about having him visit is; he starts to ask about the war time photos, I have on the wall. This gives me the opportunity to show him all of my photos, including information about my time in the POW camp. As the photo's show me with my crewmates as young men, I think he starts to see his old grandfather in a different light.

In 1999 George informs Jack of his purchase of a computer and the benefits of this more instant form of communication. Not to be left behind Jack signs up for a computer course at the local Technical college specific to Senior Citizens, he is 77. When he finally qualifies it's down to the computer shop for his first PC. Emails are sent back and forth, with details of their lives since the end of the war. Then as technology advances instant messages are exchanged. George relates his time as a P.O.W. to Jack and the forced march he was part of. At the time George made contacted Jack, he and Betty were living in Cupertino California where they moved in 1972. Later these two Veterans would advance their contact with the advent of online video communication.

Elsham Wolds Reunion

The Reunion of 1998 was to be a memorable one for all the wrong reasons. This year it was held at the "Forrest Pines Hotel" near Brigg which was a break with the tradition of using Barnetby Village Hall. At the end of the evening Shirley Westrupp, who had organised the reunion for many years made a shock announcement. RAF Elsham Wolds Association was to close forthwith. This caused an immediate uproar; an emergency meeting of members was held, they then announced that this was not going to happen. All members were informed that the reunion would take place the following August Bank holiday as usual. They thanked Shirley for her work over the years, but if it was becoming too much for her others were prepared to take over. An emergency committee was formed that night to take charge of the association, a very sad evening. During this reunion Charles Wearmouth our association President and I were talking about our time at Elsham Wolds. It was then that he mentioned a visit to Mailly le Camp in France that was taking place. This is a pilgrimage to pay our respects to the comrade who took part in the raid but did not return. When I return home I mention this to Dorothy, although she is not keen she encourages me to go, I will have to give it some thought. Life can be very coincidental at times, only a few weeks later I run into Jim Bengston in South Shields. Jim's brother was killed on the Mailly Raid, he will be going on the trip so I decide to join him.

Tonight is Wednesday 17th March 1999, I am aware that next week is the fifty fifth anniversary of the tragic Berlin Raid. The loud ringing of the phone startles me for a moment, but when I answer there is another shock for me, "Hi Jack its George Silva". He also had remembered the dates and their significances. We talked for a long time, about Berlin but also his shoot down over Chateaudun on the 28th. Somehow we got round to talking about our ailments as older people do. Thousands of miles apart in different countries we are really the same at heart. We have been exchanging voice recording by mail on a regular basis, but this phone contact is just that little bit more special. I take the opportunity to tell George of my good luck on the golf course, I have finally hit a hole in one, on one of the short holes on our local course. George congratulates me, he has not yet achieved this yet, but Betty has.

On the wall in our family room a trophy that states on 12th April 1967 on the 150yd 18th hole of a local course Betty Silva scored a hole in one. George can only hope he will get lucky one day; we play Golf at a small local course in Cupertino. We have a fixed time slot every Friday which we often play as a foursome with friends. The course is sometimes very busy with marshals hurrying us a long, when they approach our group I tell them if a wanted to run, I can stay at home to run round the block and save the $23 bucks fee. From then on they tend to leave us alone when they see us. George tells Jack he has his 11 year old grandson visiting; he cannot understand why Papa George cannot run round the yard playing soccer any more. He has been relegated to playing board games indoors. Staying in at the moment is preferable to stepping outside as the temperature is running at over 100deg F, so the air conditioning is running full time. Jack makes the comparison with England here we are lucky if the temperature in the summer reaches the high 80deg F, then jokingly asks George, "What is air conditioning".

Next day Dorothy and I are on the Ferry to Holland taking a coach trip to Brussels for a few days. We even get chance to meet up with Adrian, Ingrid and Colin, he has grown quite a lot since we last saw him. We spent the afternoon walking around the city together stopping only for food or treats for Colin. Then it's a busy few days with trips to Brussels and Waterloo. Then there is an emotional visit to the Menin Gate for the evening ceremony of wreath laying and playing of the Last Post. It's wonderful to think that this ceremony has been carried out every night since the end of the First World War. I was also staggered by the number of people, both young and old who turn out to take part. Arriving back in Wardley I have just a day or so to unpack then repack for the Mailly trip.

It's Thursday the 28th April 1999, Jim Bengston has arrived in his car, together we head of to Leeds where we will stay overnight in an hotel. Next morning we board the coach for Mailly along with a number of other Vets. As we board there is one couple already seated with a single male passenger sitting on his own. I pass down the coach to put my overcoat in the overhead rack then, the driver starts out on our journey. After a while I get up from my seat to make my way toward the single passenger, I introduce myself to Dr Bill Hossack. I mention that where I am sat there is more leg room for my long frame so if he would like to join Jim and I, his company would be welcomed. This was to be the beginning of a long friendship with an affable and knowledgeable man.

Bill has travelled a long way from his home town of MacDuff in Banff Scotland. On this trip we were to find that we both had a musical bent, though Bill had mastered a much greater range of instruments. As a Doctor in the RAF, he had experience of the stress problems that aircrew suffered, brought on by the bombing raids they flew. Joining us on this pilgrimage is another coach, it is setting off from Nottingham, it will meet up with us at Dover to continue together to Mailly. We spend the full day travelling, only stopping along the way to collect our fellow pilgrims, before finally arriving at Dover. Then it's a ferry across the Channel to Calais where we spend a night in a hotel, which is a welcome break. Next morning after an early breakfast we set off, to visit a flying bomb launch site. Only the remains of this site, with its broken launch ramp can be seen. The rest is a lunar landscape of bomb craters, some of which Jack proudly claims to have been responsible for. During the trip a video is being made to record the experiences of the veterans who took part in the raid. Jack is interviewed on the coach; he gives a graphic account of the horrors of raid on that night of the 3rd May 1944. Another member of 103 Squadron, Gordon Duckworth is on this trip, he was a flight engineer on the Mailly raid, he also recounts his experience of the raid for the video. After this visit we are back on the road across France. The signs at the side of the road flash by with the names synonymous of the First World War. A village called Vimy comes into view with a brief glimpse of the magnificent memorial erected on Vimy Ridge. Then a much larger town, Arras is seen to the South and my thoughts are of the horrors that must have taken place in this beautiful French country side. Late afternoon, we are approaching Reims, set on a hill with the Notre Dame Cathedral, standing on the summit. Onwards we go, Chalons-en-Champagne appears then Mailly le Camp, but not today ahead is our destination Troyes. After booking in at the Hotel, we enjoy a late lunch then into the old town of Troyes for a little sightseeing. The next day the actual anniversary of the raid, we arrive for the memorial service in our two coaches.

Here the French Army are on parade, with an enormous presence by the local Veterans each with their own individual Association Flags. The memorial itself is in the form of a large V shape marble slab with Black inserts depicting the Raid. In front of this stands a single propeller blade, the whole thing is set in a large gravel square, a lot of thought has gone into the design, its a fitting tribute to those lost on the raid.

Our contingent of veterans arranged itself in front of the memorial with a large RAF representation arranged behind us. There followed short speeches from the French Military and local dignitaries. Then the RAF and our Veterans replied, before we laid wreaths from the various WW2 squadrons being represented. For the next few days we toured the area, visiting crash sites of aircraft lost on the raid. What a revelation for those who took part that night, each location was commemorated by a Memorial stone. In addition an area of the churchyard was designated for the lost crew, with the Commonwealth War Graves Commission headstones set in a row. The surrounding area was lovingly tended by local people, many of which must have been only children, when the raid took place. One of the sites we visited was Courboin Communal Cemetery, here we found the headstone of my pal Jim Bengston's brother. He was with 619 Squadron Flying from Dunholme Lodge, there are eight headstones as the crew were flying with a second air bomber. He was there to gain experience of a raid first hand, but he paid the ultimate price. Thankfully for us the organiser of the trip Ken Scott could speak fluent French. So through him we express our thanks for the care the locals have taken of our comrade's graves. This will be the first of a number of trips to Mailly Jack would make.

Back home Jack is looking forward to a spot of Trout fishing as the season reopens. Dorothy has also been busy booking a few days holiday in June to Derbyshire. This would include a trip around Chatsworth House the ancestral home of the Duke of Devonshire. Early in July 99 I receive a letter from the Hospital giving me a date in early August, for another operation on my left hand. Expecting this to affect my ability to drive for a while, Dorothy and I take ourselves of to the Lake District for a few days. We are having a short break to celebrate our 34th wedding anniversary; we can't believe how quick it has gone.

Well Wednesday the 11th August arrives; I present myself at the hospital where they do all the tests prior to my operation on the next day. Dorothy calls in to see me on the Thursday afternoon about 2:00 pm but disappears later as I am given my pre-op jabs. At 3:00pm I am beginning to doze off when a Doctor arrives at my bedside. We are very sorry Mr Spark but an emergency admission has just been brought in, so we will have to reschedule your operation. I had to stay there in bed until 7:30pm to let my pre-op jabs wear off, before I could go home; Hey Ho such is life. The Doctor later offered me a new date, the 6th September but this clashed with a trip to Duxford I had planned. When I phone to explain, the hospital rescheduled my admission for 23rd November.

August Bank Holiday weekend arrives and I am at the Elsham reunion, there is a good turnout of veterans. Because Shirley Westrupp is no longer involved we are holding the Saturday morning get together in the Village Hall at Barnetby le Wold. The weekend is spent organising a new committee and appointing its officers. When I leave on the Sunday afternoon I am happy that the association is being rebuilt it will continue. This is the weekend I remember meeting David and Margaret Crawford for the first time. David was researching his cousin George Stockdale of 576 Squadron. Sadly although we served together about the same time, I had not come into contact with him. I was able however to recount my experiences of the some of the raids his cousin and I would have completed.

On the 6th September Dorothy and I travelled with the Air Gunner Association to see the newly extended Duxford Air Museum in Cambridge. The coach dropped the men of at the museum before taking our wife's for a boat trip on the river, then into the city for a bit of retail therapy. Since my last visit they have added the American section and what a spectacular display it was. I spent a great deal of time taking photographs to send to George Silva.

All too soon my Hospital appointment comes round as I report to admissions as required on the 23rd November. I only hope that this time it will go ahead as planned. Sure enough it's done; I am back home with Dorothy. Having had the other hand done before, I am well aware that I must be careful not to do anything with it for a long time. Sadly after a few months, I begin to realise that although the operation has been successful, I still have limited grip in the fingers. This will put an end to my golfing, though I can still hold a fishing rod thank goodness.

The end of August 2000 arrives and I am off to the Elsham Reunion at Barnetby le Wold. I will travel by train as the long drive is becoming very tiring. Dorothy is not accompanying me, but I will be meeting up with Dr Bill Hossack who I met on the Mailly trip. This time we are back at the Barnetby Village Hall and although the numbers are depleted slightly we had a great time. It would take another year before the membership recovers. Saturday night we enjoyed an excellent meal then we got down to the serious business of chatting to people.

Some we already knew others we had to introduce ourselves to before we realised who they were. I took lots of photos of people I served with and having group photo's taken including myself. There was also time to enjoy a few glasses of something alcoholic. Sunday morning I am up at the airfield, the here I spend time browsing through the exhibits in the museum run by Robin Lingard. His collection ranges from RAF uniforms of the era maps and logbooks too replica instrument panel from a Lancaster, Halifax and Wellington bombers. There are also numerous photograph albums of individual airmen, crews and buildings showing the Elsham Wolds base during the war. After the memorial service plus the flypast by the Lancaster up at the airfield, Bill and I made our way to

Barnetby Station. Here we would catch the train to Doncaster where we would change to connect for Newcastle for me and Edinburgh for Bill. Standing on the station platform where I had arrived for the first time over fifty five years ago was a little eerie. I then decided to use up the last two frames, on the roll of film in my camera, to record the station as it is now. The train arrives then in no time at all we arrived at Doncaster, we grab our bags, leaving the train to cross to the North bound platform.

When the Edinburgh train arrived, we boarded and settled down for the hour or so ride to Newcastle. Thinking about the film in my camera I decided to remove it. To my horror I could not find the camera, I must have left it on the train at Doncaster which would terminate at Manchester Airport. When I arrived home I rang the train company who took my details promising to ring back. Sadly they reported that nothing had been handed in or found. It's lost I thought and although disappointed I forgot about it. The following Saturday evening we were watching TV when the phone rings, a ladies voice says, "Hello is that Mr Spark", "Yes" I replied, "Well I think I have your camera".

"Where are you ringing from" I asked, "Truro" came the reply. I was dumbstruck, apparently her twenty year old son had found it on the train, he had also spotted my name and address sticker on the underside. As he had a name, he decided not to hand it in but contact me later. He continued to his meeting in Manchester, where he stayed for a few days, before travelling home to Truro. When he arrived home his mum unpacked his bag and found Jacks camera, which prompted the phone call. The camera was duly returned; Jack duly sent the young man a cheque to cover the postage including something to buy a drink or two as a reward.

In September 2000 Jack was contacted by the 'Fly Past Magazine' who wants to publish his story of the last of the Berlin Raids. This was to be part of a Bomber Command Special issue for January 2001. The story titled 'Back with a Bang' gave a detailed account of the raid with photos of his crew. There was also a mention of his subsequent contact with George Silva.

The approaching winter of that year also brought to Jack attention his advancing years. Golf had become more demanding for him to play, due to a contracting tendon in his left hand, making it difficult to hold a club. An operation on the hand on 23rd November brought some relief, but he realised his golfing days were numbered. The end of November brought a further shock for Jack; a letter arrives from Margaret Barker in Canada. His crew mate Norman Barker had passed away on the 21st of the month in Missiisauga (Toronto) aged 85. His passing brought back a flood of memories about the War years with all we had endured together at that time. I remember post-war Norman had worked for the Famous

Players Theatres he was also a recognised water colour artist. My letter of condolence to Margaret and her family seemed so inadequate.

It was about this time that Jack was also contacted by Ian Mclachlan. Ian was writing a book recalling the stories of the Eighth Air Force Bomber crews. He had already made contact with George Silva who had told him about his own contact with Jack. Ian was fascinated by the two Veterans story which he wanted to include it in the book even though Jack was not a US Vet. This book was published in 2004 and included a photo of George's aircraft 'The Passionate Witch II' spiralling out of control on the Chateaudun raid. This photo was taken by an aircraft in George's formation to be used to log the lost of the Witch.

April 2001 has arrived and Dorothy and Jack spend a few days in Scotland. We travelled to Loch Lomond and its surrounding district. I remember one part of the area had been a military establishment but had been converted to a shopping complex. Dorothy had a great time; there were a huge range of products reflecting Scotland's crafts and heritage. On an evening there were also the delights of locally caught Salmon or Venison with all the trimming. Whilst I am normally a beer drinker, I did sample some of the surrounding areas Whisky, in moderation.

The rest of the year slips by with my usual trip to the August Bank Holiday Reunion. Our membership is recovering with our numbers up again; there is also a rise in new people who are family of crew members who had served at Elsham.

In the March of 2002 Jack was introduced to the daughter of a friend at the fishing club. This young lady Emily Gibson was compiling a School project on the Second World War; her father asked Jack if he would help. When it was completed Emily sent Jack a copy of the finished project for his comment he read it carefully and offered a few additional facts for her consideration Afterwards she reported back that her work had received a special commendation. It also resulted in Jack being asked to visit schools in the area to give talks about his war in bomber command. History to these young people, were words in a book or moving images on a Video. But now they had the opportunity to listen to someone who was there, someone they could actually talk to. Jack was also surprised by some of the questions they asked, not just about the fighting, but how they lived and coped day to day.

It's October 2002 and Jack is approaching his eightieth birthday, Dorothy has decided we will have a quite dinner together to celebrate. When the day arrives we set off for the restaurant but Dorothy wants to call at her brother's house on the way. Bill's wife Norma welcomes us at the door; I follow them through to the lounge, then it all dawns on me I have been duped. The whole of the family are there in the room singing Happy Birthday, both of Dorothy's brothers and their wives are there with their children. The dining room tables are groaning with the weight of food and drink on them. Dorothy produced my camera, photos of the assembled family are taken, it was an evening to remember.

Two weeks have passed by, Dorothy and I are off to the Newcastle Metro Centre, we have some shopping to do. Dorothy has the rolls of film from my birthday party in her handbag, which we will take to be developed. We drive to the local Heworth Metro Rail station where we leave the car in the park. As we stand waiting for the train, Dorothy is talking about which shops we need to visit. Then the train arrives we walk forward to board, then Dorothy stumbles and falls against the side of the carriage. With the help of another passenger we lift her to her feet then help her to a seat on the train. What a stupid thing to do, she protests as she dusts herself down. I can see that one of her knee's is scuffed but It's not serious I am told. We spent the next couple of hours slowly walking round the shops before Dorothy complains her knee is becoming sore. The shopping trip is cut short, we head off home, when we arrive the knee is bathed in warm water and she takes a couple of painkillers. Next morning the knee is badly bruised so I insist that we visit the local hospital's A and E department. Dorothy reluctantly agrees and goes to get ready to leave. When she does not return Jack goes looking for her, only to find her slumped on the floor. He immediately calls for an ambulance, when they arrive they find Dorothy is unconscious; she is rushed to the Hospital, here I am left in the waiting room for the doctors to do their job. After what seems an eternity, they call me into a side room where I am informed that Dorothy has suffered a blood clot from the knee injury. They are doing their best but things are very serious, I sit in a daze unable to take it all in. Despite the best effort of the doctors, Dorothy never regains consciousness and passes away. My world falls apart for the fourth time in my life. I cannot comprehend how so simple an injury can result in such a devastating outcome. Dorothy's family rally round to give me support, I remember the nieces being particularly so. They ring me on a regular basis to talk for ages, urging me to remember the good times we had had together. There is a steady stream of family and friends to help me through this ordeal. Autumn turns to winter, Christmas has lost it magic, the New Year is just an end the horrors of 2002. I slowly work my way a day at a time into 2003 getting used to having to do the things Dorothy did every day.

As Winter turns into Spring, an offer to travel to Mailly le Camp in France again. At first I am not interested, but Dorothy's family suggest it is just the break I need. Reluctantly I agree so on the 1st May I join the coach at Newcastle with Charles Wearmouth, President of Elsham Wolds Association for the long run to France. Our first stop is Darlington where we pick up David and Margaret Crawford who I remember from the

Elsham reunions. The next stop is Wetherby where we collect Fred and Betty Spencer, Fred was one of the ground crew at Elsham who I know very well from previous reunions. Along the way to Dover we make further stops to pick up other people, some aircrew, some relatives of aircrew lost on the raid. The atmosphere was very friendly, with some of the young relatives wanting to hear all about the raid from me, as I had taken part in it. To my great surprise the attitude of the French people was heart warming. We visited crash sites around the area and lay wreathes on the graves of our comrades who did not return.

One village Euilly had taken our comrades to heart, graves were well tended and their names have been added to the local War Memorials. A local mayor summed it up by saying "Your fallen Hero's are our fallen Hero's", I felt very humbled and grateful. The country around Euilly was beautiful the hillsides are covered with the vines that produce the Champagne the area is famous for. It's here I meet up with my friends David and Margaret Crawford again who introduce me to David and Elaine Frampton. David Frampton's father served with one of the Pathfinder Squadrons so they are here to see some of the raids his dad was involved in. They then tell me they are both Army Vets, who have served two tours of Northern Ireland before serving in Berlin for many years. A very interesting young couple, I will come to know well in the future. Our final part of the tour is the memorial service on the anniversary of the raid. This was conducted within the French Army camp at Mailley where they treat us royally; there was the usual full turnout of army regulars. But the most memorable feature was the huge compliment of French Veterans from the War with their individual Standards held aloft. They formed three ranks filling one side of the parade ground in front of the memorial itself. The British contingent is arranged facing the memorial with the official RAF representatives alongside. This memorial itself consists of a large Granite slab in the form of a V with a Lancaster propeller and hub mounted in front. Speeches were made by all sides, National anthems were played. The RAF Veterans then began laying wreaths on the memorial. Afterwards we were all treated to a wonderful meal in the Officers Mess with the obligatory glass of wine. One of the funny moments of the lunch in the Officers mess hall came at the end of the meal, a few of the Vets including myself made a visit to the Gents toilet. Standing in a row doing what comes naturally, we are shocked to find two female officers march in to occupy the cubicles behind us. This communal usage is common in France but was a surprise for us old RAF men. That evening in the hotel we recounted the last few days' events and the memories created.

All of these memories made the long trip back to the channel the following day seem so much quicker than the outward trip. The final leg of the journey to Newcastle sees Jack exchange phone numbers with David and Margaret Crawford. A week later Jack rings Margaret to arranged for them both to visit him at home, then to go for a meal in South Shields, this is to be the start of a long friendship. This year also see's Jack being asked to make a recording for posterity by "The Second World War Experiences Centre" in Wetherby. He is visited by the Centres people to talk about his time in the RAF during the war. The result is a double CD which was released in late 2003.

August has arrived with the Reunion only couple of weeks away. I was intending to travel by train but David has invited me to travel in the car with him and Margaret. On the Friday afternoon they duly arrive from Thornaby, before we set off for Elsham. Midway we stop for a bite to eat at the 'Black Bull' in Wetherby. "Here I get the chance to try their Steak and Kidney Pudding washed down with a glass of John Smiths best." This stopping point will become a regular event every August Reunion and the November Remembrance meeting. Later we sign in at the Guest house in Barnetby le Wold which is run by the local Doctor, Ajay Vora and his wife Angela. The evening is spent at their home, here we are in for a shock, the intervening year has been a one of upheaval. The committee is in disarray, Ajay and Angela have had to take temporary control to stabilise the association. Despite these problems a new committee is formed at the AGM and the association goes from strength to strength over the coming years.

These two people, Ajay and Angela Vora will be the backbone of the association for many years to come. Working alongside of them is another rock of the association, Jennie Mackay. Jennie's dad, John or Jack Mackay was part of the ground crew at Elsham, he was another staunch supporter of the association. Together we would always be known as young Jack and old Jack but I cannot remember which of us is which. At Ajay's welcoming party I find my pal Bill Hossack with his friend Margaret Roxburgh, who have travelled down from Scotland. The following midday, Saturday is the buffet reception at the village hall which is bussing with Vets swopping tales of the war. The evening dinner is a time for meeting with old friends but I notice that some are no longer with us. The President Charles Wearmouth is also missing due to ill health. One new member I am introduced to is Group Captain Don Hiller (retired) from Grantham. Don and his wife Marjorie have spent many years in the RAF travelling around the world. Don was a Engineering Officer at the time when the RAF were flying aircraft like the futuristic Victor, Valliant and Vulcan, all part of Britain's V bomber force. Another two people I would become good friends with over the next few years.

The New Year of 2004 sees the publication of Ian Mclachlan Book, 'Eighth Air Force Bomber Story's'. A few days later, George is on the phone to ask if I have my copy. "Yes" was my reply, we both commented on what a wonderful job he has done of telling our story. We spent the next half hour talking about how we were doing and what we were planning for the coming year. I spent some time relating to George my previous trips to Mailly and the upcoming trip in May.

This year's trip to Mailly will be without Charles Wearmouth, who is not well. I have been asked to stand in for him as the Elsham representative, which I gladly accept. Amongst those attending this year are a number of grandchildren of veterans, they show a great deal of interest in the events of the night of the 3rd May 1944. Jack and the other veterans are repeatedly being asked questions about the events of that night. As we visit the local villages, the extent of the losses begins to dawn on them, 280 young men have been killed on the raid. One of them comments that the coach we are travelling in holds 70 people, so four coaches would represent the number of people lost, a sobering comparison. I remember at the end of the trip on the way home in England, these young people took time to thank the veterans as they left the coach. They would no doubt have lots of stories to relate to their school pals back home. Sadly Charles Wearmouth passes away in the May after we return from Mailly. Charles was one of this world's gentlemen; he was always approachable to answer peoples questions. He was quiet spoken, but with a passion for Bomber Command and the people who served in it. As a proud Cumbrian, he would have been pleased to see Jack Spark elected as the new President of Elsham Wolds Association in the August.

During the 2004 Reunion Don Hiller and Bill Hossack suggest to David Crawford that he should start documenting Jacks war stories. We are visiting Jack at least twice a week, so when we are there I ask him if I can record our conversations about the war. He has no objections, so every time we visit, I switch my mobile phone to record then leave it running until we leave. From his initial war stories and service history, he expands to cover his school days including his family. Later my mobile phone would be replaced by my compact camera which will be used to video Jacks stories. At this time I also realise that our weekly talks with George Silva are also something special. In response I start to make notes about his time in the USAAF especially about his time as a POW. George talked about a book he has sent to Jack called, Kriegie Memories by Ben Phelper. This book gives a comprehensive account of how it was in Stalag 17B including numerous photo's. George expanded on the Kriegie book to give his version of his time in Stalag 17B including how the Forced March had affected him. Every week we talk to George and Betty drawing comparisons with our lives in our respective countries. George would talk about the garden birds in Cupertino, which would include Humming birds, Oriole's and Flycatchers. Jack by comparison would be putting out seeds for the Sparrows, Robins, Blackbirds and a range of Finches.

One of their major comparisons was healthcare costs; George was amazed to hear that Jack did not have to pay for his Medication or for Hospital Operations costs. But when it came to Petrol (Gas) costs for their cars, George at the time was paying $1.30 for a gallon. Jack on the other hand was paying the equivalent of $5.30 per gallon in Britain due to Government Taxes.

The spring of 2005 sees Jack invited to visit Don and Marjorie Hiller for the weekend at Grantham. He arrives on the Friday afternoon then they spend the evening having a meal at a local restaurant. Next morning after a leisurely breakfast Jack is taken to view some of the sights of the area. Don is a retired Group Captain and officer of the Mess at RAF Cranwell's Collage, he springs a surprise on Jack when they stop at Cranwell for lunch. I remember Jack recalls, "We finished a first class meal, then visited Cranwell's library of aviation and technical books". In the corner of one room stands a large desk with a plush chair, "It's Bomber Harris's desk" comments Don "In a flash I am seated in the great mans chair, to have a photo taken, what a memory for me."

As the new president of Elsham Wolds Association, Jack is now more involved in the organisation of the reunions. Part of this includes the distribution of the newsletter produced by David Fell. This is a mine of information about 103 Squadron going back to the First World War. But also covers both Squadrons operations during WW2, this young man has a mountain of photographs and Operational records.

It's now the spring of 2006, soon it will be the anniversary of the Dunsfold crash. I have decided to give both Jack and George a present; a friend of mine Alfred Alderson is an accomplished painter who is also a military historian. I have commissioned Alf to complete two painting for me. One is Jacks Lancaster PM-M the other is Georges B17 Passionate Witch.

Two weeks before the anniversary I post George's painting to him in California. The other I keep in the car for when I visit Jack. A week or two later, as we are talking to George on the webcam he produces his painting. I then give Jack his painting of the Lancaster. Both of them are delighted with the presents; Jacks goes up on the wall that very night.

The New Year becomes a full one with a return visit to Mailly where there will be a sad reunion for Jack. We have arrived at a Church in the village of Trouan-le-Petit to pay our respects to airmen lost on the raid. To one side of the churchyard are twelve headstones an arranged in a single row. Six are from 50 Squadron plus six from 625 Squadron. Wreathes are laid then we work our way down the row reading the dedications. Then Jack spots one stone in particular, the name Reg Tailby comes as a shock. He sadly recounts to us his training with Reg at Stormy Down, how he had a one year old son. I always hoped that Reg had survived the war, but here he has lain all this time. We had unknowingly both taken part in the Mailly raid, but Reg had made the ultimate sacrifice, a cruel reminder of the war for Jack.

The August Reunion this year see's a new member all the way from Texas in the USA where he was a preacher. John and Joan Curnow had just found out about the Elsham Wolds association existence, they joined then flew to be at their first reunion. John was a Navigator in 103 Squadron in 1943 but was shot down on a raid to Munich where he was taken POW. I bought a copy of his book about his war called "SHOT DOWN". Later he spoke with Jack who was amazed to find he had spent some of his training at Millom in Cumbria. He also talked about his time walking in the hills around the Lake District, Jack old stomping ground, it's a small world.

Over the years I have listened to Jacks stories and those of the other aircrews, wondering how they coped. But on the Sunday up at the airfield I was to experience something special for me. John and Joan Curnow are standing with Jack and I waiting for the Lancaster to make its appearance. I asked John if he had been to Trenton in Canada to see the Canadian Lancaster. "Yes" he replied "But it was being serviced so I did not see it fly. In fact he said I have not seen or heard a Lancaster since the March of 1943". At this point over Johns shoulder I could see the BBMF Lancaster coming in low towards us "Is your camera switched on John" I said, "She's here". John turned then lifted his camera, click, click, click it went. The Lancaster roars overhead then, passes out of sight behind the Water Company building. John turned back to me and puts his hand on my shoulder. His mouth opens, but he just could not speak, tears were running down his cheeks. When he regains his voice, all he could say was; "For that moment I was back on the field in 43 watching a Lancaster". I have never forgotten that emotional moment, I suppose I never will. John and Joan would make a number of visits to Elsham Wolds over the coming years.

January 2007, Jack receives a letter from a Mr P.J Grimm who is Chairman of the Air War Study Group 1939-45 in Holland. He has asked me to give a talk about 103 Squadrons last raid on Berlin and our crew's involvement. My invite has been prompted by my old friend Adrian, who has arranged for me to stay with his family while I am there. The talks will involve a number of speakers on different subjects at the Dutch Air Base at Gilze Rijen. By the strangest of coincidences Saturday the 24th March will be the anniversary of our raid. This will require copious notes and thorough preparation on my part. On the 22nd March I fly out to Holland, Adrian picks me up at the airport. When I arrive at his home

Ingrid is there to greet me along with Colin who has grown a great deal. I feel totally at home with this young family, who treat me as one of their own. The following day Adrian shows me some of the work he is doing to research some of the aircraft and crews lost over Holland during the War. He is part of a very dedicated group of volunteers compiling this information. One other topic being discussed this weekend will be a talk about the US 8th Air force's support, during the unsuccessful Operation Market Garden in 1944.

Then the time came for me to give my presentation about our night over Berlin. I started by asking what people in the room were doing last night. Because last night 63 years ago, on the 23th March 1944 I was setting out to bomb Berlin on the morning of the 24th. This I thought made a very poignant start to my talk, which was very well received. The get together afterwards, brought forward more questions along with a lot of kind comments. I find it amazing the amount of interest there still is in the history of the Second World War, especially here in Holland. All too soon I was back on the plane to Newcastle and home.

We are into June 2008 I am travelling down to Grantham with Margaret and David; it's one of our regular trips to meet friends. There will be the usual gang of about twenty for a weekend of good company and fine dining, after which Jack will entertain every one, with his mountain of stories from the war.

On the Sunday Don Hiller has made arrangements for seven of us to have lunch at Cranwell. After a splendid lunch Jack decides to sit in the lounge to read the Sunday papers. We slip upstairs to see the library; Don shows Margaret the displays of memorabilia relating to Laurence of Arabia. At the same time David sits in Bomber Harris's chair to have his photo taken at the great mans desk. When they all eventually troop down stairs to the lounge, Jack is not immediately visible. Then we notice a large group of young airmen from all over the world sat in a semi circle around Jack. Sitting like an elderly sage he is recounting his tales of life on a bomber station during the War, including some of his funny stories. We had to just about drag him away from these enthusiastic young officers, such was their interest in Jack. They finally realised Jack had to leave, but not before they profusely thanked him as they shook his hand. It was a memorable event for all of us who witnessed this special moment for Jack.

Back in Cupertino California George Silva had been wondering about what had happened to the artist Harold Rhoden who had made the sketch of him in Stalag 17b. "My daughter Gloria contacted the History Detectives on PBS for help". They in turn wanted to tell Georges story in one of their broadcasts. This included his meeting up with Fletcher Rhoden, Harold's Son who brought me a sketch of his Dad which still hangs in my home. Harold had qualified as a Lawyer after the war but sadly he, his wife and daughter were all killed in a plane crash in 1989. Having survived the war I found this news so sad, the world can be a cruel place at times.

We have been on the Skype today talking to George Silva who tells us of a group called the History Detectives, operating in the USA. They have contacted George about his time in the Air force during the War and as a POW in Germany. The program will be shown in early 2009 and will be on the internet, to view we are looking forward to watching his interview.

In august we attend the Elsham Reunion where I find myself sat with Bill Hossack and Ajay Vora, both are Doctor friends of myself and Jack. They both ask if I have noticed any changes in Jacks behaviour which puzzles me. Having not seen Jack for a year they immediately notice his memory lapses that Margaret and I have become accustomed to over time. It's something we will have to aware of for the future.

One week into January 2009 Jack hears from George Silva that Betty his wife is not well and has been getting worse. She is going to be moved into a nursing home for a while, George will visit every day but cannot stay with her. George is very upset; this will be the first time they have been apart in over 50 years. We can only offer our hope that things will improve for her in the future. He has the support of daughters Lisa and Gloria who will be there for them both.

Spring arrives, I begin noticing Jacks memory lapses, but I am not prepared for what is to happen. We were on one of our regular Thursday night visits to Jacks home. I have a few queries about some of his school days his answers are immediate and clear. But when I ask about his fishing expeditions a few years ago he becomes confused and unsure. Then he stops talking, looks me full in the face and asks "How long have I been like this David". His question pole axes me; I have to bite my lip. Then somehow I reply, "We all suffer from these occasional forgetful moments mate". He smiled at me then says "I suppose we do"; he then changes the subject. This moment of self realisation that things were not right in his life was for me so sad.

The autumn is approaching and we are to visit Jack this evening when his sister in law Norma phones to say he has been admitted to Hospital. When we arrive there, we meet up with his brother in law Darly and his wife Pamela. They are waiting to see Jack so we sit chatting; apparently he had missed taking some of his medication. Finally we are admitted to the ward to find Jack is quite chirpy, he is being treated so should be allowed home in a few days. Then he will need community support, to ensure he takes his medication regularly. One thing I notice in the hospital; is that his care though excellent is somewhat impersonal. To improve this, on my next visit I am armed with a printout of his story of the Berlin raid. One copy I drop on the nursing station worktop, another I put on the empty doctors desk. The following day, Jack tells me the nurses and doctors are asking him about his war service. He asks how they found out about it; I have to admit to making him a star on the ward. In the weeks that followed Jack would receive help from Social Services, with daily visits to ensure he is taking his medication. They also see that he has hot meals every day.

The new year of 2010 start badly with the news that George Silva's wife Betty has passed away at the end of January. Jack telephones George to convey his condolences; they had been married for 54 years. George is now moving to live with his daughter Lisa, in San Jose California. In Wardley, Gateshead Jack is managing to cope, but it is decided that it would be better if he could be assessed for his future needs.

To that end, he moves to one the specialist review centres in Gateshead. In the August I attend the reunion with Bill Hossack then, on the Sunday we travel back home to Thornaby. Here we collect my wife Margaret before setting off to visit Jack. When we arrive at the centre Jack is delighted to see Bill; we spend a couple of hours talking to Jack and reminiscing. Then sadly we have to leave to drop Bill at Newcastle Station, but not before I take a group photo. Bill is pleased to have seen Jack but saddened at the decline in his old friend. Margaret and I continue to visit Jack as his birthday approaches, we are thinking about what we can buy for him. A few days before his birthday his sister in law Norma telephones to say Jack has had a fall which has resulted in a broken arm. The break is not serious but he is in Hospital, Margaret and I visit to find him surprisingly cheerful. I again distribute a copy of his Berlin Raid article to the ward staff, so they can relate to his war service. On the 22nd of October he celebrates his 88th Birthday with the Doctors and nurses singing happy birthday to him. A few days later there is a sudden deterioration in his condition due to his other health issues. Margaret and I are planning to visit next day, when Norma telephones to give us the bad news that Jack had passed away that morning.

It's a sad time when someone close passes away but at the same time there are all the necessary formalities to complete. Norma and Bill ask me to produce a potted history of Jack; the funeral will be a humanist one, which will reflect Jacks life. Margaret and I now visit the South Shields Gazette to place a memorial notice in the paper on behalf of ourselves and George Silva. The News editor when he hears of Jacks demise asks for any photos; he takes a copy of my concise history of Jack. The following Thursday they do a full page spread in a "Last Respects" section of the paper dedicated to local Hero's.

The funeral itself was well attended by family and friends. There is a large contingent from RAF Elsham Wolds making the 300 mile round trip. Don and Marjorie Hiller along with David and Elaine Frampton travel from Grantham. Also in attendance is Jacks old friend Dr Bill Hossack, who has made the 600 mile round trip from Macduff in the North of Scotland for the funeral. An RAF Standard bearer was in attendance and the last post was sounded at the end of the service. A fitting tribute to a great man my wife and I had the privilege of calling a friend.

I now have the difficult task of telephoning George to tell him of Jack's passing but each time I am greeted by an answering machine. Eventually I leave our telephone number with a message for George. Later that week his Daughter Lisa phones to inform Margaret that George has moved to San Jose to live with her family. At the time George's health was not good but she would give him our best wishes then give him the news of Jacks passing. He had been a little puzzled at not being able to contact Jack. Christmas comes Margaret and I send George a Christmas card along with a large Calendar, showing views of the Lake District Jack's favourite area of Cumbria. It was some time after this that George moved to live with his daughter Gloria and her husband Art in Tempe Arizona.

In the June of 2014 I receive the Elsham Wolds Magazine which includes a notice of the passing of Ron Walker in Canada in January 2014 at the age of 96. Ron retired from Allstate Insurance of Canada as Director of Industry Relations after a multi-decade career. He was most proud of his efforts to promote vehicle safety standards and was a champion of both the installation of seat belts and air bags.

Chateaudun Memorial trip

August 2015 saw another chapter added to the story of the Passionate Witch, when a group of 452nd Bomb Group relatives travelled to Chateaudun in France. These included Julie Blichmann, niece of Carl Blichmann & her husband Ted Fore, Jim & Robbie Thomas Daughter of Gerald Poplett & Terri & Rick Moore Cousin of Fremont Granade. There to greet them was Stephanie Lopez & Pascal Bulois. These French people   have researched the history of the Americans who helped liberate France from the Germans. They not only set up the visit but also organised the accommodation for everyone in a local hotel. They were wonderful hosts who we have remained in touch with.

The visit itself saw the family members witness the unveiling of a Stele (a vertical stone monument) commemorating the names of those aircrew who lost their lives on the raid to

Chateaudun on 28th March 1944. The actual stone is erected on a building in the French Camp "Kellerman". After the ceremony they would be treated to French hospitality, an excellent lunch with examples from the local vineyards to sample. Later they would be taken to the site of the Passionate Witch Crash, though it was now covered by a barracks on the Chateaudun airfield, The aircraft itself would have been long ago removed, but the memories of what had happened would be fresh in their minds. Later they would also be treated to visits to some local Chateaus & to visit other American monuments to the fallen in the area. One of the days included the group visiting a WW2 exhibition where they could climb into Jeep, Tanks & other vehicles. It was a visit that was a mixture of pleasure & sadness, but something that we were all pleased to have taken part in.

In 2016 I became a member of the 452nd Bombardment Group only to sadly find that George Silva had passed away in 2015. Through social media I finally make contact with Gloria Silva Mack who has kindly provided me with a historical document created by George. This has helped to complete Georges place in the history of the WW2 Bomber War which I have tried to represent alongside Jack Spark's place in the same War.

So ends the story of Jack Spark, George Silva their lives and the crews they served with during WW2.

Over the years I have listened to the stories of the War recounted by veterans from a number of countries. At first they can sound exciting, but then the horror behind them becomes apparent. Only then do we start to realise the sheer courage they displayed. They saw firsthand the losses of air crews every day, but still they continued to climb aboard their aircraft and set out on the next mission. Jack always admitted to being scared on every raid he flew and I am sure George would say the same. They were just ordinary young men doing extraordinary things with a hope of creating a better world. Our duty is to not let their sacrifice be a waste.

As part of my poetry group I wrote the following about Elsham Wolds Airfield and its people.

Elsham Wolds Bomber Boys

They came with the dawn, in innocence drawn
To fight off the Hun, until victory was won
But winnings not soon, as they will find
Only death and destruction, to pray on the mind
Their posting is One Group, in Bomber Command
A newly built airfield, fresh hewn from the land
High on the hill, it's Elsham Wolds Drome
This bleak remote Base, is to be their new home
How long they will live here's, in the lap of the gods
Their whole reason for living, is beating the odds
Just ordinary young men, performing extraordinary deeds
To face down Jerry, a whole world to be freed
They're Just a sprog crew, with a great deal to learn
The respect of their fellows, they will have to earn
There's thirty long trips, to drop bombs by the ton
Then they'll get a respite, their tour will be done
They first flew the Wimpy, in 41-42
Then came the Halifax, which needed more crew
Only five months later, came the Queen of the sky
The beautiful Lancaster, a real joy to fly
Were a family of seven, and we fly close to heaven
But our life can be hell, as we brave shot and shell
Night fighters, flak, and the dreaded searchlight
They're all out to get us, and cancel our night
Aircrews at the sharp end are facing the flak
But the ground crews are waiting, till they come back
Then they'll service their kites, making sure they're fit
To go back tomorrow, they're doing their bit
Were back in our billets, and it's cold in my bed
Though the pot belly stove, is glowing bright red
Fun in the billets, there's a little horseplay
But we'll all be quiet, for young Bob to pray
Young Bob Thomas, was Browning's rear gunner
Only nineteen years old, the girls thought a stunner
But the last Raid to Berlin, he met his end
Fighting off a 109, defending his friends
The airfield abounds, with people filling a need
Cooks in the kitchen, preparing our feed
There's Packers of chutes, we hope we won't use
And the MT drivers, who will ferry our crews
Doc Henderson's our medic, his first name is Bob

At curing our ache's he's the best in the job
He looks for the Twitch, a sure sign of strain
Then he'll give you a rest, before you fly again
Our free time is spent, in Scunny's Oswald bar
The 'Barnetby Flyer', will get us that far
But if we should miss it, we'll not get our flagon
The Doc he will take us, in the stations Blood Wagon
We have a night off and the urge for a Jig
So get out the bikes, were all off to Brig
We'll down a few jars, in the Gladiator or Bull
Then it's into the dance we're all on the pull
The Base had its characters, now you will see
There was Cy Grant the lawyer, and talent had he
He would sing News calypso's, on national TV
Then there's Don Charlwood, a writer so bright
He went back to Oz, to pen 'No Moon Tonight'
The 'Mad Belgian' Van Rolleghem, Seventy missions he flew
He would be an Air Marshall, in his own air force too
There was Winco Ken Wallis, of autogyro fame
He gave James Bond, that Little Nell plane
There's old Jack and young Jack, Spark and Mackay
One on the ground, the other up in the sky
There were others, not famous, they just did their bit
On Cenotaph stones, you can find their names writ
She was Tall and Elegant, she stole young men's hearts
A Bomber Command legend, more than the sum of her parts
M Mother flew 140 trips; they're all marked on her card
But still she ended her days, in a breakers scrap yard
She was a Lancaster Bomber that flew like a dream
So thank you Roy Chadwick and the Avro design team

David Crawford (Watching)

Acknowledgements

Bill & Norma Young for Jack Spark's family photographs & letters exchanged with George Silva.

Australian National Archives A705, 166/43/698 for the report of the Atlas Mountains Dakota crash.

Adrian van Zantvoort for the Luftwaffe night fighter report of the loss of 576 Squadron Lancaster ME810.

Adrian van Zantvoort for photographs & letters exchanged with George Silva & Jack Spark.

Art & Gloria Silva Mack for George Silva's historical record "You must be a Yank".

Jessica Thayer Kidwell for Dick Thayer's war diary entries, family details & photographs.

Julie Blichmann for photographs & corrected details of Carl H. "Herbie" Blichmann.

Candace Cook daughter of Robert Cook Skipper of the Passionate Witch for Bob's peace time history.

Howard Keller 452nd Bombardment Group for Mission and Crew Statistics for the Passionate Witch.

Ben H Phelper for a photograph of George Silva's hut in Stalag 17b shown in Kriegie Memories.

David Fell for historical details & losses for 103 & 576 Squadrons.

The National Archives RAF Squadron Operational Records for 1944 for 103 & 576 Squadrons.

To all of those Aircrew & Ground crew who served at Elsham Wolds & provided input.

Printed in Great Britain
by Amazon

38479838R00136